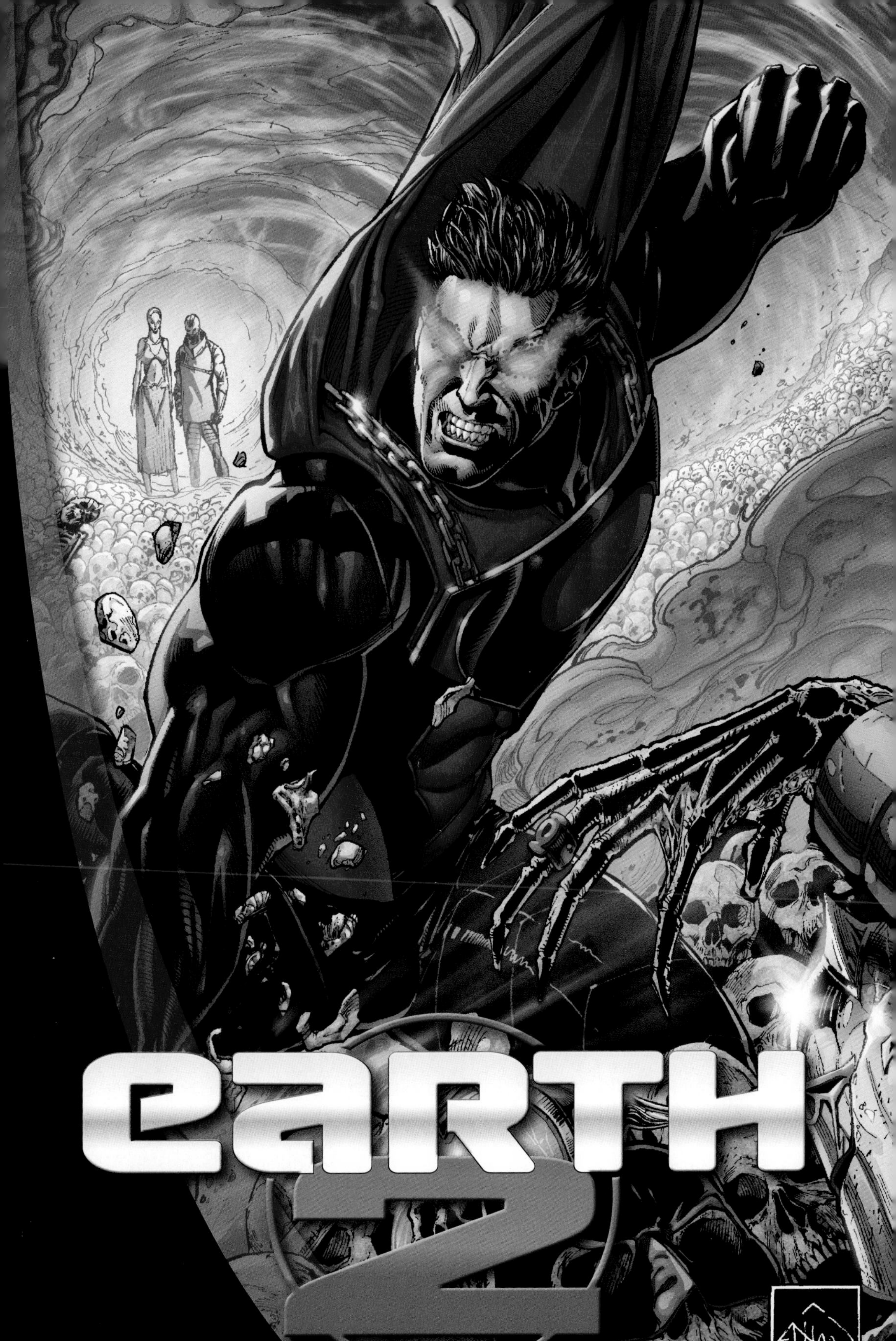
EARTH
2

VOLUME 4 **THE DARK AGE**

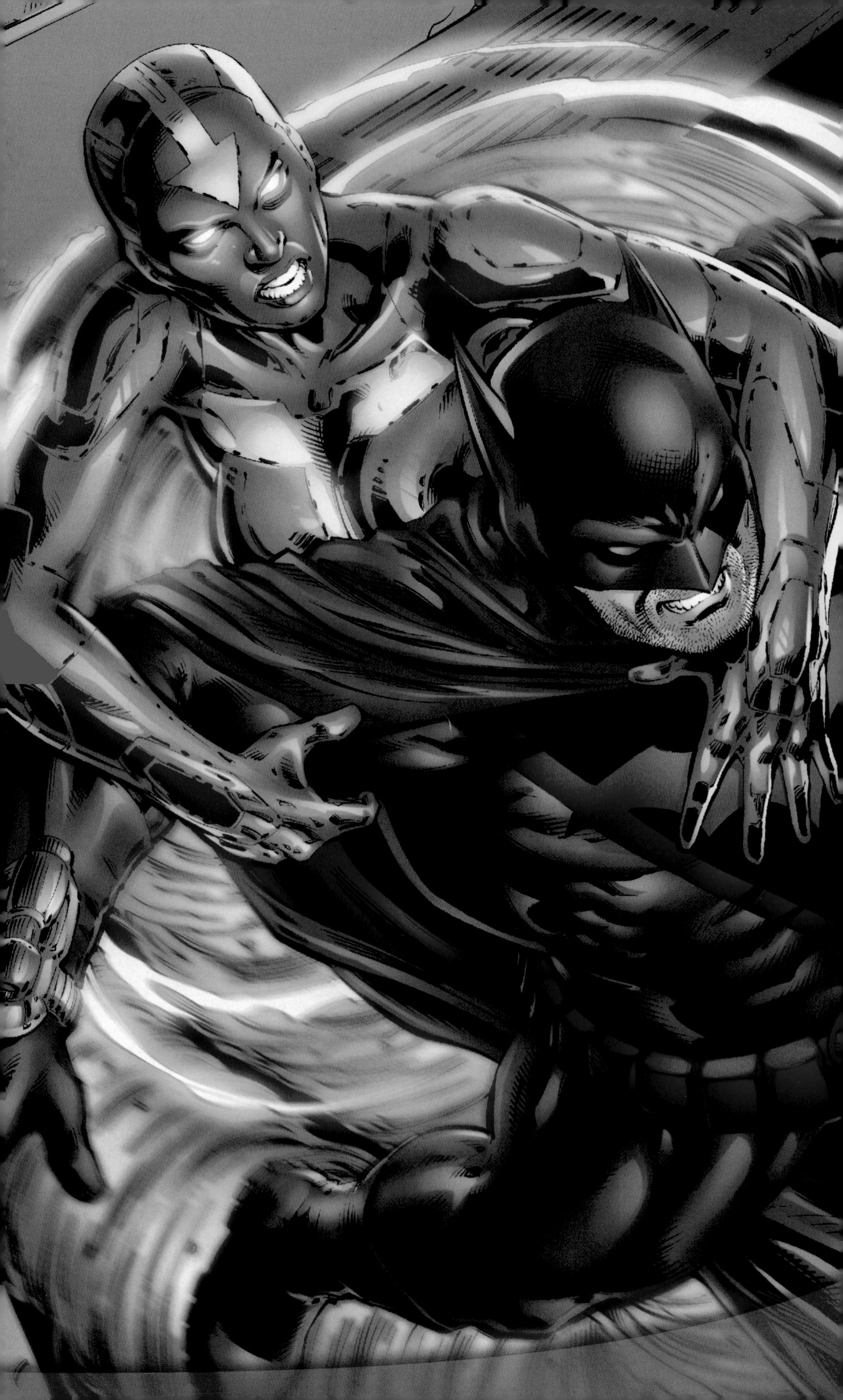

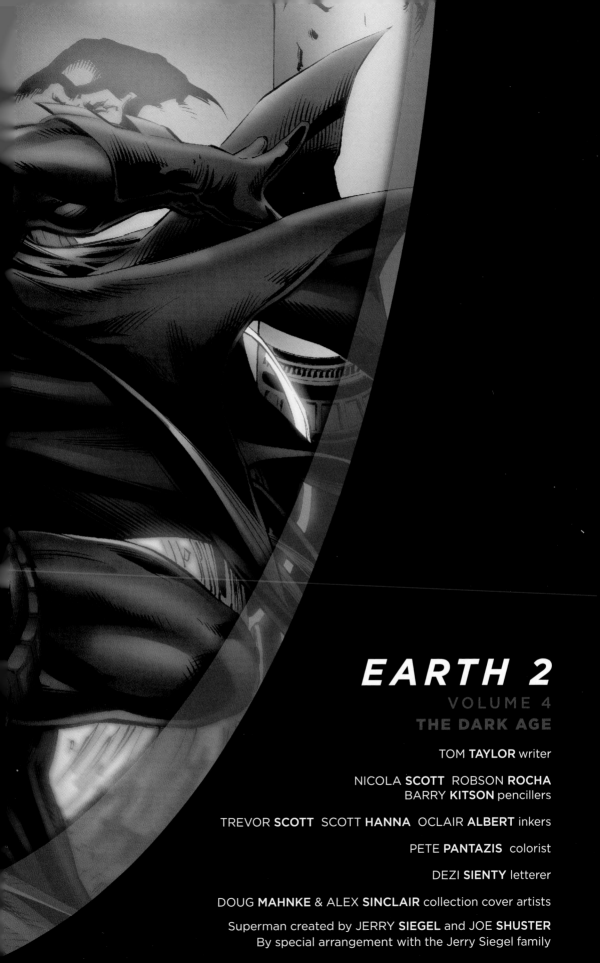

EARTH 2
VOLUME 4
THE DARK AGE

TOM **TAYLOR** writer

NICOLA **SCOTT** ROBSON **ROCHA**
BARRY **KITSON** pencillers

TREVOR **SCOTT** SCOTT **HANNA** OCLAIR **ALBERT** inkers

PETE **PANTAZIS** colorist

DEZI **SIENTY** letterer

DOUG **MAHNKE** & ALEX **SINCLAIR** collection cover artists

Superman created by JERRY **SIEGEL** and JOE **SHUSTER**
By special arrangement with the Jerry Siegel family

MIKE COTTON Editor – Original Series ANTHONY MARQUES Assistant Editor – Original Series
ROBIN WILDMAN Editor ROBBIN BROSTERMAN Design Director – Books

BOB HARRAS Senior VP – Editor-in-Chief, DC Comics

DIANE NELSON President DAN DIDIO and JIM LEE Co-Publishers GEOFF JOHNS Chief Creative Officer
AMIT DESAI Senior VP – Marketing & Franchise Management AMY GENKINS Senior VP – Business & Legal Affairs
NAIRI GARDINER Senior VP – Finance JEFF BOISON VP – Publishing Planning
MARK CHIARELLO VP – Art Direction & Design JOHN CUNNINGHAM VP – Marketing
TERRI CUNNINGHAM VP – Editorial Administration LARRY GANEM VP – Talent Relations & Services
ALISON GILL Senior VP – Manufacturing & Operations HANK KANALZ Senior VP – Vertigo & Integrated Publishing
JAY KOGAN VP – Business & Legal Affairs, Publishing JACK MAHAN VP – Business Affairs, Talent
NICK NAPOLITANO VP – Manufacturing Administration SUE POHJA VP – Book Sales
FRED RUIZ VP – Manufacturing Operations COURTNEY SIMMONS Senior VP – Publicity Bob Wayne Senior VP – Sales

EARTH 2 VOLUME 4: THE DARK AGE

Published by DC Comics. Copyright © 2014 DC Comics. All Rights Reserved.

Originally published in single magazine form as EARTH 2 17-20, EARTH 2 ANNUAL 2 Copyright © 2013, 2014 DC Comics. All Rights Reserved.
All characters, their distinctive likenesses and related elements featured in this publication are trademarks of DC Comics. SCRIBBLENAUTS
and all related characters and elements are trademarks of and © Warner Bros. Entertainment Inc. The stories, characters and incidents
featured in this publication are entirely fictional. DC Comics does not read or accept unsolicited ideas, stories or artwork.

DC Comics, 1700 Broadway, New York, NY 10019
A Warner Bros. Entertainment Company.
Printed by RR Donnelley, Salem, VA, USA. 9/5/14. First Printing.
ISBN: 978-1-4012-5001-0

Library of Congress Cataloging-in-Publication Data

Taylor, Tom, 1978- author.
Earth 2. Volume 4, The Dark Age / Tom Taylor, Nicola Scott, Trevor Scott.
pages cm.
Summary: "Once thought dead, Superman now returns to Earth to do the destructive bidding of Darkseid! The Wonders of Earth 2 have
struggled to keep the forces of Brutal and Darkseid at bay. But now with the return of Superman, they can no longer stand up to the wake of
destruction he brings. But now, with the emergence of a new and mysterious Batman, comes the hope that he may know how to defeat the
rogue Man of Steel before Earth 2 is destroyed completely"— Provided by publisher.
ISBN 978-1-4012-5001-0 (hardback)
1. Graphic novels. I. Scott, Nicola, illustrator. II. Scott, Trevor, illustrator. III. Title. IV. Title: Dark Age.
PN6727.T293E27 2014
741.5'973—dc23
2014014908

SUSTAINABLE
FORESTRY
INITIATIVE

Certified Chain of Custody
20% Certified Forest Content,
80% Certified Sourcing
www.sfiprogram.org
SFI-01042
APPLIES TO TEXT STOCK ONLY

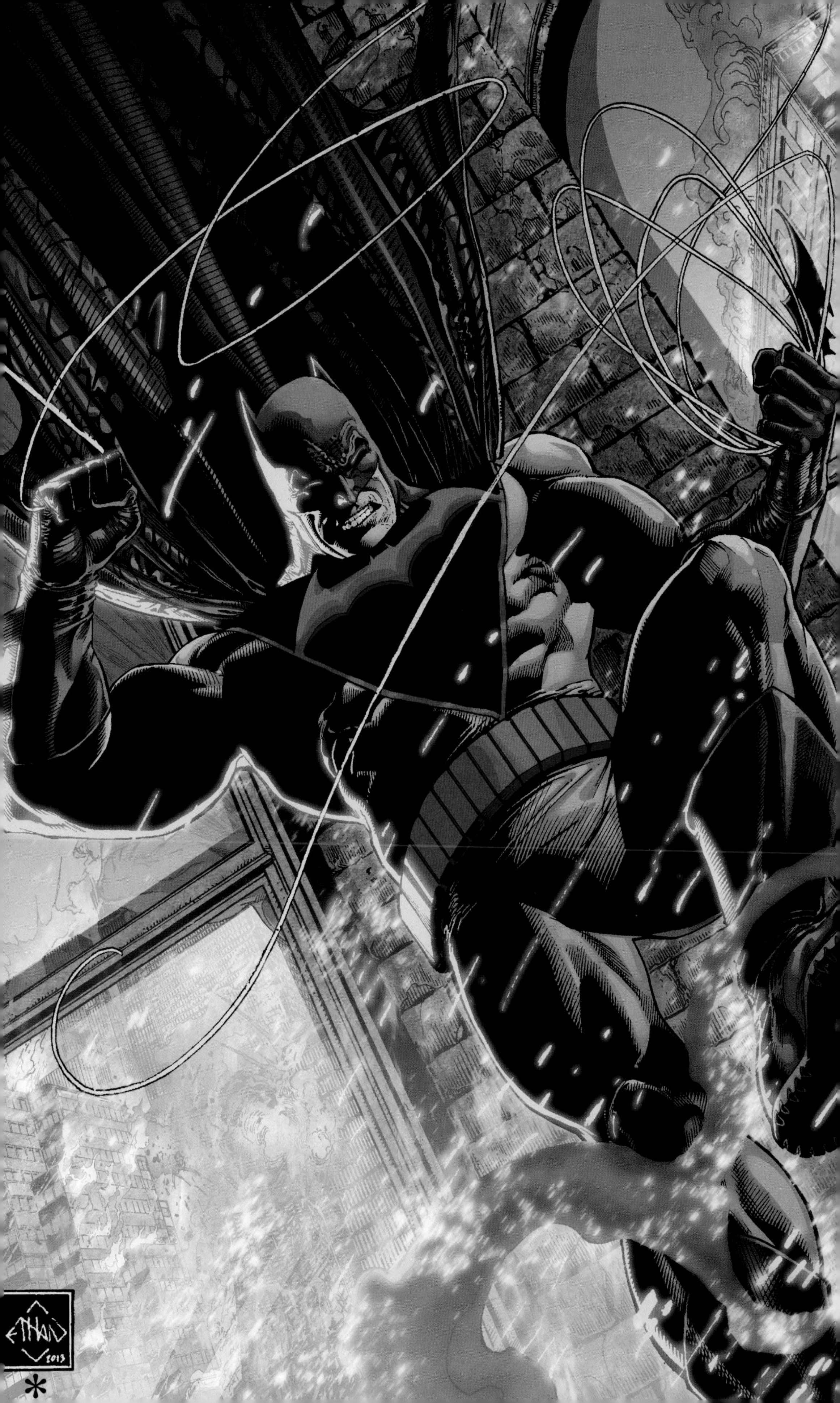

THE DARK AGE
PART 1

TOM TAYLOR
writer

NICOLA SCOTT
penciller

TREVOR SCOTT
inker

ETHAN VAN SCIVER & HI-FI
cover artists

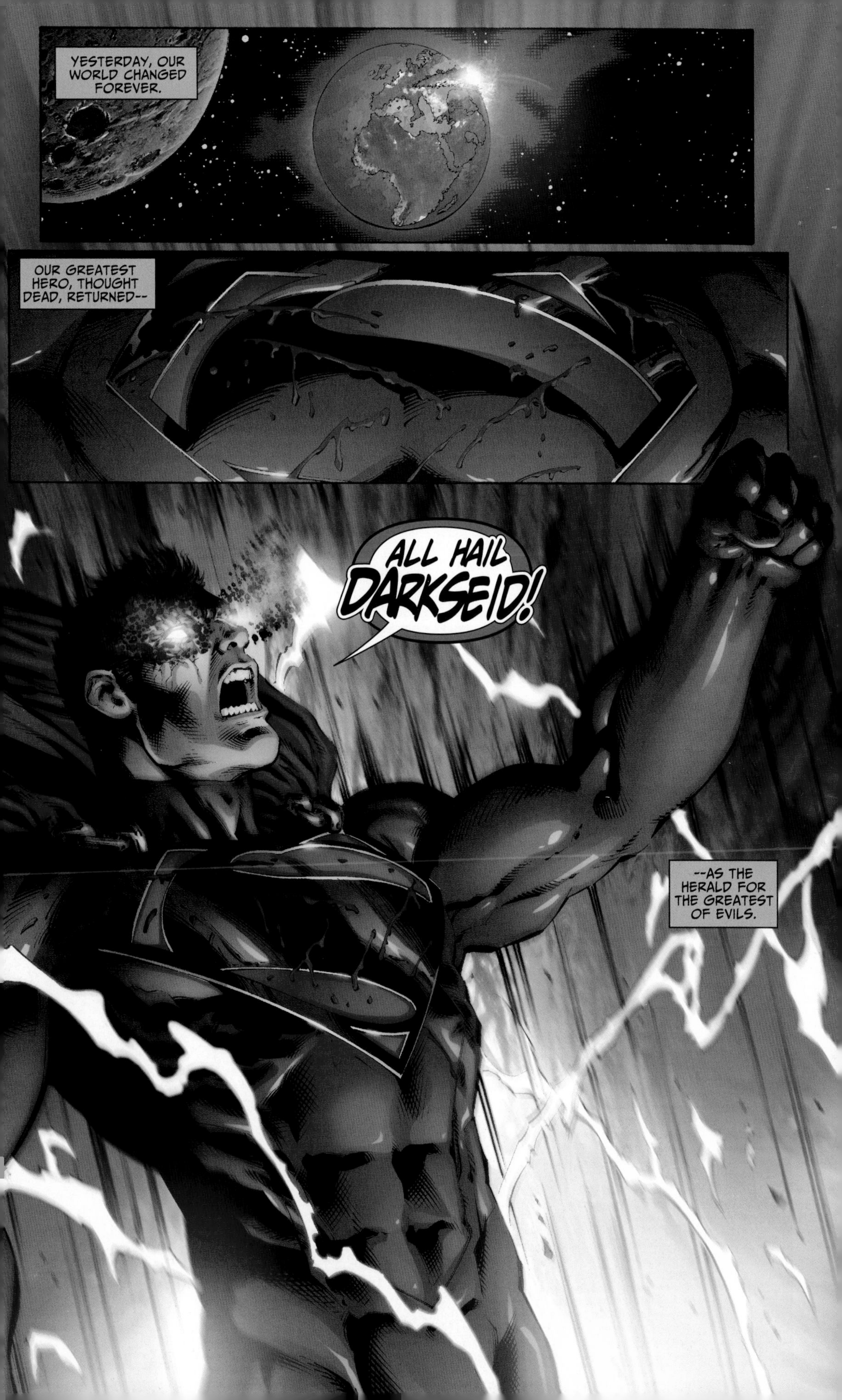
YESTERDAY, OUR WORLD CHANGED FOREVER.
OUR GREATEST HERO, THOUGHT DEAD, RETURNED--
ALL HAIL DARKSEID!
--AS THE HERALD FOR THE GREATEST OF EVILS.

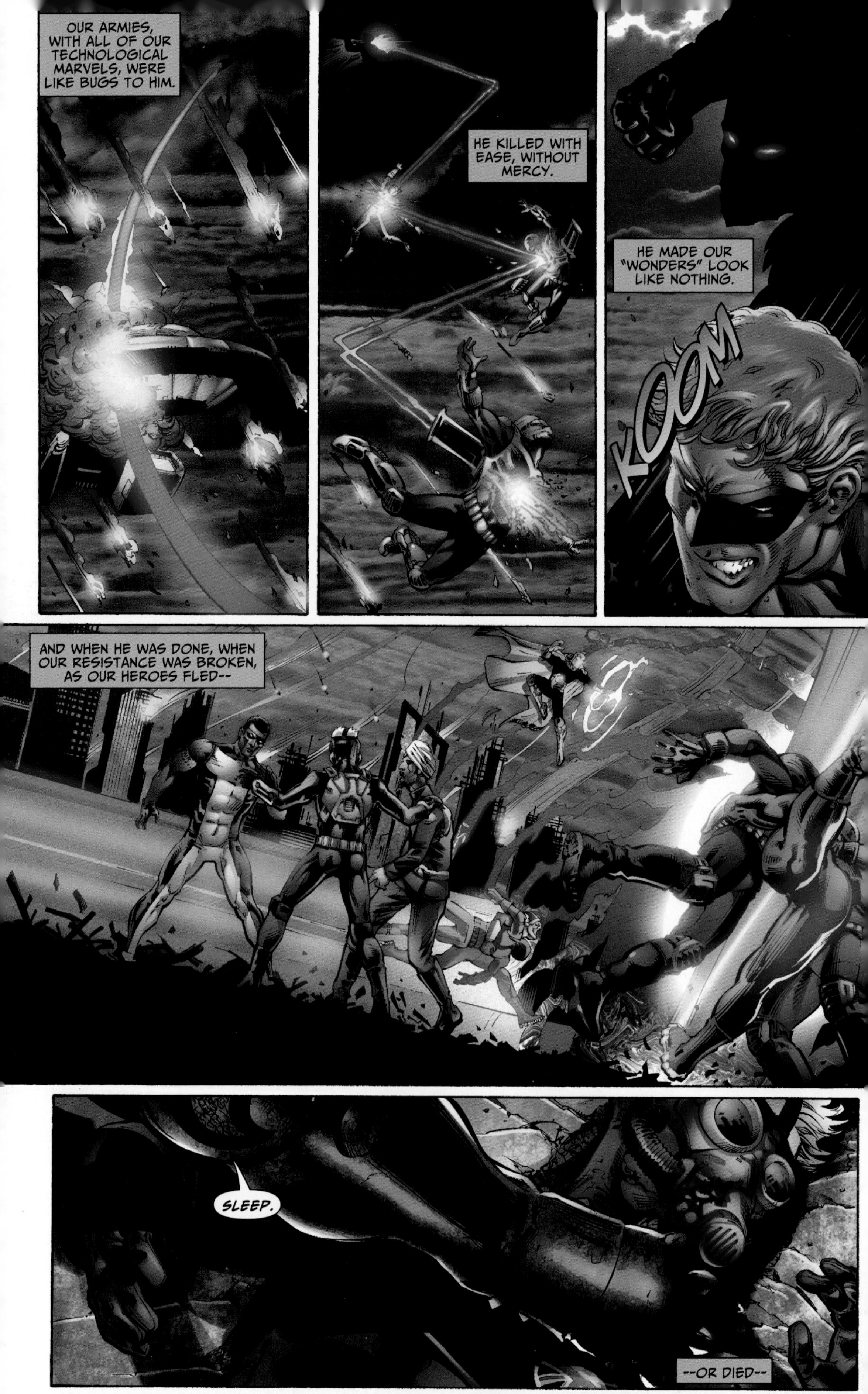
OUR ARMIES, WITH ALL OF OUR TECHNOLOGICAL MARVELS, WERE LIKE BUGS TO HIM.
HE KILLED WITH EASE, WITHOUT MERCY.
HE MADE OUR "WONDERS" LOOK LIKE NOTHING.
KOOM
AND WHEN HE WAS DONE, WHEN OUR RESISTANCE WAS BROKEN, AS OUR HEROES FLED--
SLEEP.
--OR DIED--

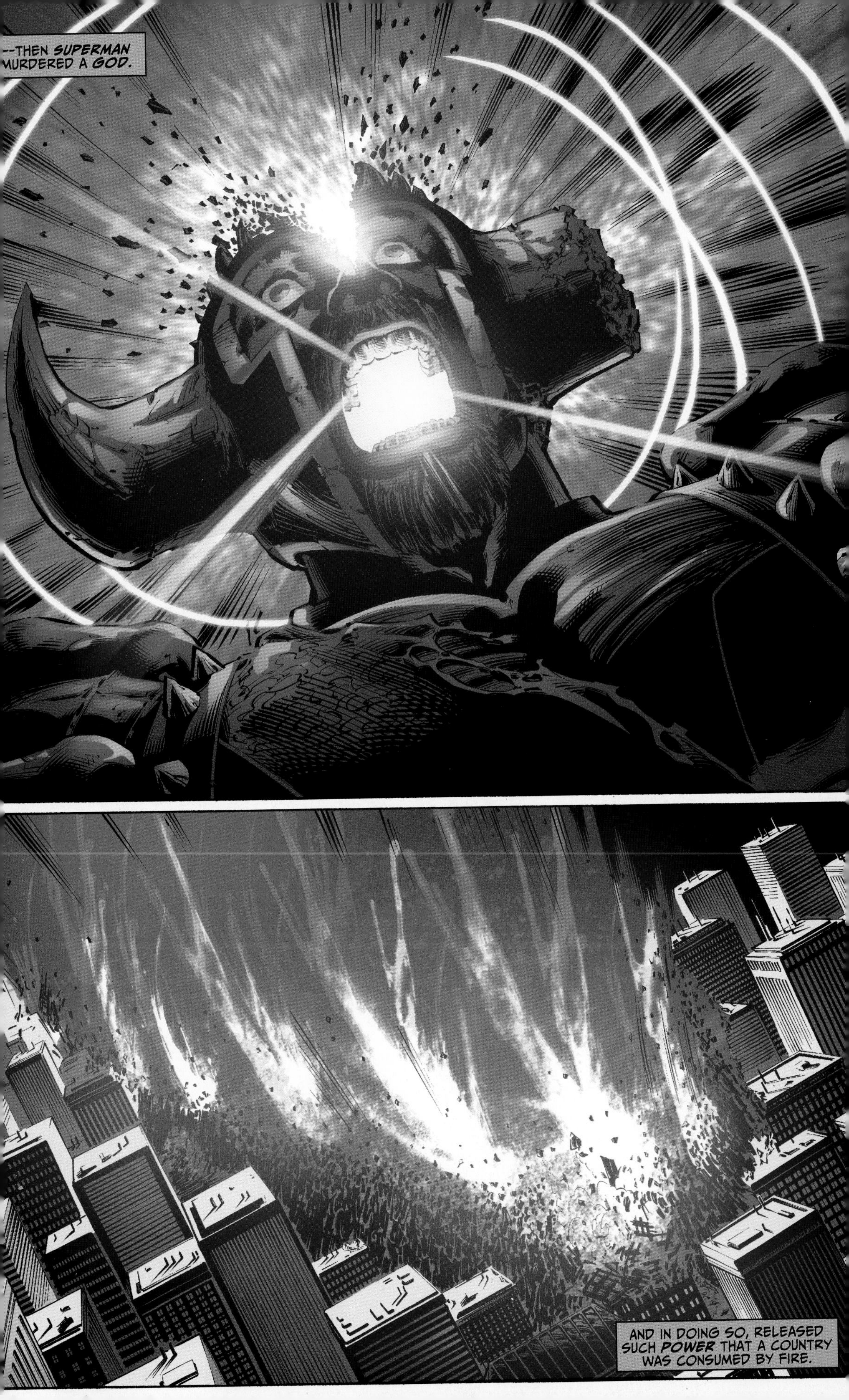
--THEN SUPERMAN MURDERED A GOD.
AND IN DOING SO, RELEASED SUCH POWER THAT A COUNTRY WAS CONSUMED BY FIRE.

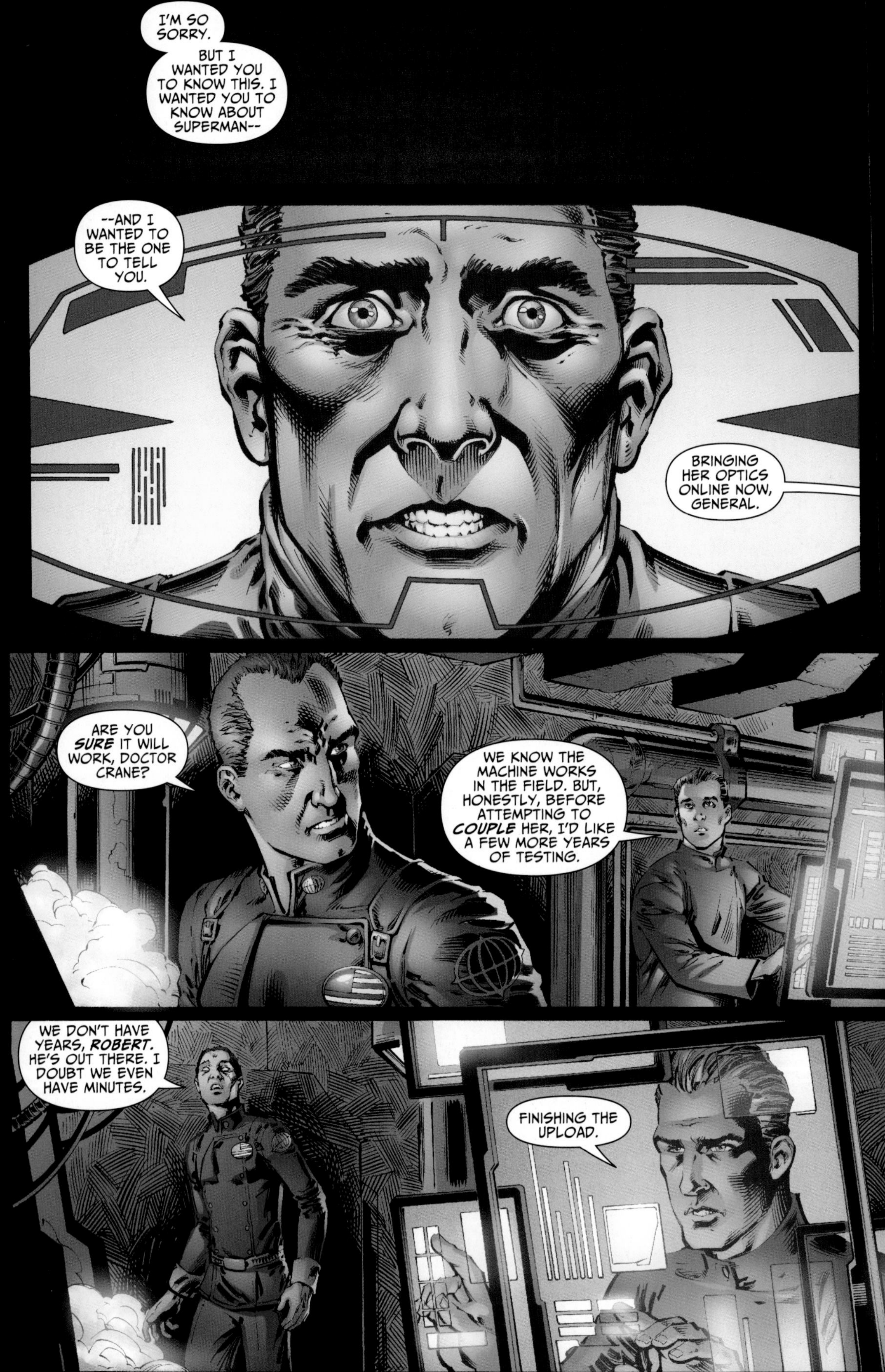

I'M SO SORRY.
BUT I WANTED YOU TO KNOW THIS. I WANTED YOU TO KNOW ABOUT SUPERMAN--
--AND I WANTED TO BE THE ONE TO TELL YOU.
BRINGING HER OPTICS ONLINE NOW, GENERAL.
ARE YOU SURE IT WILL WORK, DOCTOR CRANE?
WE KNOW THE MACHINE WORKS IN THE FIELD. BUT, HONESTLY, BEFORE ATTEMPTING TO COUPLE HER, I'D LIKE A FEW MORE YEARS OF TESTING.
WE DON'T HAVE YEARS, ROBERT. HE'S OUT THERE. I DOUBT WE EVEN HAVE MINUTES.
FINISHING THE UPLOAD.

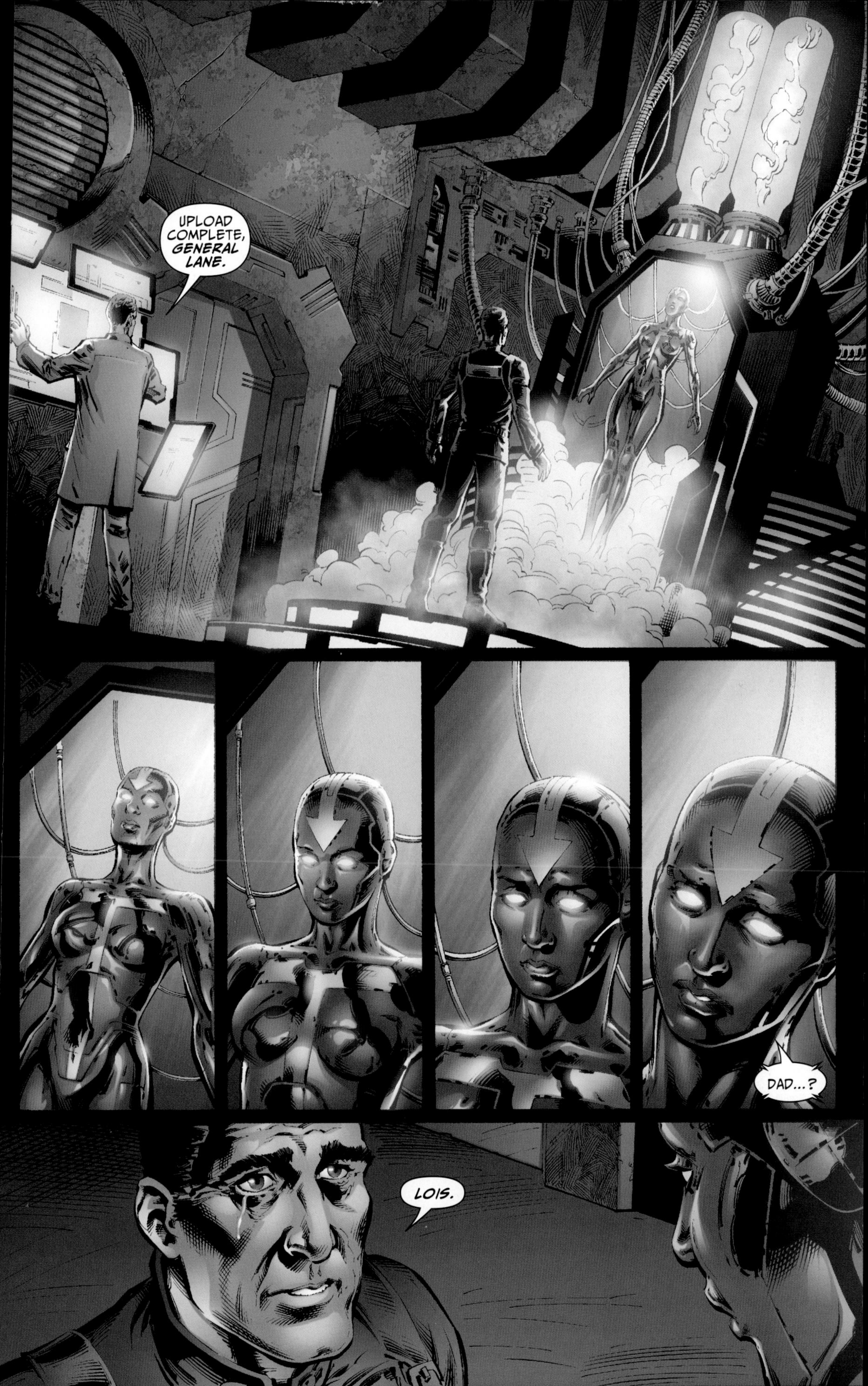
UPLOAD COMPLETE, GENERAL LANE.
DAD...?
LOIS.

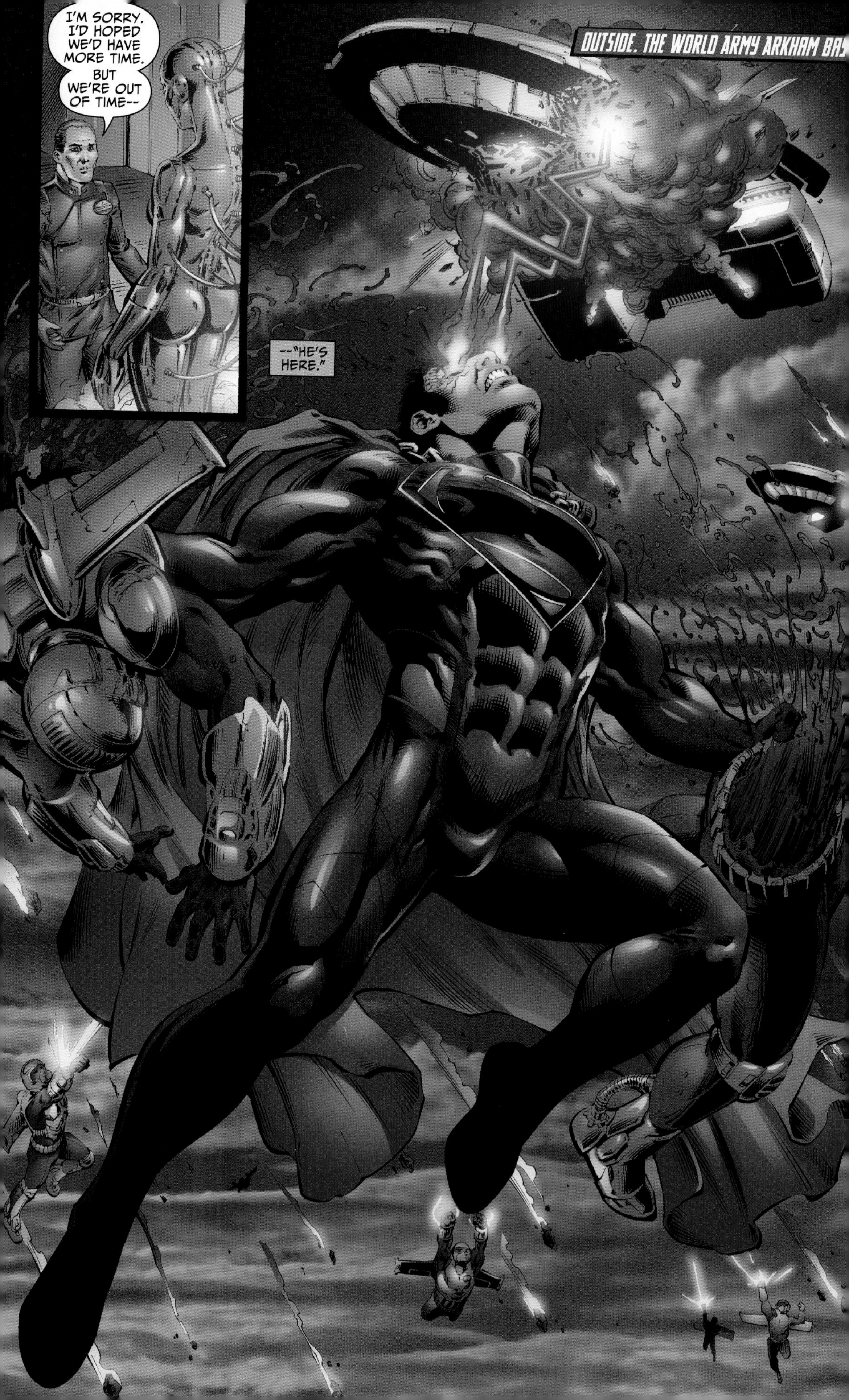
I'M SORRY. I'D HOPED WE'D HAVE MORE TIME. BUT WE'RE OUT OF TIME--
OUTSIDE. THE WORLD ARMY ARKHAM BAS
--"HE'S HERE."

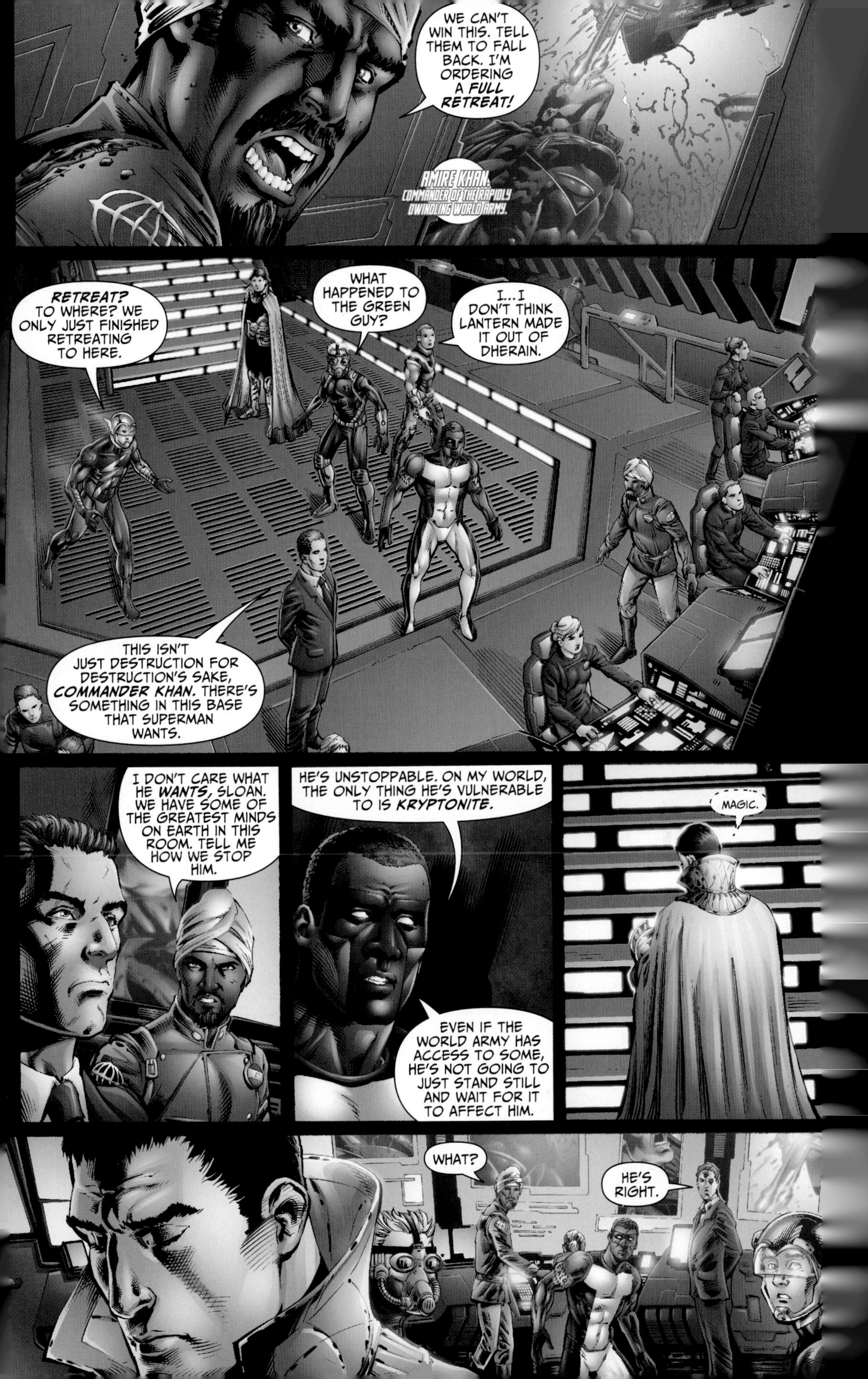
WE CAN'T WIN THIS. TELL THEM TO FALL BACK. I'M ORDERING A FULL RETREAT!
AMIRE KHAN. COMMANDER OF THE RAPIDLY DWINDLING WORLD ARMY.
RETREAT? TO WHERE? WE ONLY JUST FINISHED RETREATING TO HERE.
WHAT HAPPENED TO THE GREEN GUY?
I...I DON'T THINK LANTERN MADE IT OUT OF DHERAIN.
THIS ISN'T JUST DESTRUCTION FOR DESTRUCTION'S SAKE, COMMANDER KHAN. THERE'S SOMETHING IN THIS BASE THAT SUPERMAN WANTS.
I DON'T CARE WHAT HE WANTS, SLOAN. WE HAVE SOME OF THE GREATEST MINDS ON EARTH IN THIS ROOM. TELL ME HOW WE STOP HIM.
HE'S UNSTOPPABLE. ON MY WORLD, THE ONLY THING HE'S VULNERABLE TO IS KRYPTONITE.
EVEN IF THE WORLD ARMY HAS ACCESS TO SOME, HE'S NOT GOING TO JUST STAND STILL AND WAIT FOR IT TO AFFECT HIM.
MAGIC.
WHAT?
HE'S RIGHT.

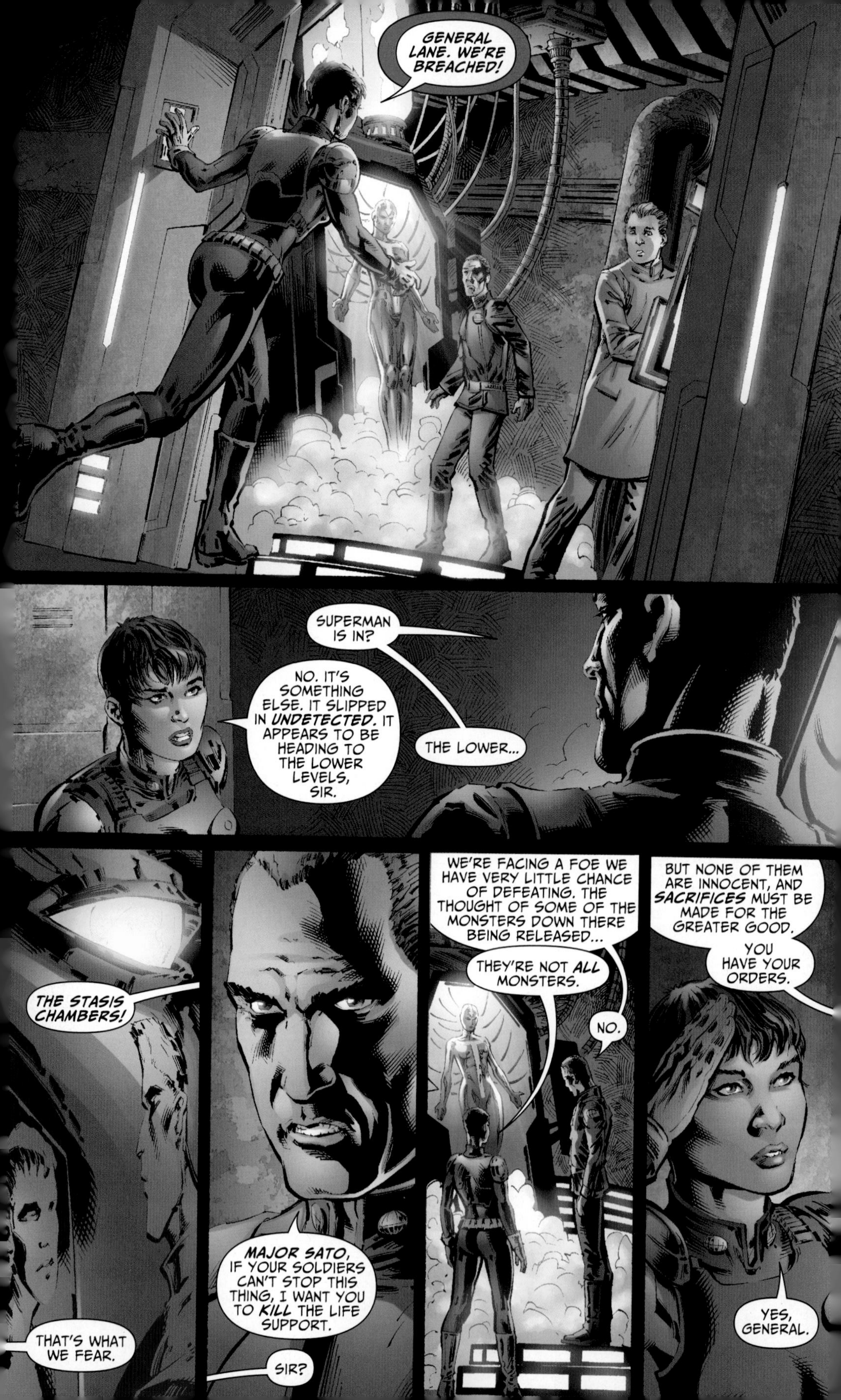
GENERAL LANE. WE'RE BREACHED!
SUPERMAN IS IN?
NO. IT'S SOMETHING ELSE. IT SLIPPED IN UNDETECTED. IT APPEARS TO BE HEADING TO THE LOWER LEVELS, SIR.
THE LOWER...
THE STASIS CHAMBERS!
THAT'S WHAT WE FEAR.
MAJOR SATO, IF YOUR SOLDIERS CAN'T STOP THIS THING, I WANT YOU TO KILL THE LIFE SUPPORT.
SIR?
WE'RE FACING A FOE WE HAVE VERY LITTLE CHANCE OF DEFEATING. THE THOUGHT OF SOME OF THE MONSTERS DOWN THERE BEING RELEASED...
THEY'RE NOT ALL MONSTERS.
NO.
BUT NONE OF THEM ARE INNOCENT, AND SACRIFICES MUST BE MADE FOR THE GREATER GOOD.
YOU HAVE YOUR ORDERS.
YES, GENERAL.

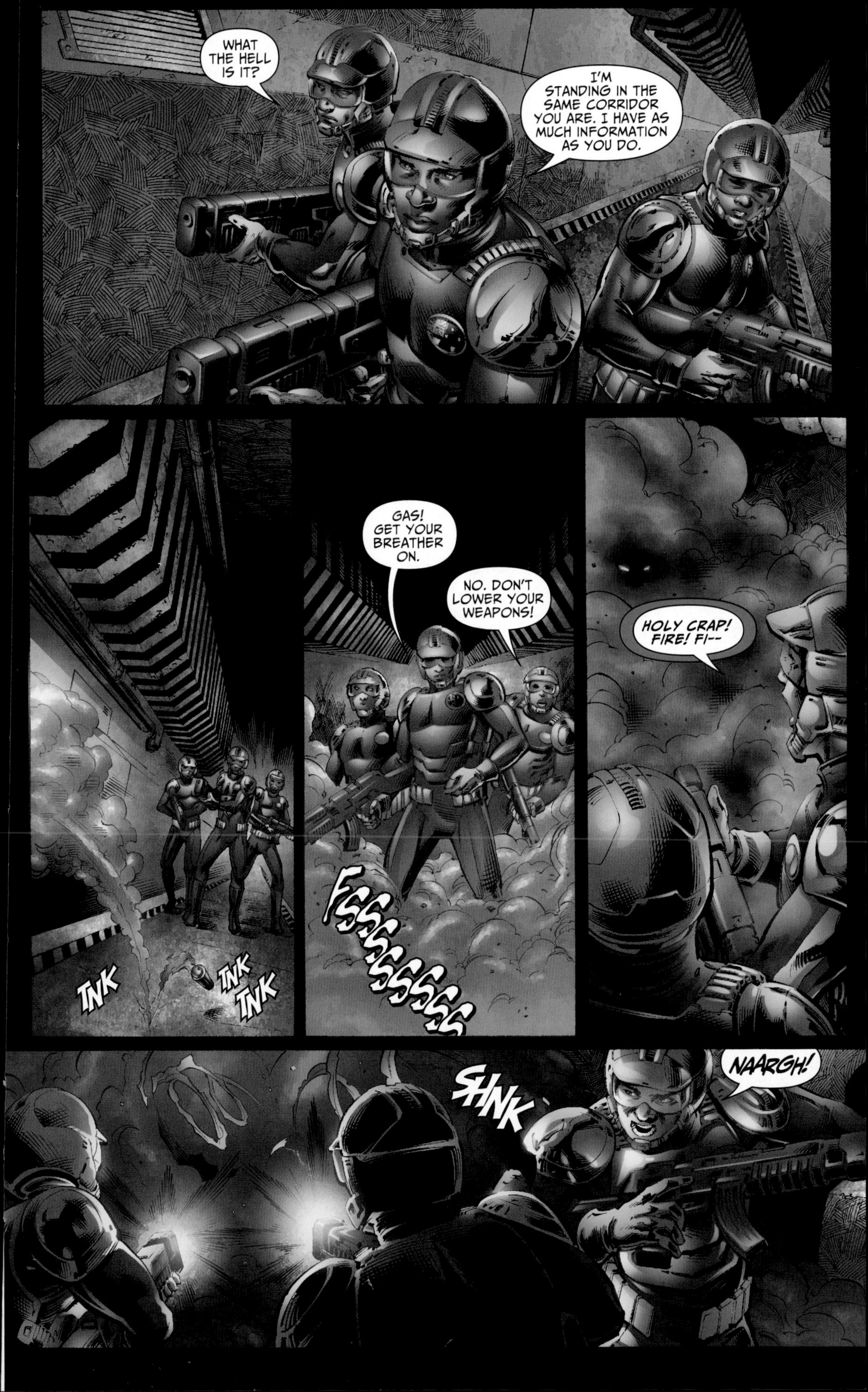
WHAT THE HELL IS IT?
I'M STANDING IN THE SAME CORRIDOR YOU ARE. I HAVE AS MUCH INFORMATION AS YOU DO.
TNK
TNK
TNK
GAS! GET YOUR BREATHER ON.
NO. DON'T LOWER YOUR WEAPONS!
FSSSSSSSSS
HOLY CRAP! FIRE! FI--
SHNK
NAARGH!

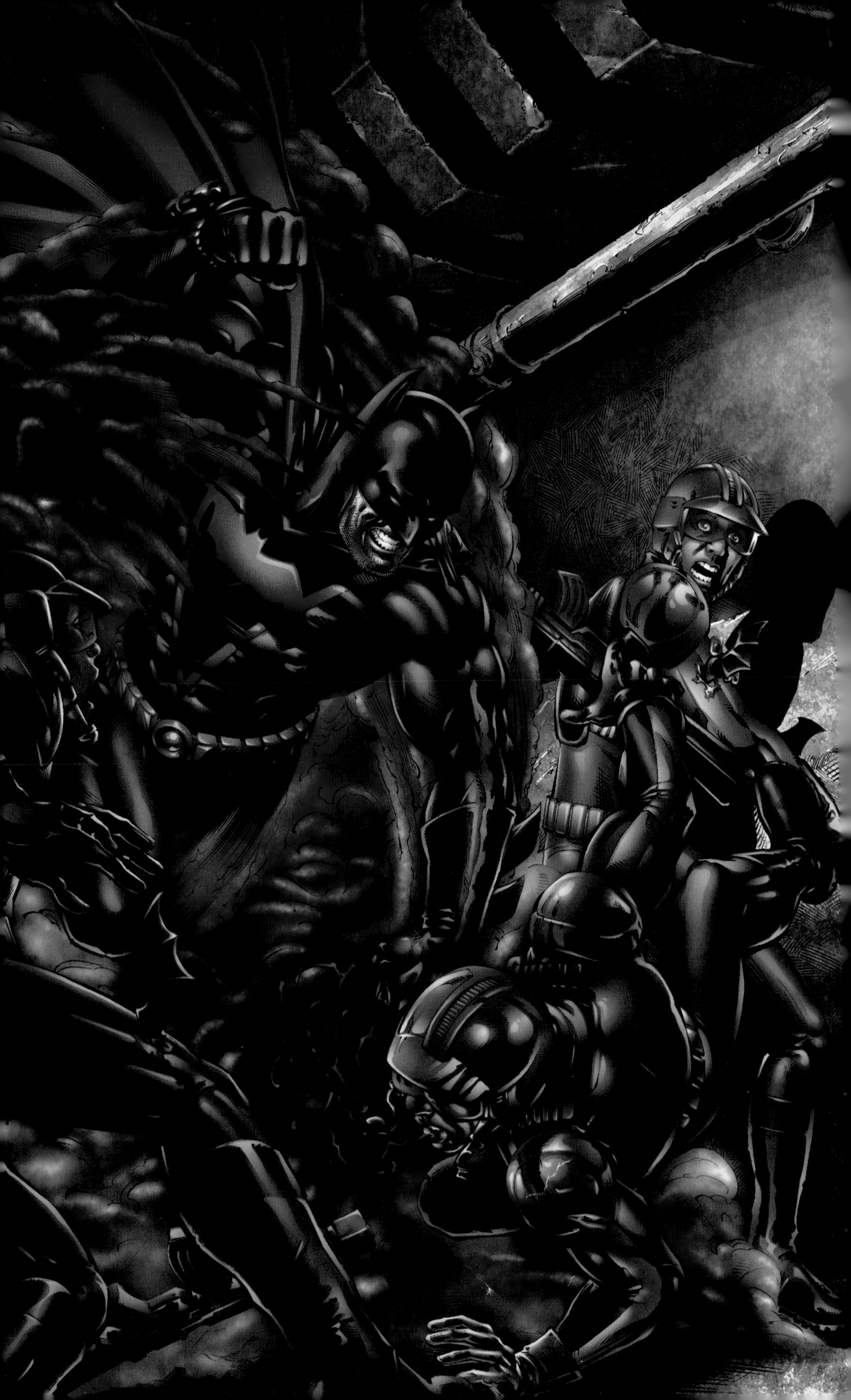

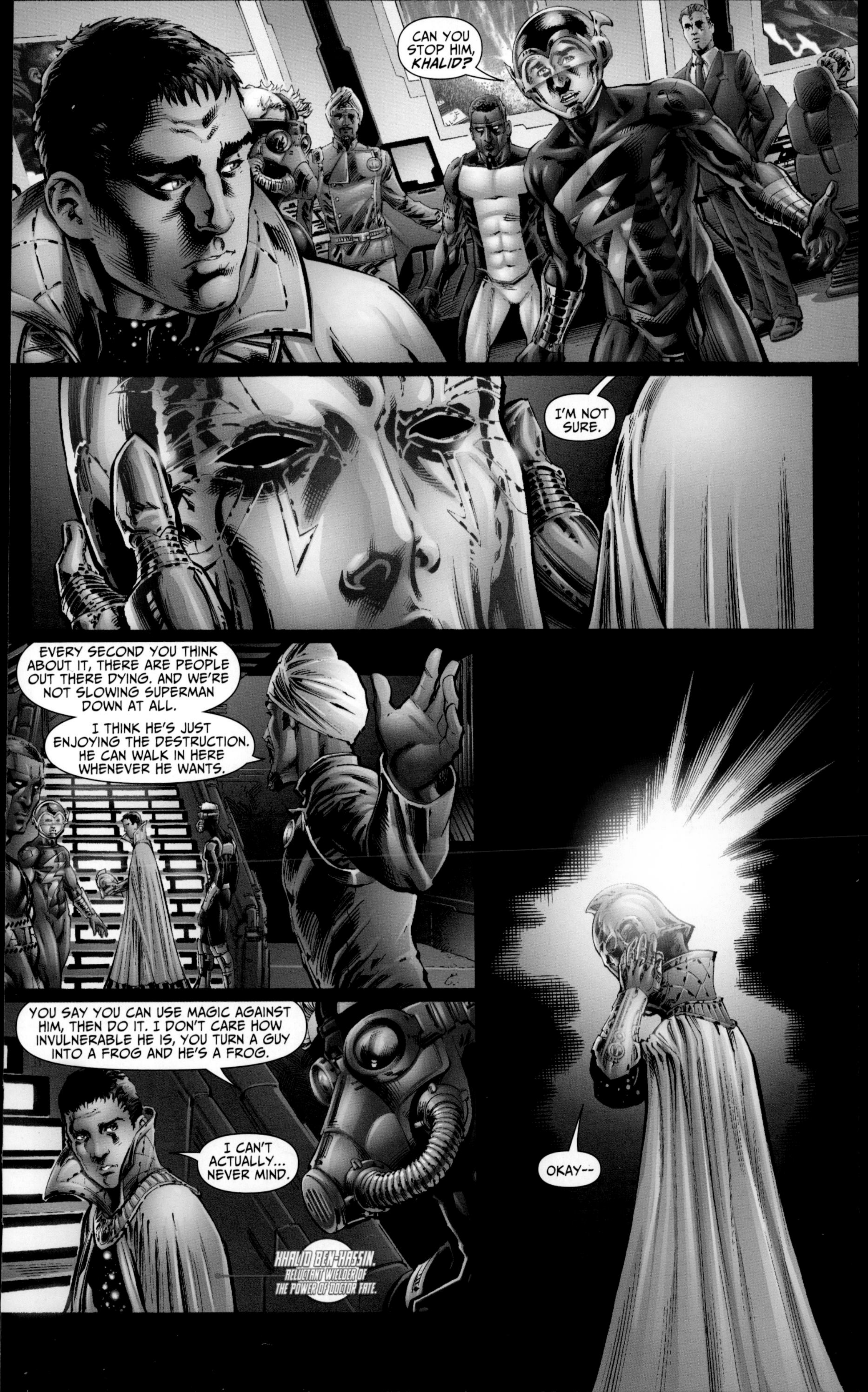
CAN YOU STOP HIM, KHALID?
I'M NOT SURE.
EVERY SECOND YOU THINK ABOUT IT, THERE ARE PEOPLE OUT THERE DYING. AND WE'RE NOT SLOWING SUPERMAN DOWN AT ALL.
I THINK HE'S JUST ENJOYING THE DESTRUCTION. HE CAN WALK IN HERE WHENEVER HE WANTS.
YOU SAY YOU CAN USE MAGIC AGAINST HIM, THEN DO IT. I DON'T CARE HOW INVULNERABLE HE IS, YOU TURN A GUY INTO A FROG AND HE'S A FROG.
I CAN'T ACTUALLY... NEVER MIND.
KHALID BEN-HASSIN.
RELUCTANT WIELDER OF THE POWER OF DOCTOR FATE.
OKAY--

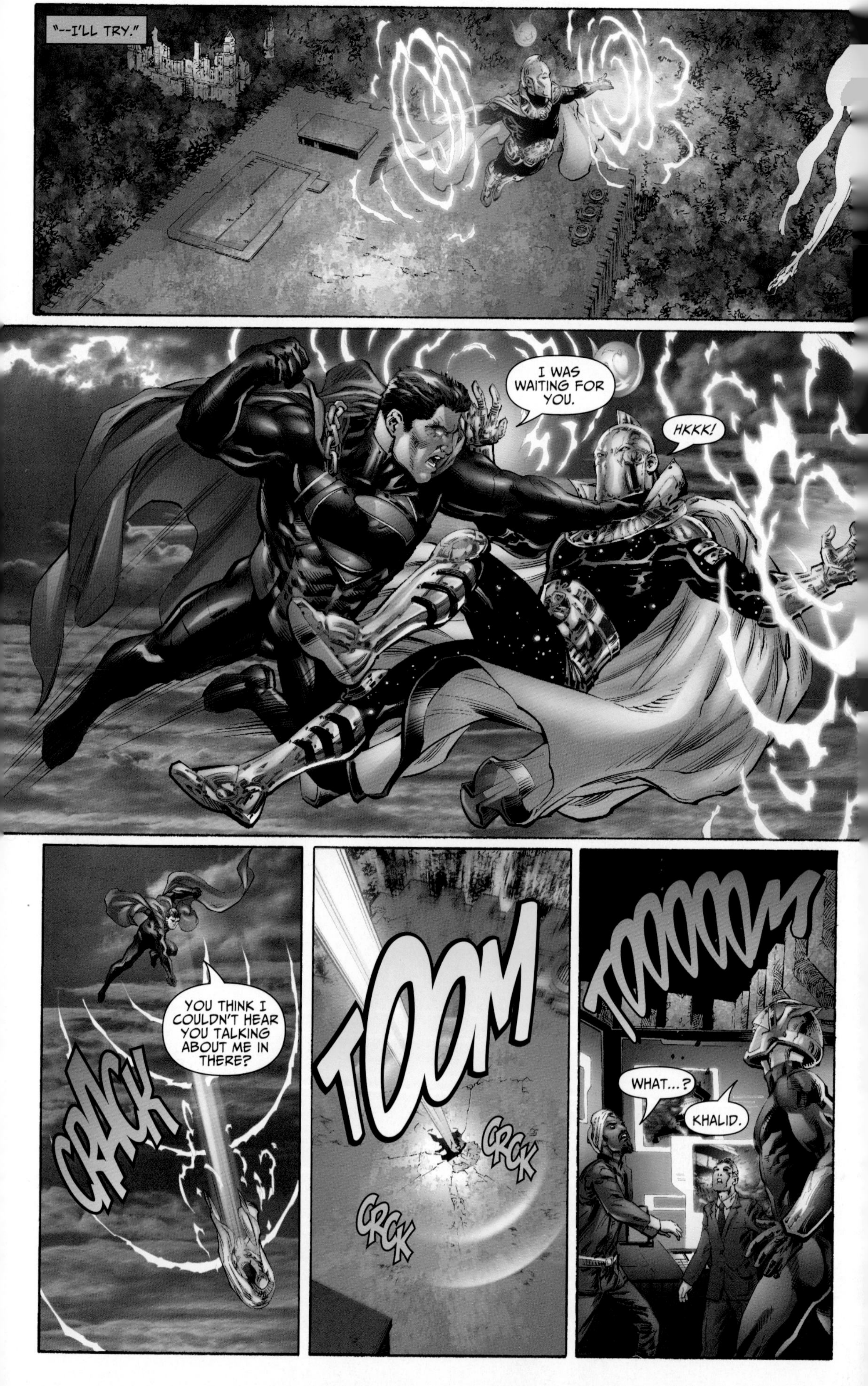
"--I'LL TRY."
I WAS WAITING FOR YOU.
HKKK!
YOU THINK I COULDN'T HEAR YOU TALKING ABOUT ME IN THERE?
CRACK
TOOM
CRCK
CRCK
TOOOOOM
WHAT...?
KHALID.

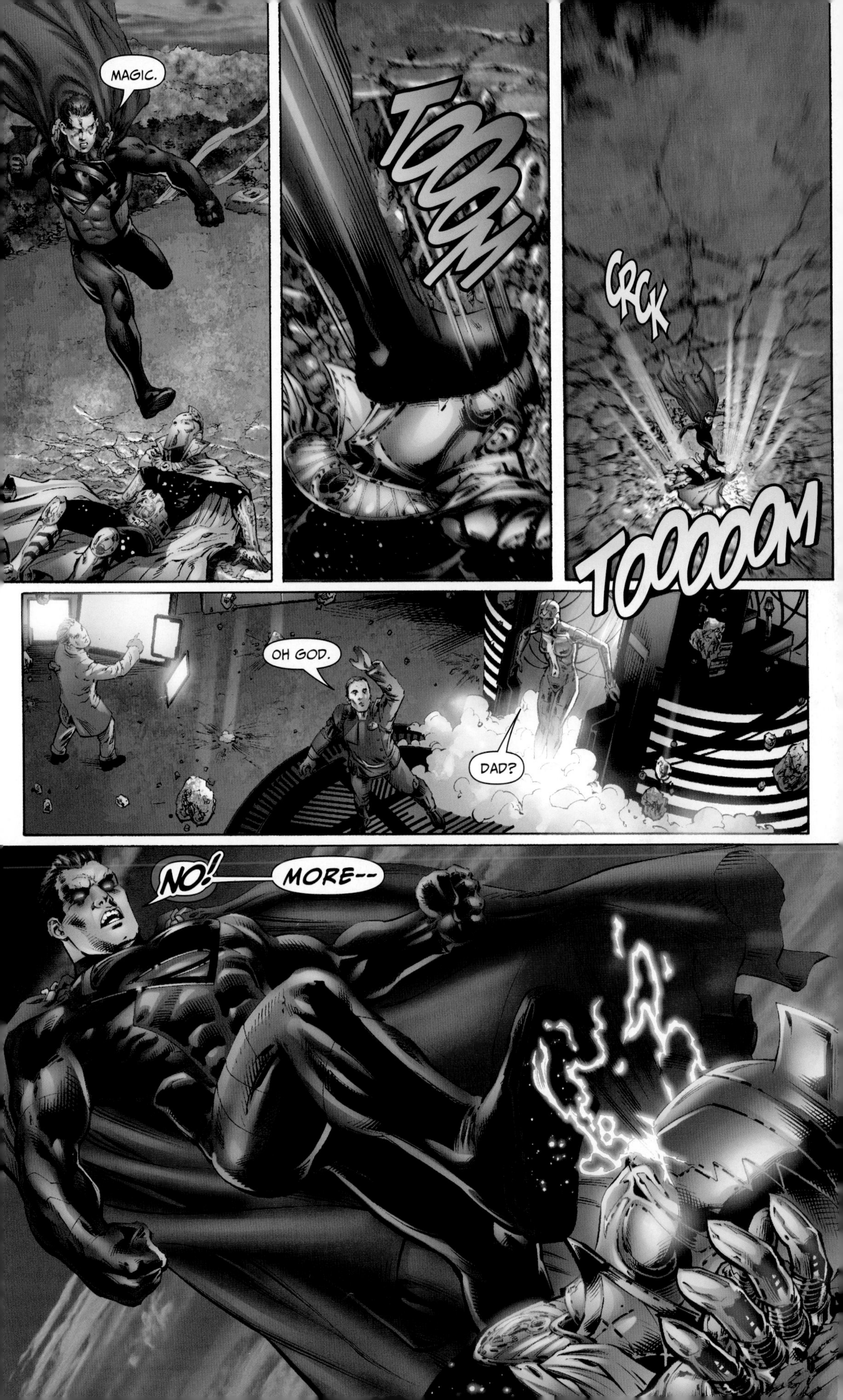
MAGIC.
TOOOM
CRCK
TOOOOOM
OH GOD.
DAD?
NO!
MORE--

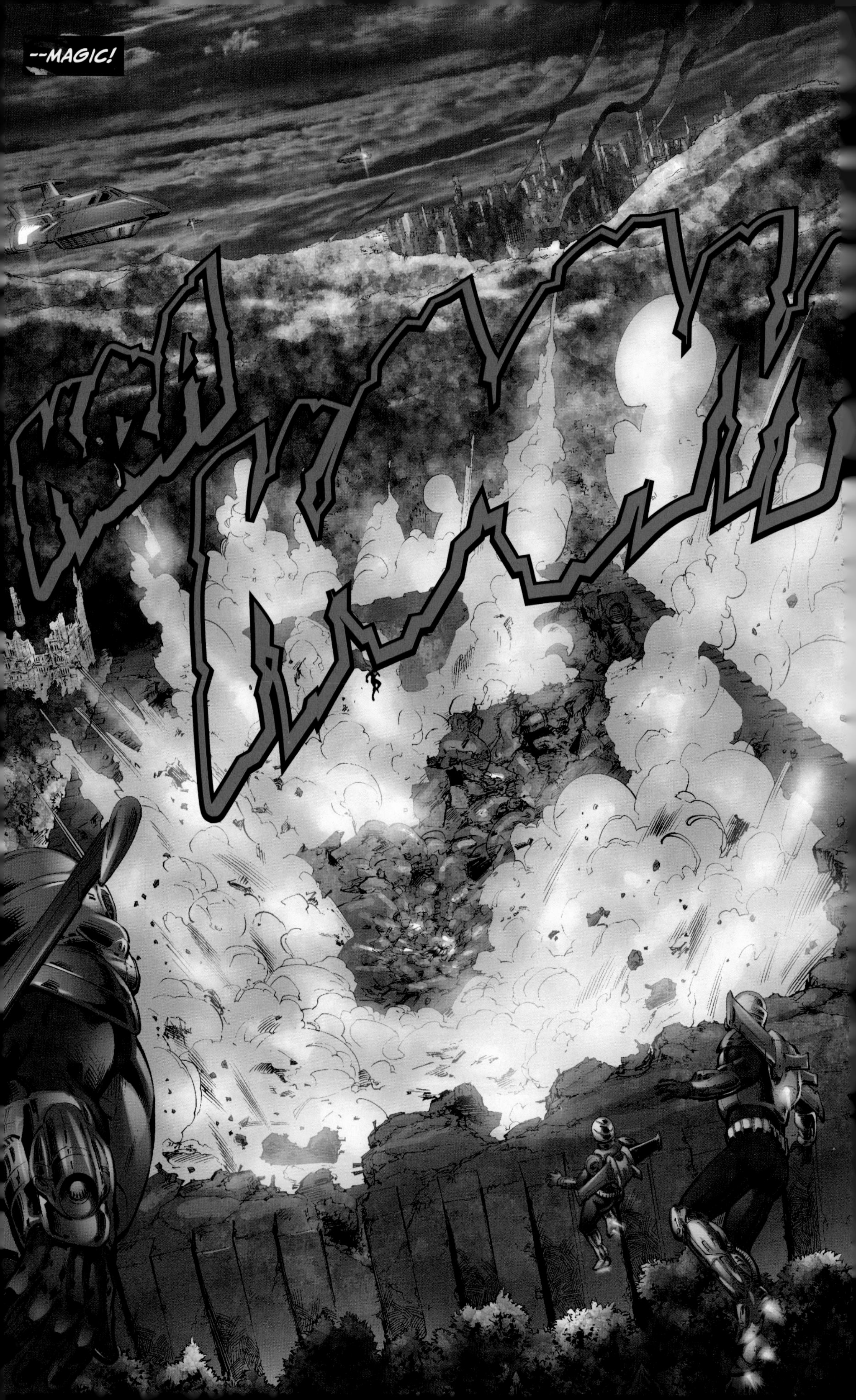
--MAGIC!

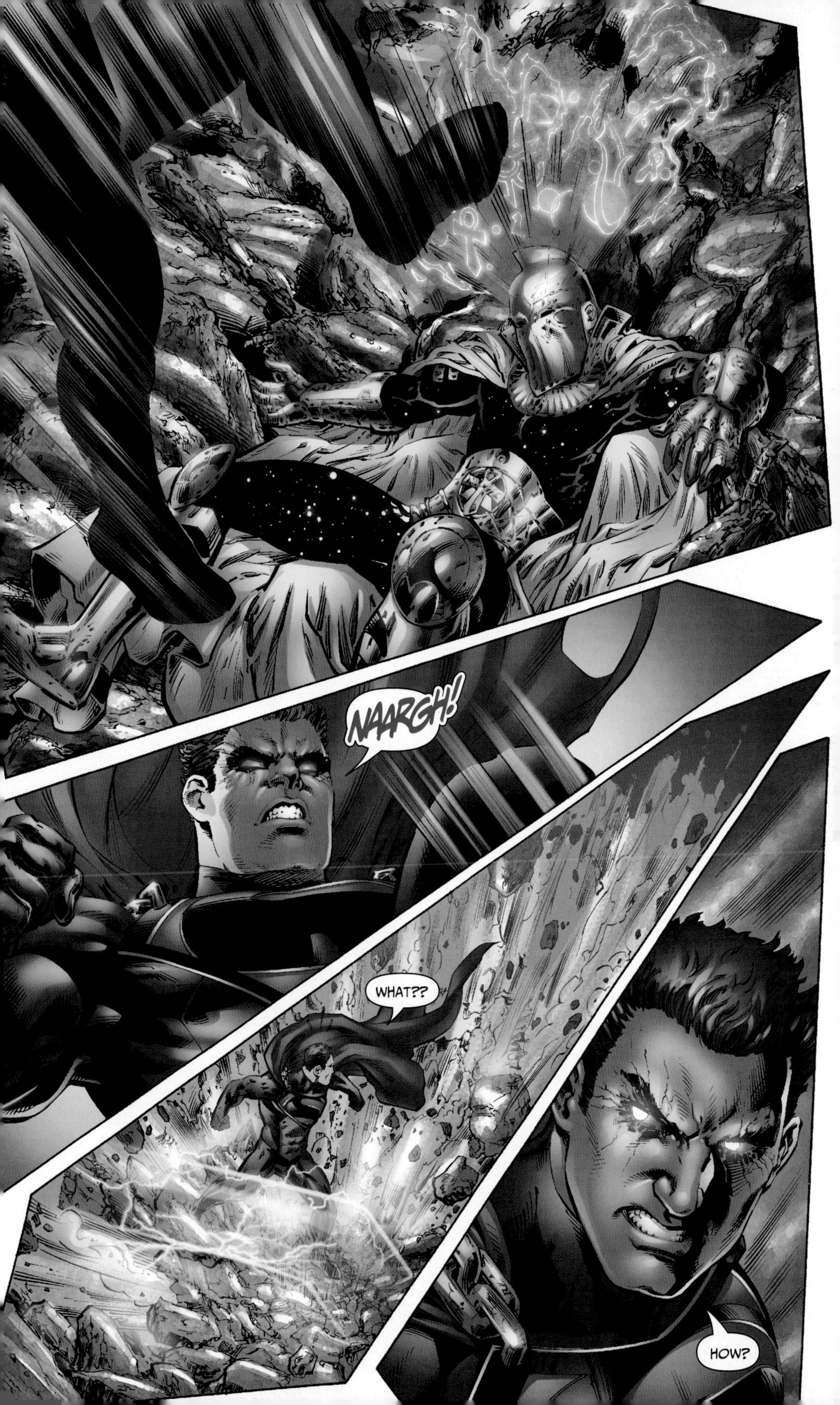
NAARGH!
WHAT??
HOW?

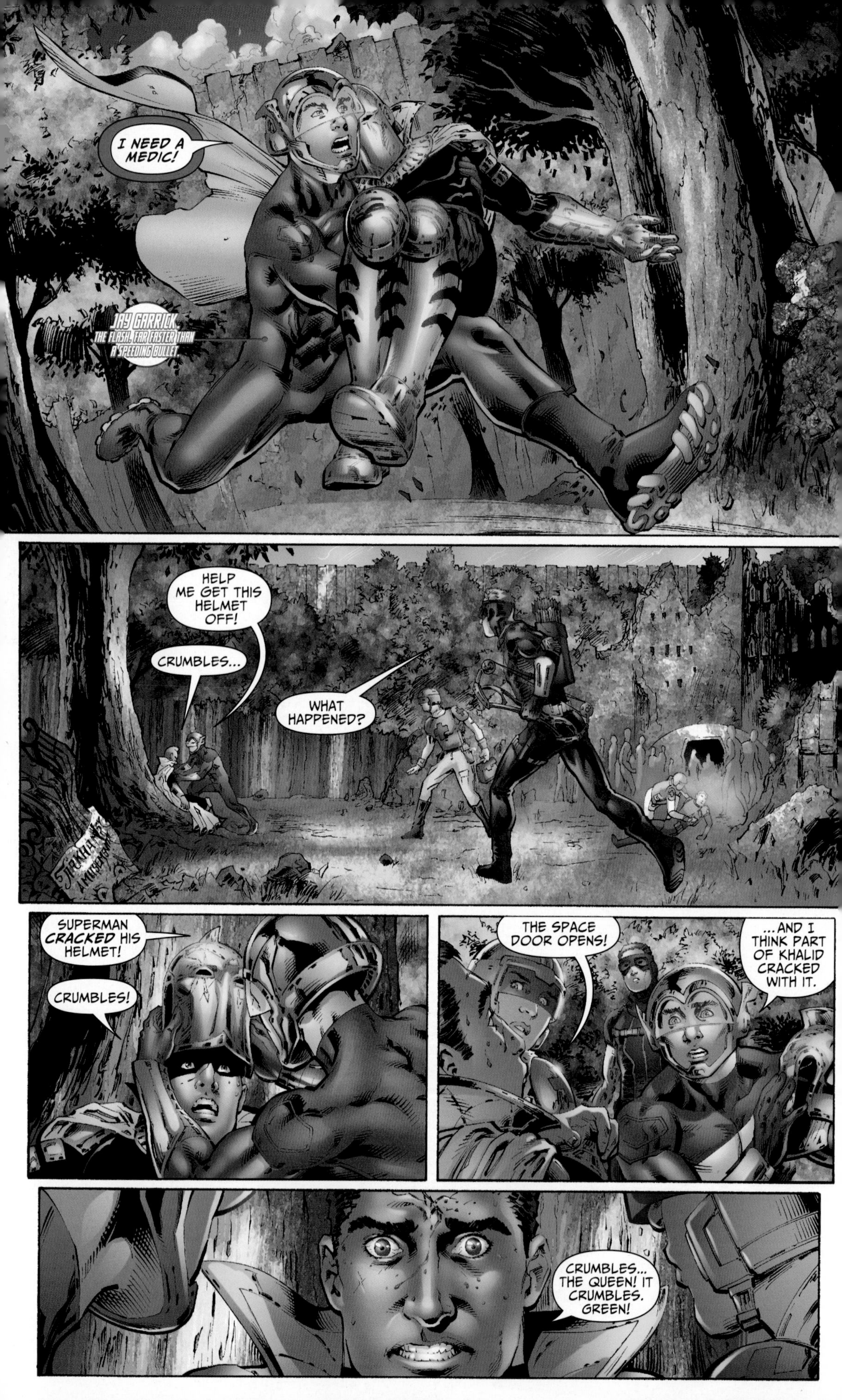
I NEED A MEDIC!
JAY GARRICK. THE FLASH. FAR FASTER THAN A SPEEDING BULLET.
HELP ME GET THIS HELMET OFF!
CRUMBLES...
WHAT HAPPENED?
SUPERMAN CRACKED HIS HELMET!
CRUMBLES!
THE SPACE DOOR OPENS!
...AND I THINK PART OF KHALID CRACKED WITH IT.
CRUMBLES... THE QUEEN! IT CRUMBLES. GREEN!

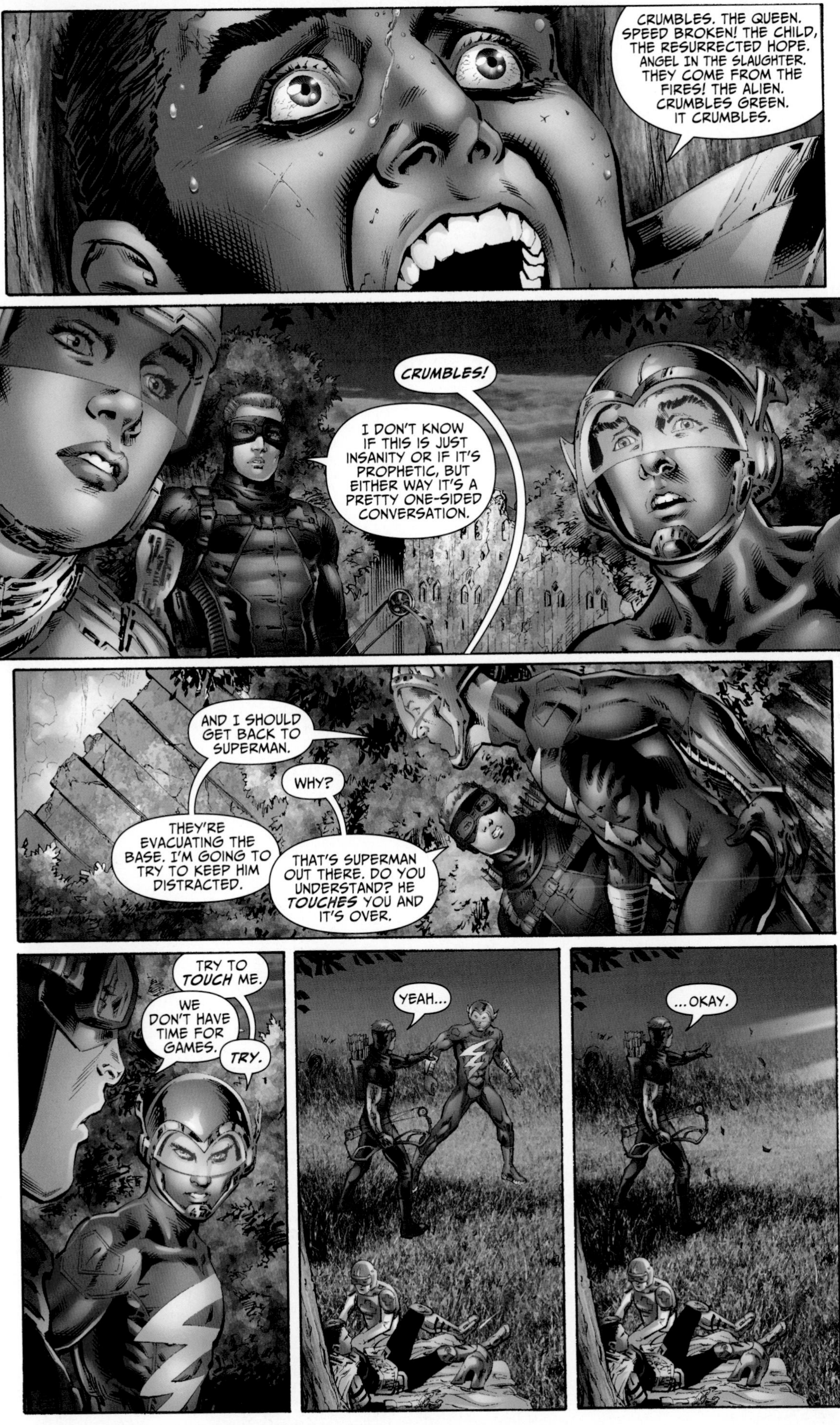
CRUMBLES. THE QUEEN. SPEED BROKEN! THE CHILD, THE RESURRECTED HOPE. ANGEL IN THE SLAUGHTER. THEY COME FROM THE FIRES! THE ALIEN. CRUMBLES GREEN. IT CRUMBLES.
CRUMBLES!
I DON'T KNOW IF THIS IS JUST INSANITY OR IF IT'S PROPHETIC, BUT EITHER WAY IT'S A PRETTY ONE-SIDED CONVERSATION.
AND I SHOULD GET BACK TO SUPERMAN.
WHY?
THEY'RE EVACUATING THE BASE. I'M GOING TO TRY TO KEEP HIM DISTRACTED.
THAT'S SUPERMAN OUT THERE. DO YOU UNDERSTAND? HE TOUCHES YOU AND IT'S OVER.
TRY TO TOUCH ME.
WE DON'T HAVE TIME FOR GAMES.
TRY.
YEAH...
...OKAY.

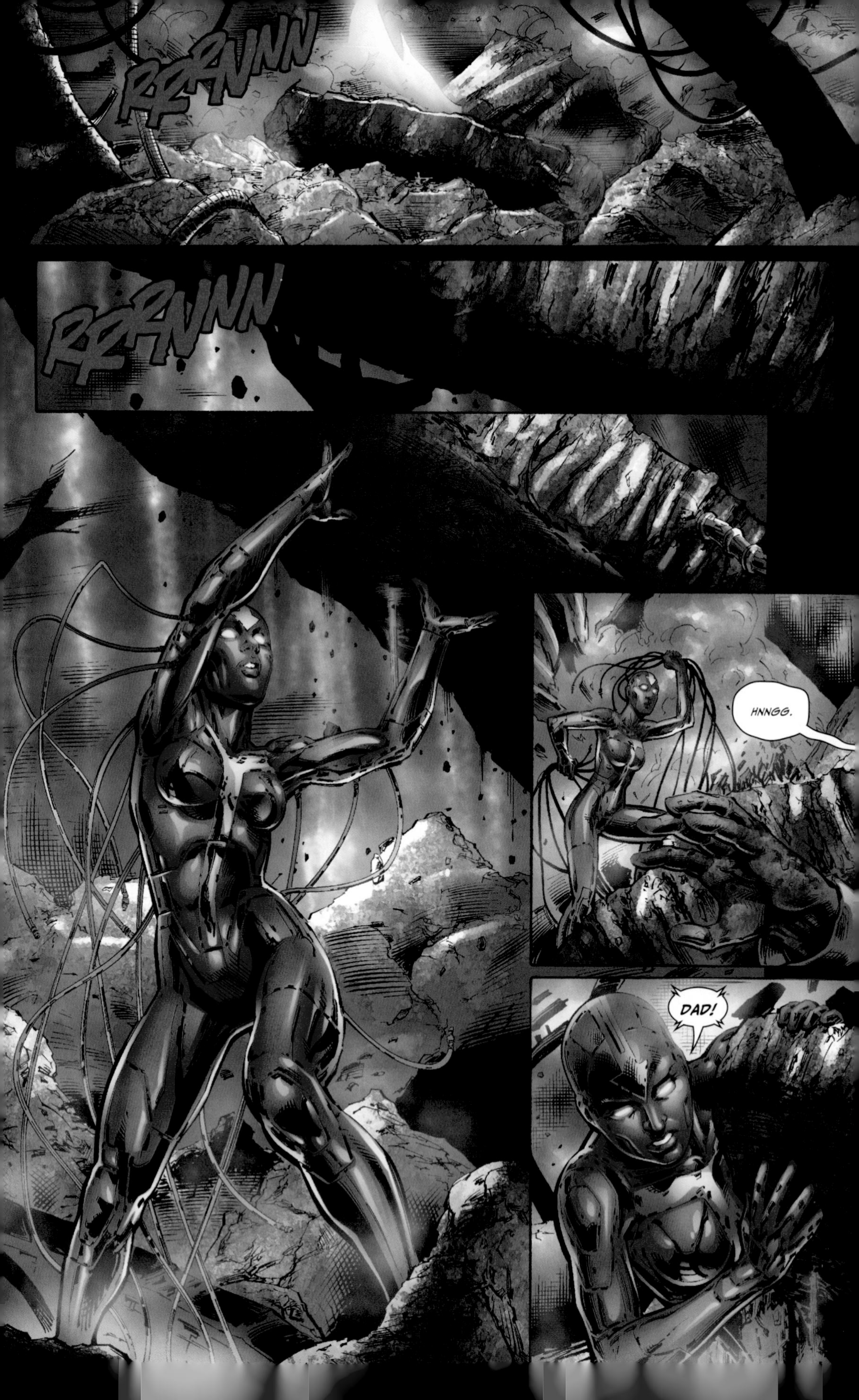
RRRNNN
RRRNNN
HNNGG.
DAD!

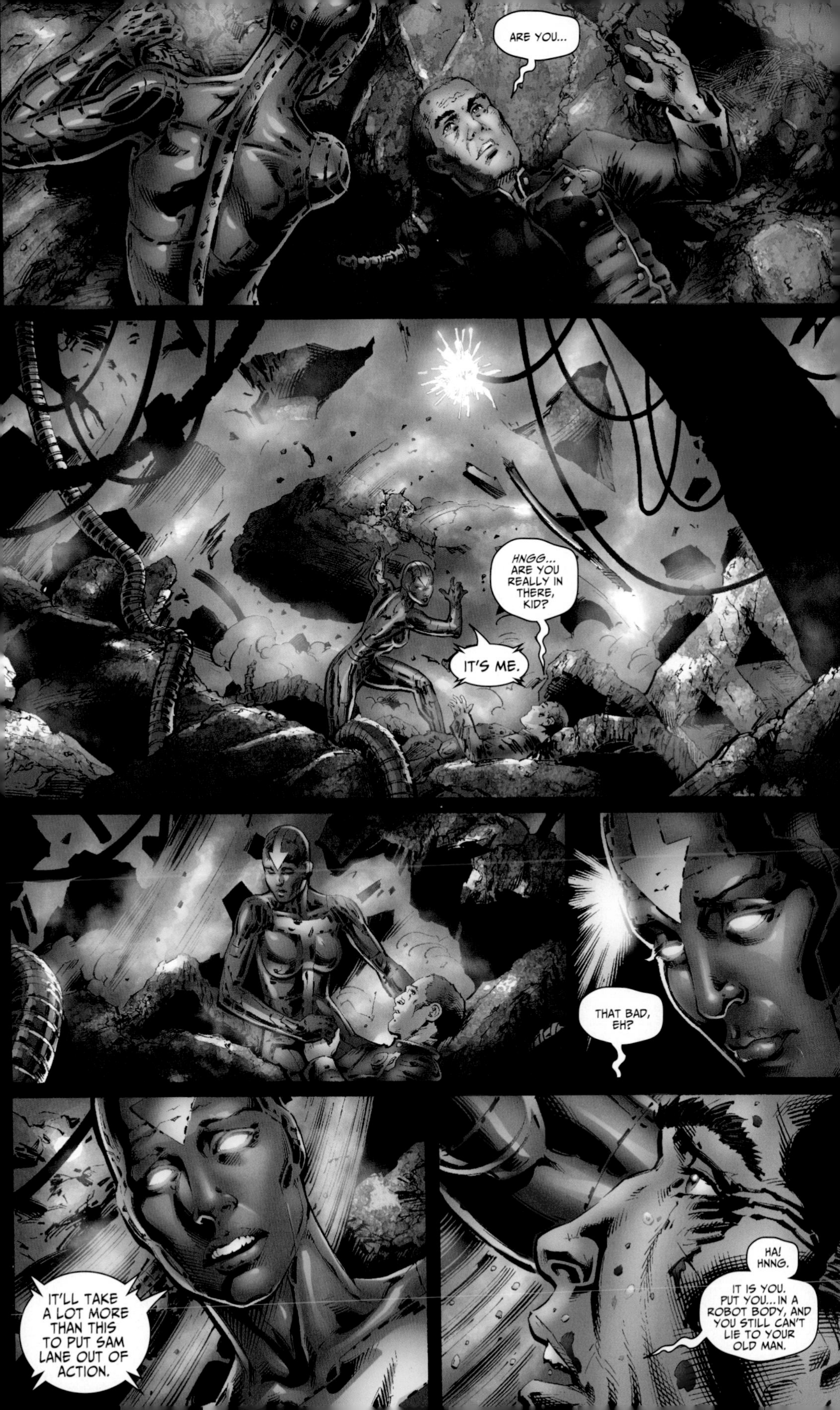
ARE YOU...
HNGG... ARE YOU REALLY IN THERE, KID?
IT'S ME.
THAT BAD, EH?
IT'LL TAKE A LOT MORE THAN THIS TO PUT SAM LANE OUT OF ACTION.
HA! HNNG.
IT IS YOU. PUT YOU...IN A ROBOT BODY, AND YOU STILL CAN'T LIE TO YOUR OLD MAN.

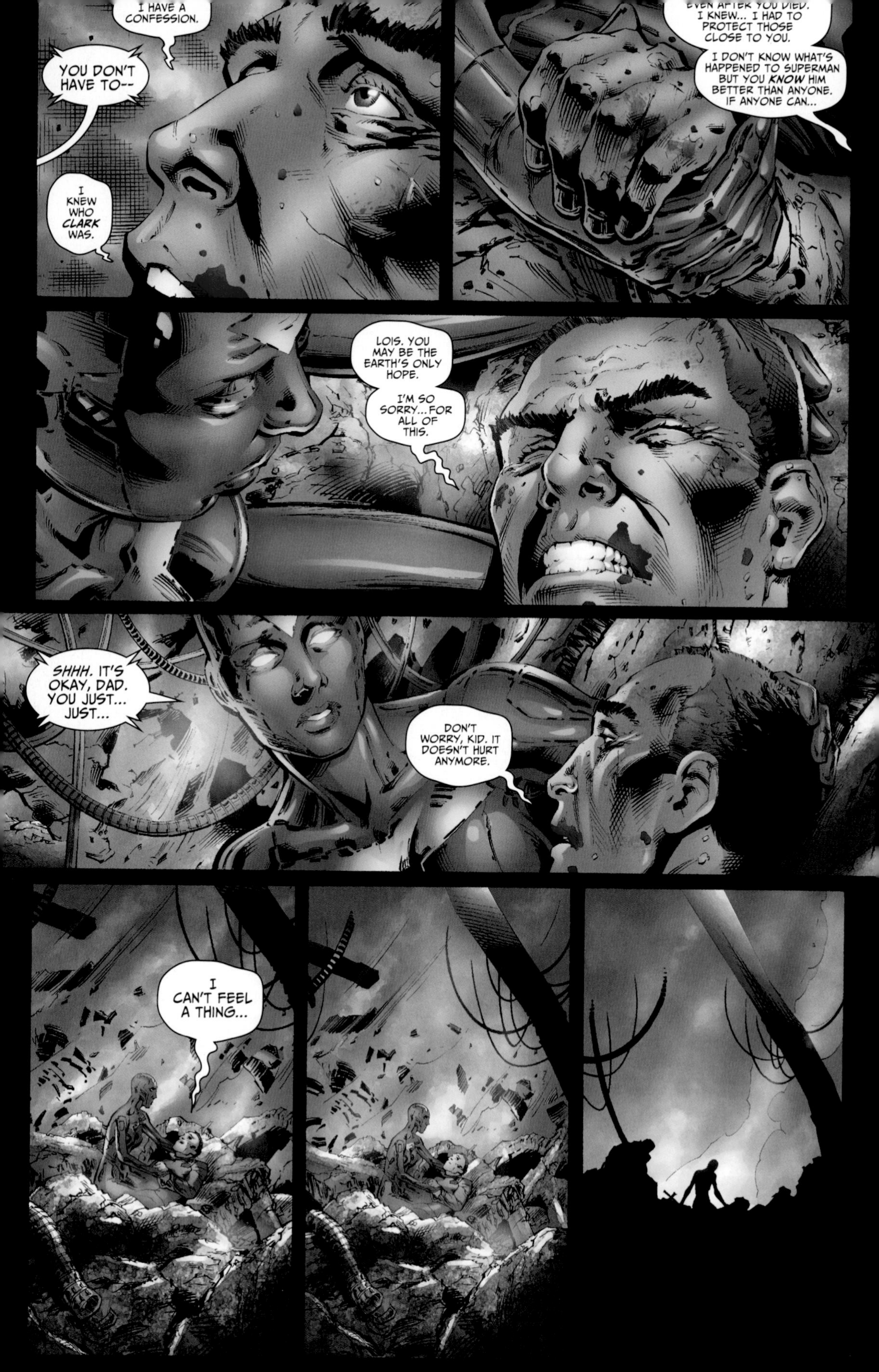
I HAVE A CONFESSION.
YOU DON'T HAVE TO--
I KNEW WHO CLARK WAS.
EVEN AFTER YOU DIED. I KNEW... I HAD TO PROTECT THOSE CLOSE TO YOU.
I DON'T KNOW WHAT'S HAPPENED TO SUPERMAN BUT YOU KNOW HIM BETTER THAN ANYONE. IF ANYONE CAN...
LOIS. YOU MAY BE THE EARTH'S ONLY HOPE.
I'M SO SORRY...FOR ALL OF THIS.
SHHH. IT'S OKAY, DAD. YOU JUST... JUST...
DON'T WORRY, KID. IT DOESN'T HURT ANYMORE.
I CAN'T FEEL A THING...

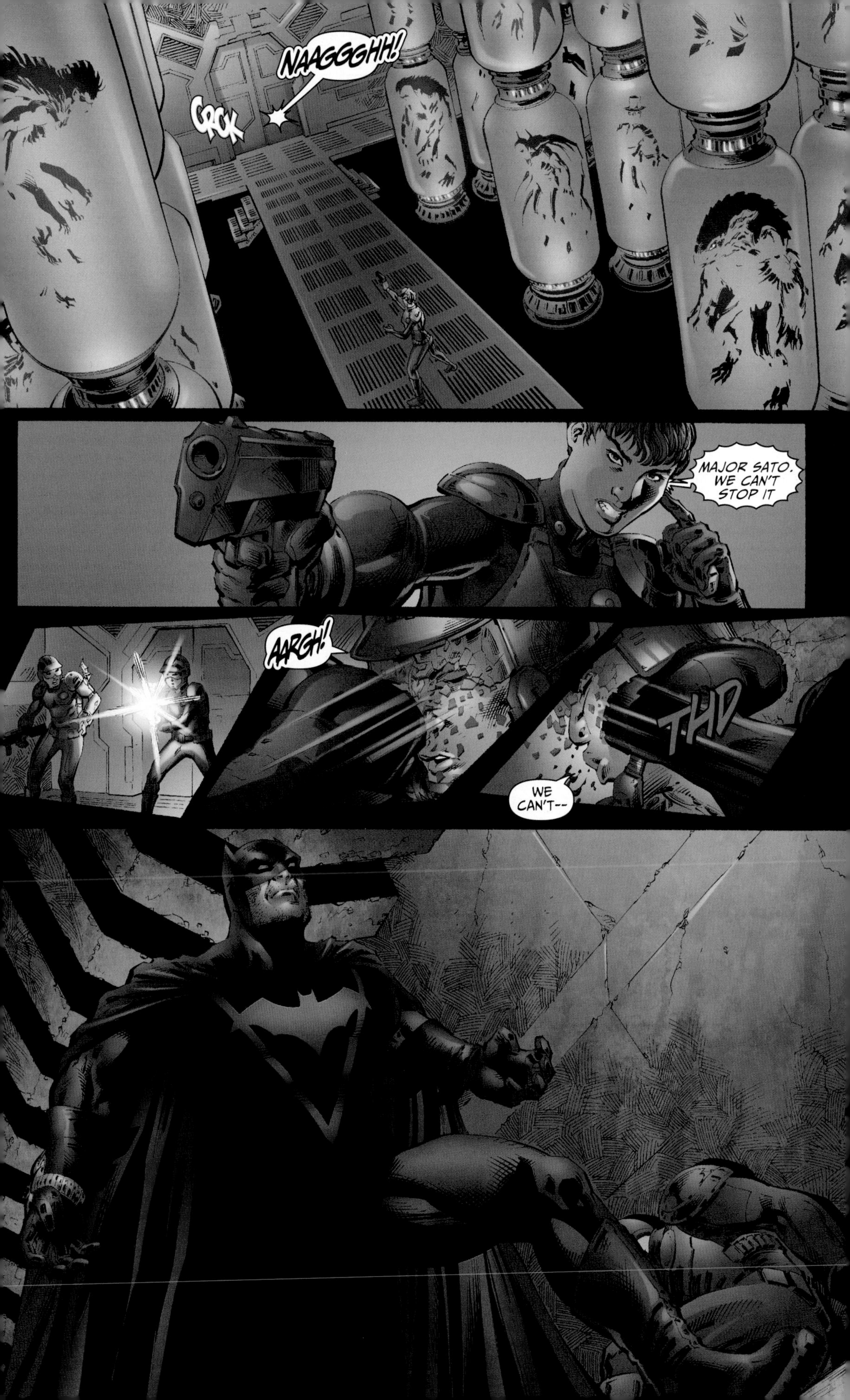
GROK
NAAGGGHH!
MAJOR SATO. WE CAN'T STOP IT
AARGH!
THD
WE CAN'T--

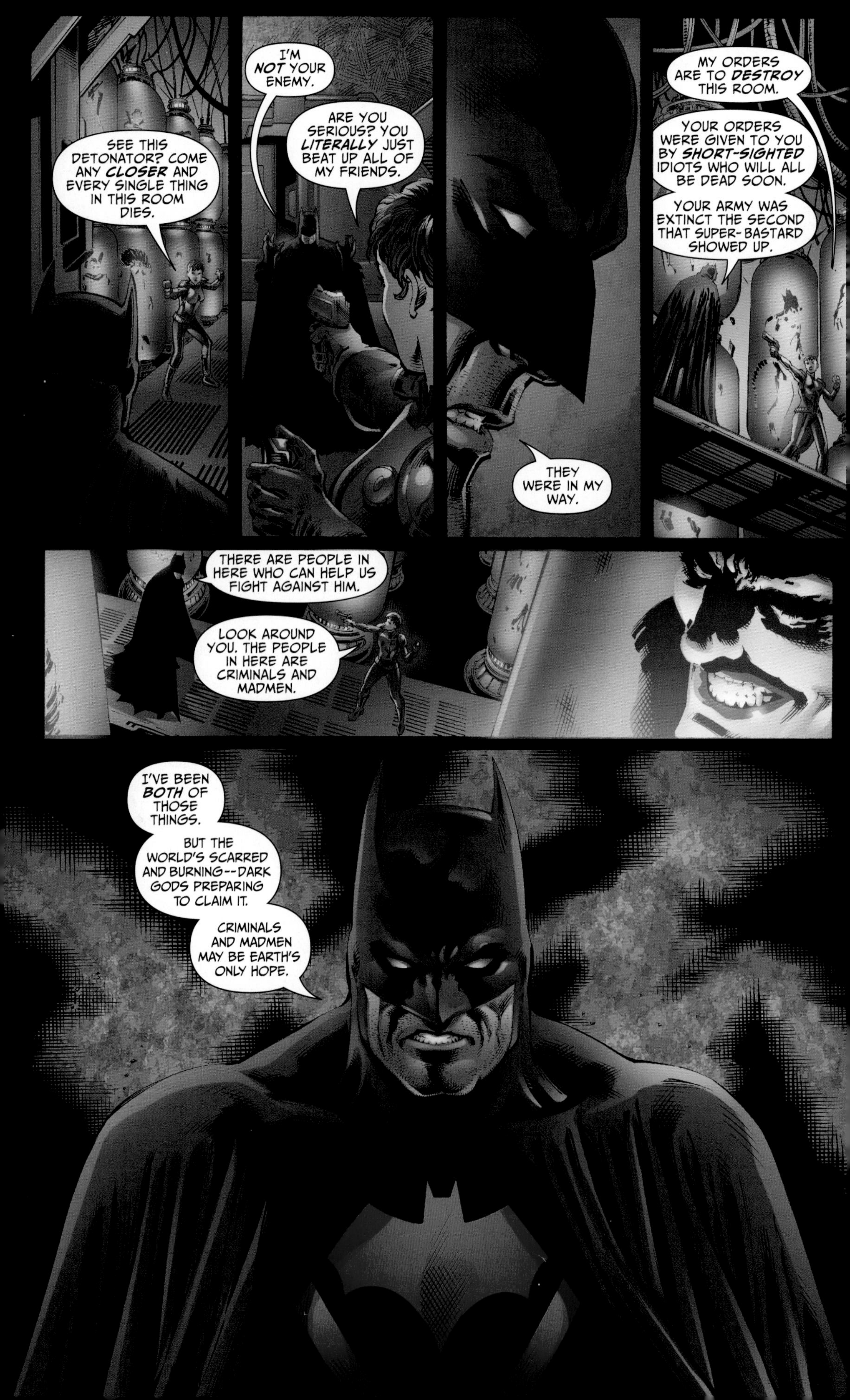

SEE THIS DETONATOR? COME ANY CLOSER AND EVERY SINGLE THING IN THIS ROOM DIES.
I'M NOT YOUR ENEMY.
ARE YOU SERIOUS? YOU LITERALLY JUST BEAT UP ALL OF MY FRIENDS.
THEY WERE IN MY WAY.
MY ORDERS ARE TO DESTROY THIS ROOM.
YOUR ORDERS WERE GIVEN TO YOU BY SHORT-SIGHTED IDIOTS WHO WILL ALL BE DEAD SOON.
YOUR ARMY WAS EXTINCT THE SECOND THAT SUPER-BASTARD SHOWED UP.
THERE ARE PEOPLE IN HERE WHO CAN HELP US FIGHT AGAINST HIM.
LOOK AROUND YOU. THE PEOPLE IN HERE ARE CRIMINALS AND MADMEN.
I'VE BEEN BOTH OF THOSE THINGS.
BUT THE WORLD'S SCARRED AND BURNING--DARK GODS PREPARING TO CLAIM IT.
CRIMINALS AND MADMEN MAY BE EARTH'S ONLY HOPE.

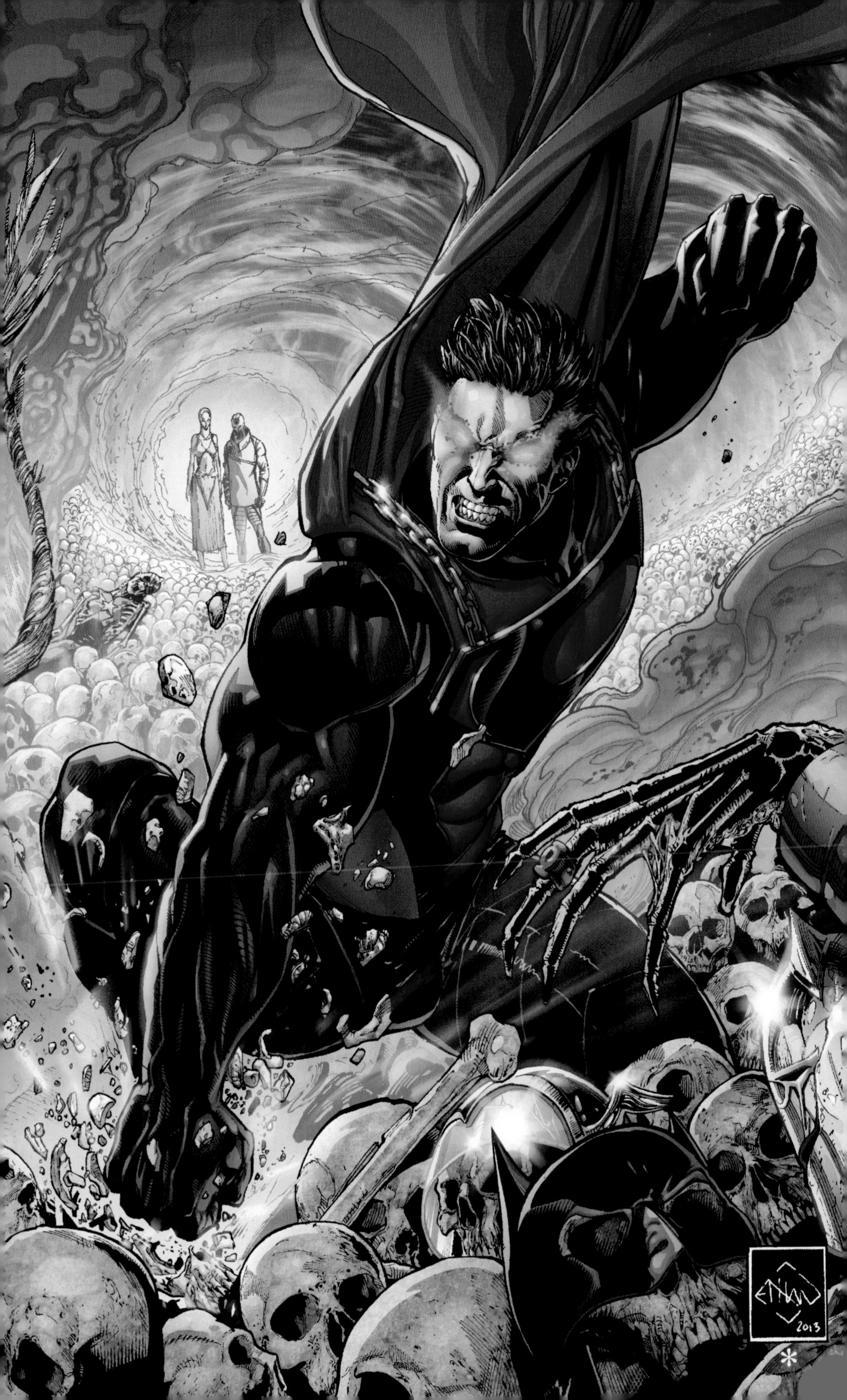

THE DARK AGE
PART 2

TOM TAYLOR
writer

NICOLA SCOTT
penciller

TREVOR SCOTT
inker

ETHAN VAN SCIVER & HI-FI
cover artists

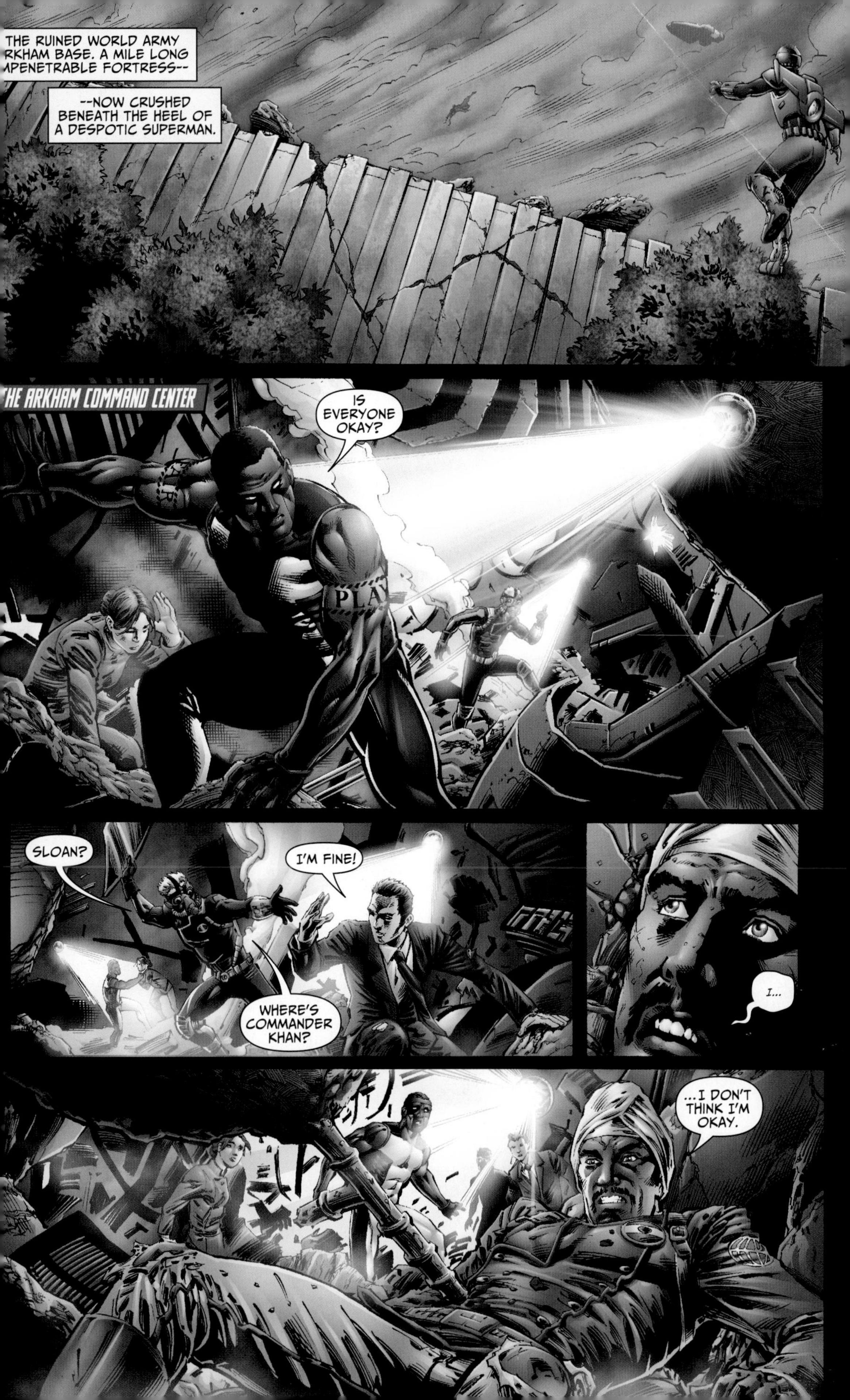
THE RUINED WORLD ARMY
RKHAM BASE. A MILE LONG
MPENETRABLE FORTRESS--
--NOW CRUSHED BENEATH THE HEEL OF A DESPOTIC SUPERMAN.
THE ARKHAM COMMAND CENTER
IS EVERYONE OKAY?
PLA
SLOAN?
I'M FINE!
WHERE'S COMMANDER KHAN?
I...
...I DON'T THINK I'M OKAY.

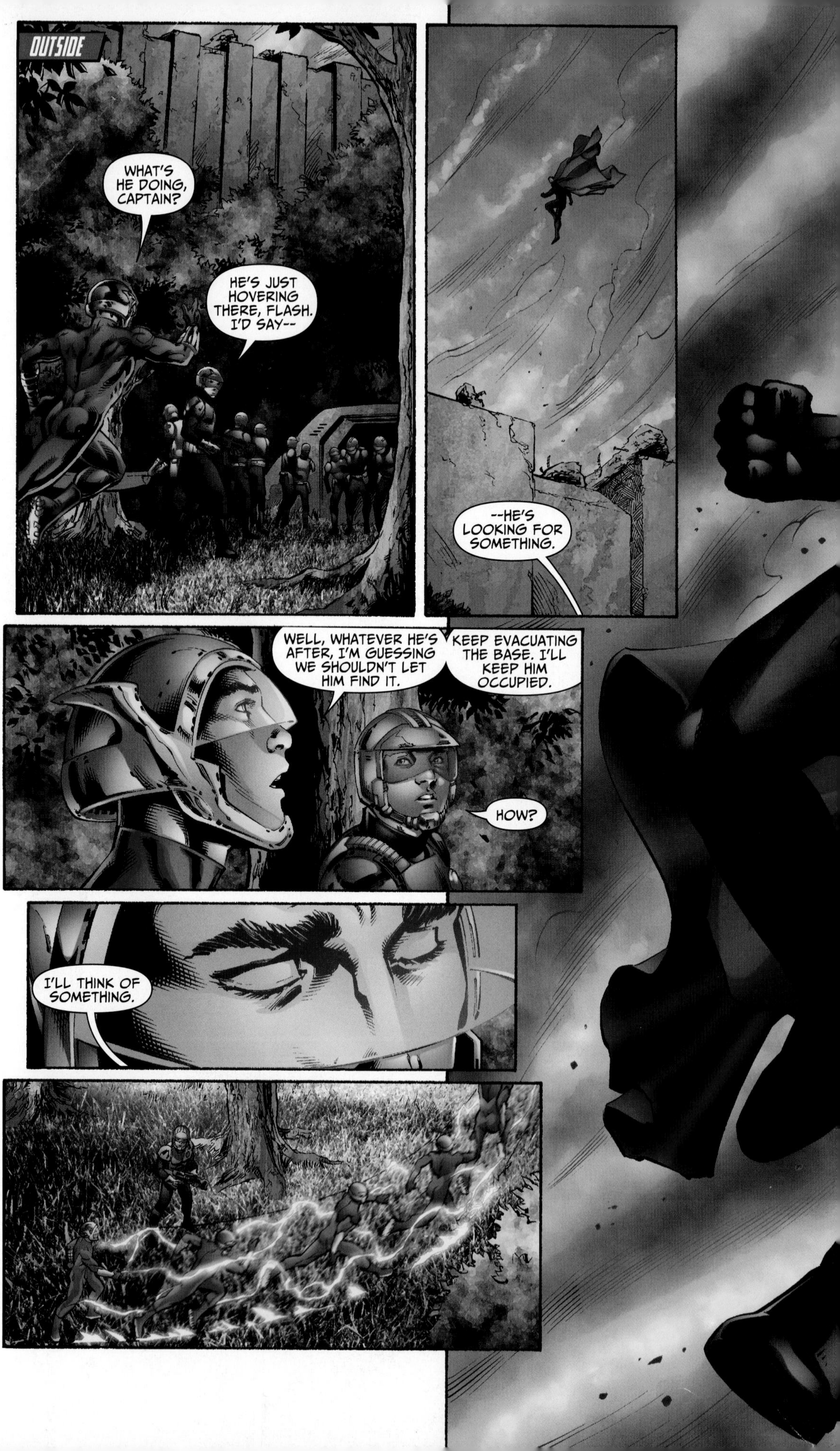
OUTSIDE
WHAT'S HE DOING, CAPTAIN?
HE'S JUST HOVERING THERE, FLASH. I'D SAY--
--HE'S LOOKING FOR SOMETHING.
WELL, WHATEVER HE'S AFTER, I'M GUESSING WE SHOULDN'T LET HIM FIND IT.
KEEP EVACUATING THE BASE. I'LL KEEP HIM OCCUPIED.
HOW?
I'LL THINK OF SOMETHING.

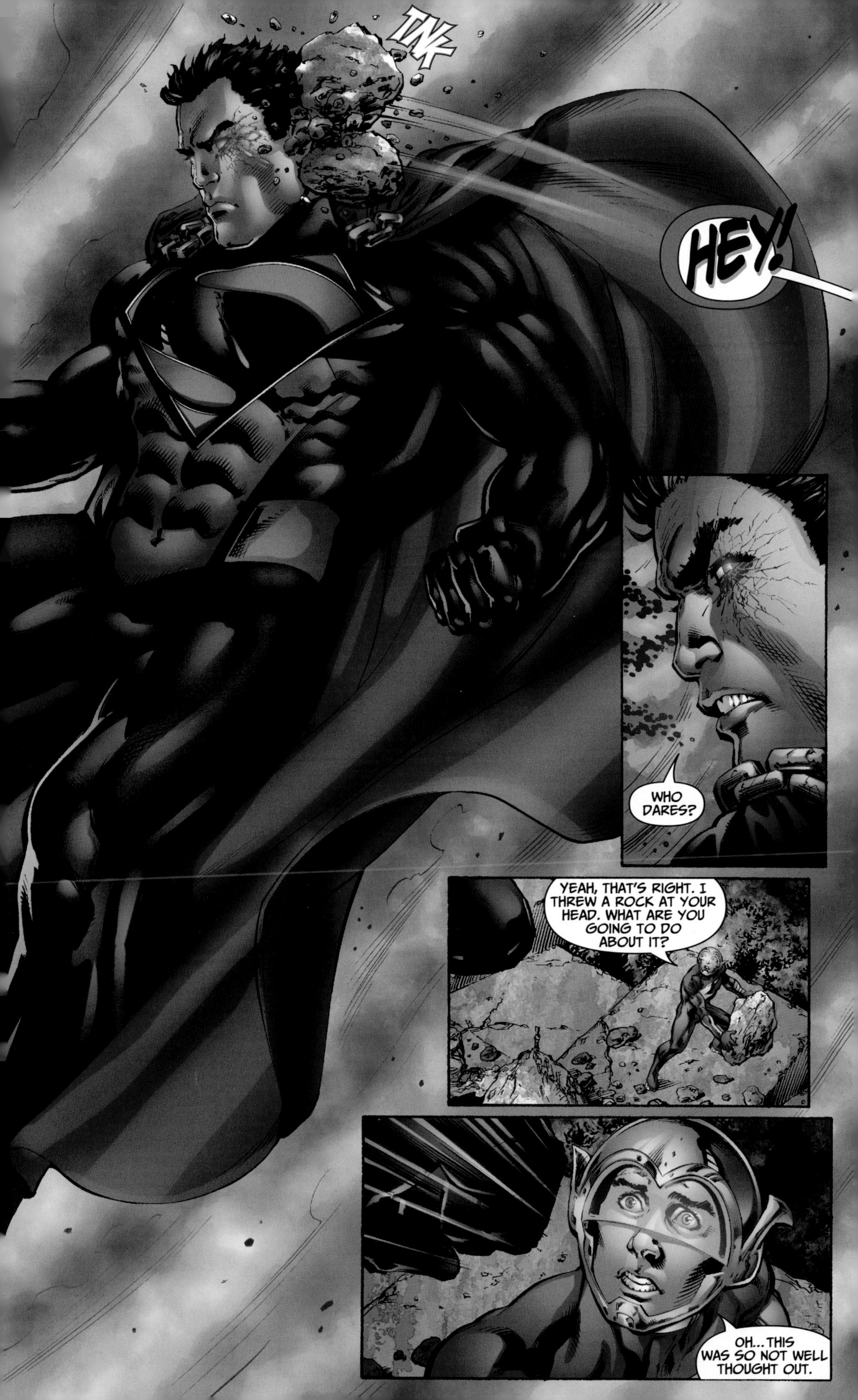
TNK
HEY!
WHO DARES?
YEAH, THAT'S RIGHT. I THREW A ROCK AT YOUR HEAD. WHAT ARE YOU GOING TO DO ABOUT IT?
OH...THIS WAS SO NOT WELL THOUGHT OUT.

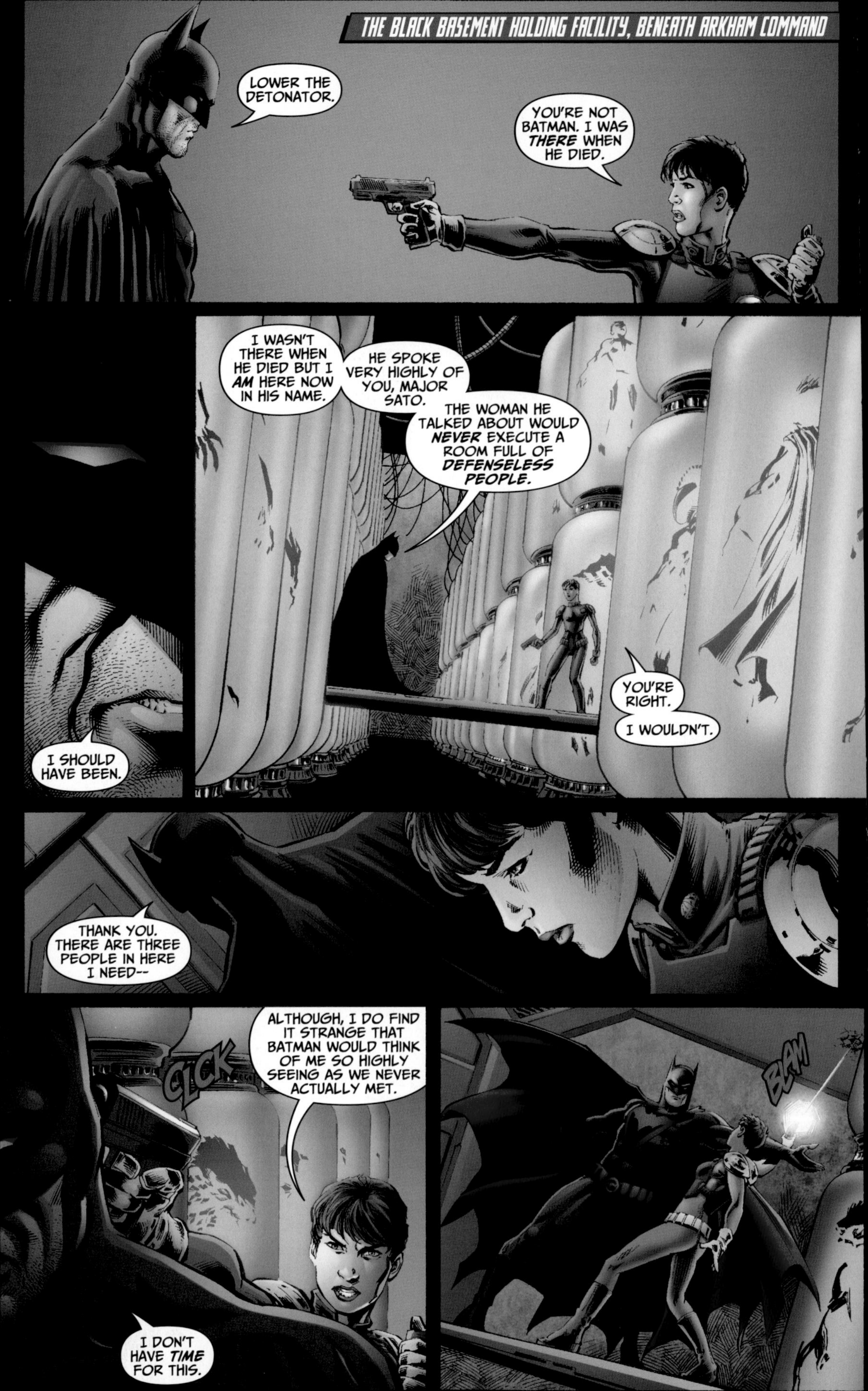
THE BLACK BASEMENT HOLDING FACILITY, BENEATH ARKHAM COMMAND
LOWER THE DETONATOR.
YOU'RE NOT BATMAN. I WAS *THERE* WHEN HE DIED.
I WASN'T THERE WHEN HE DIED BUT I *AM* HERE NOW IN HIS NAME.
I SHOULD HAVE BEEN.
HE SPOKE VERY HIGHLY OF YOU, MAJOR SATO.
THE WOMAN HE TALKED ABOUT WOULD *NEVER* EXECUTE A ROOM FULL OF *DEFENSELESS PEOPLE.*
YOU'RE RIGHT.
I WOULDN'T.
THANK YOU. THERE ARE THREE PEOPLE IN HERE I NEED--
CLCK
ALTHOUGH, I DO FIND IT STRANGE THAT BATMAN WOULD THINK OF ME SO HIGHLY SEEING AS WE NEVER ACTUALLY MET.
I DON'T HAVE *TIME* FOR THIS.
BLAM

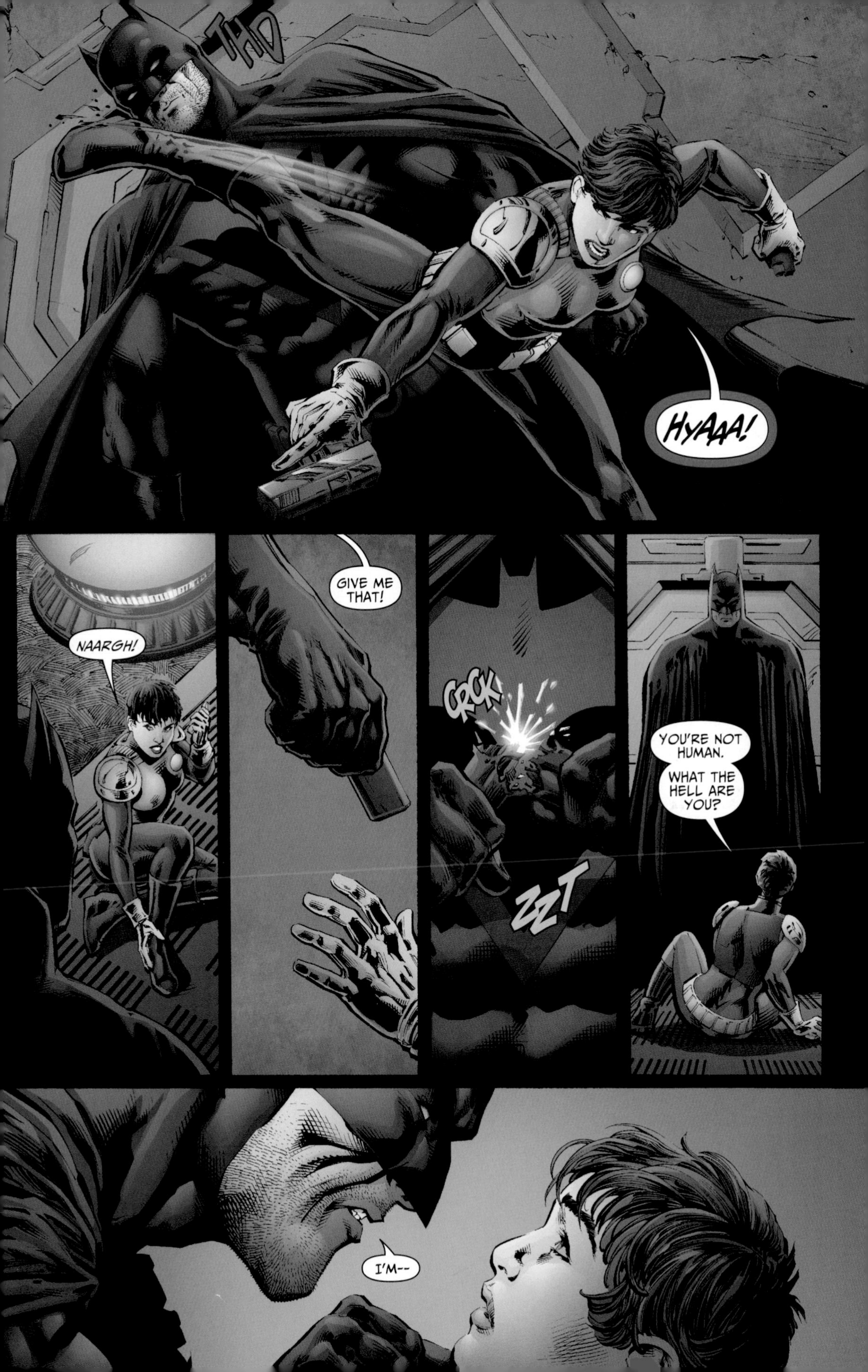
THD
HYAAA!
NAARGH!
GIVE ME THAT!
CROK
ZZZT
YOU'RE NOT HUMAN.
WHAT THE HELL ARE YOU?
I'M--

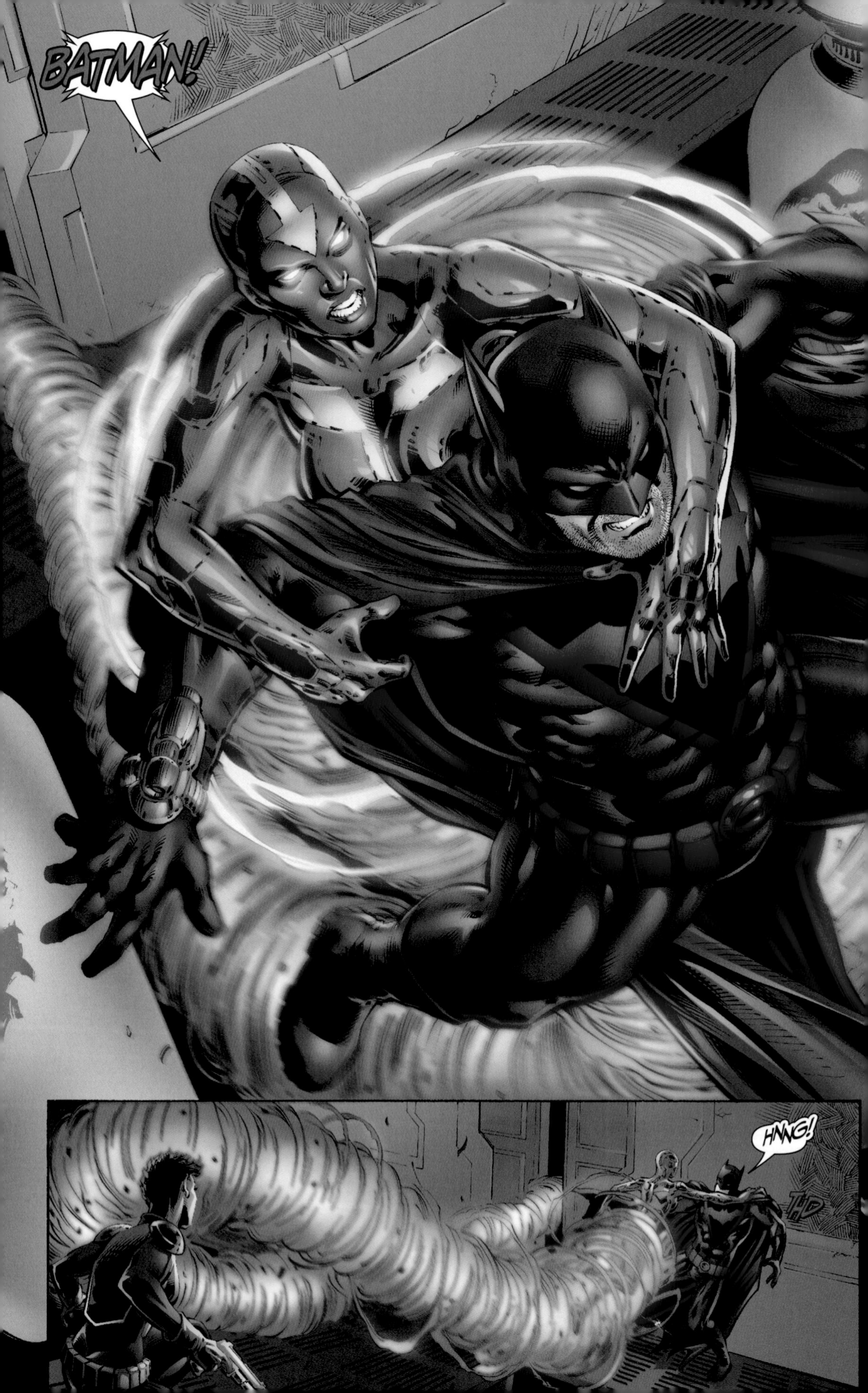
BATMAN!
HNNG!

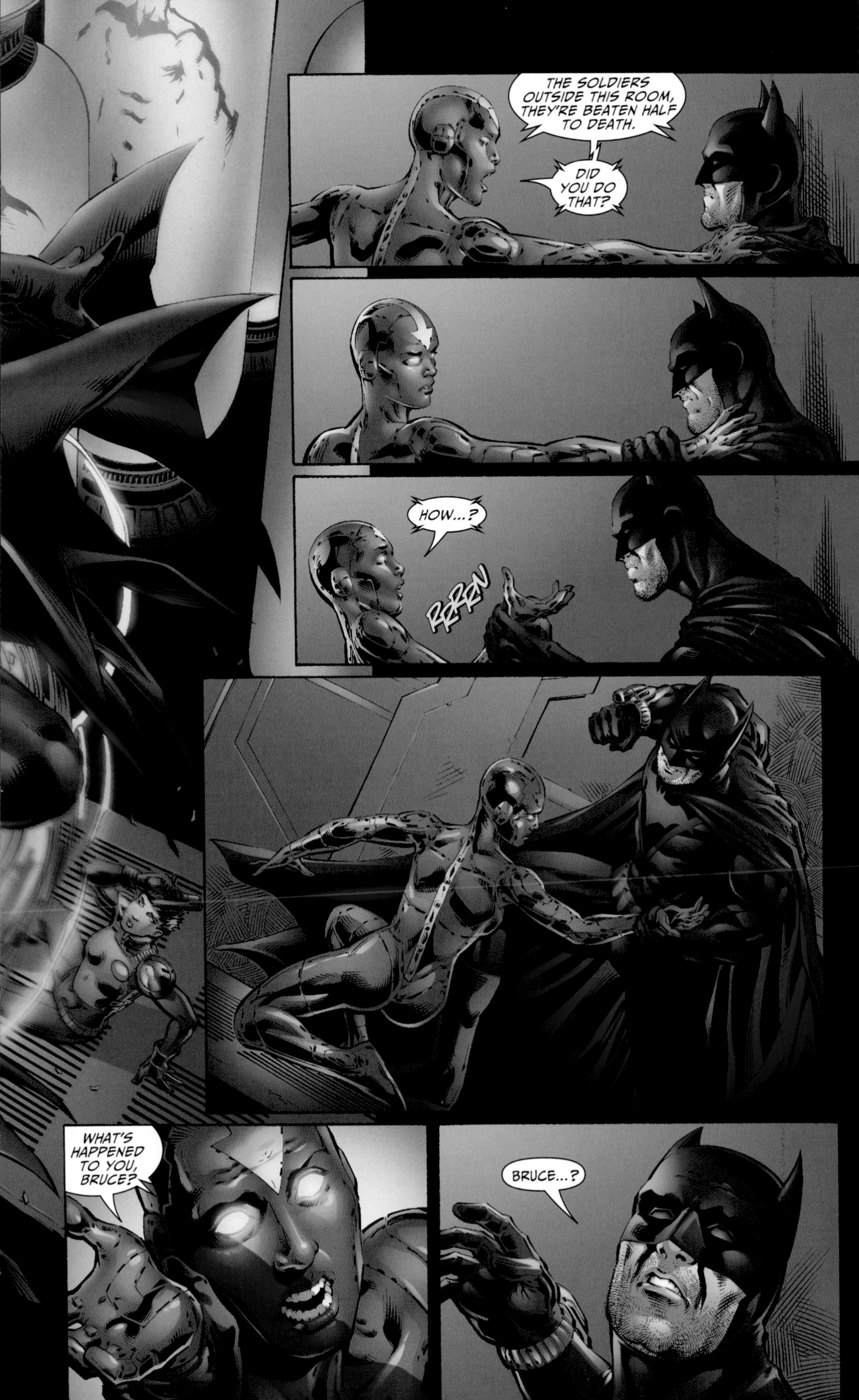
THE SOLDIERS OUTSIDE THIS ROOM, THEY'RE BEATEN HALF TO DEATH.
DID YOU DO THAT?
HOW...?
RRRN
WHAT'S HAPPENED TO YOU, BRUCE?
BRUCE...?

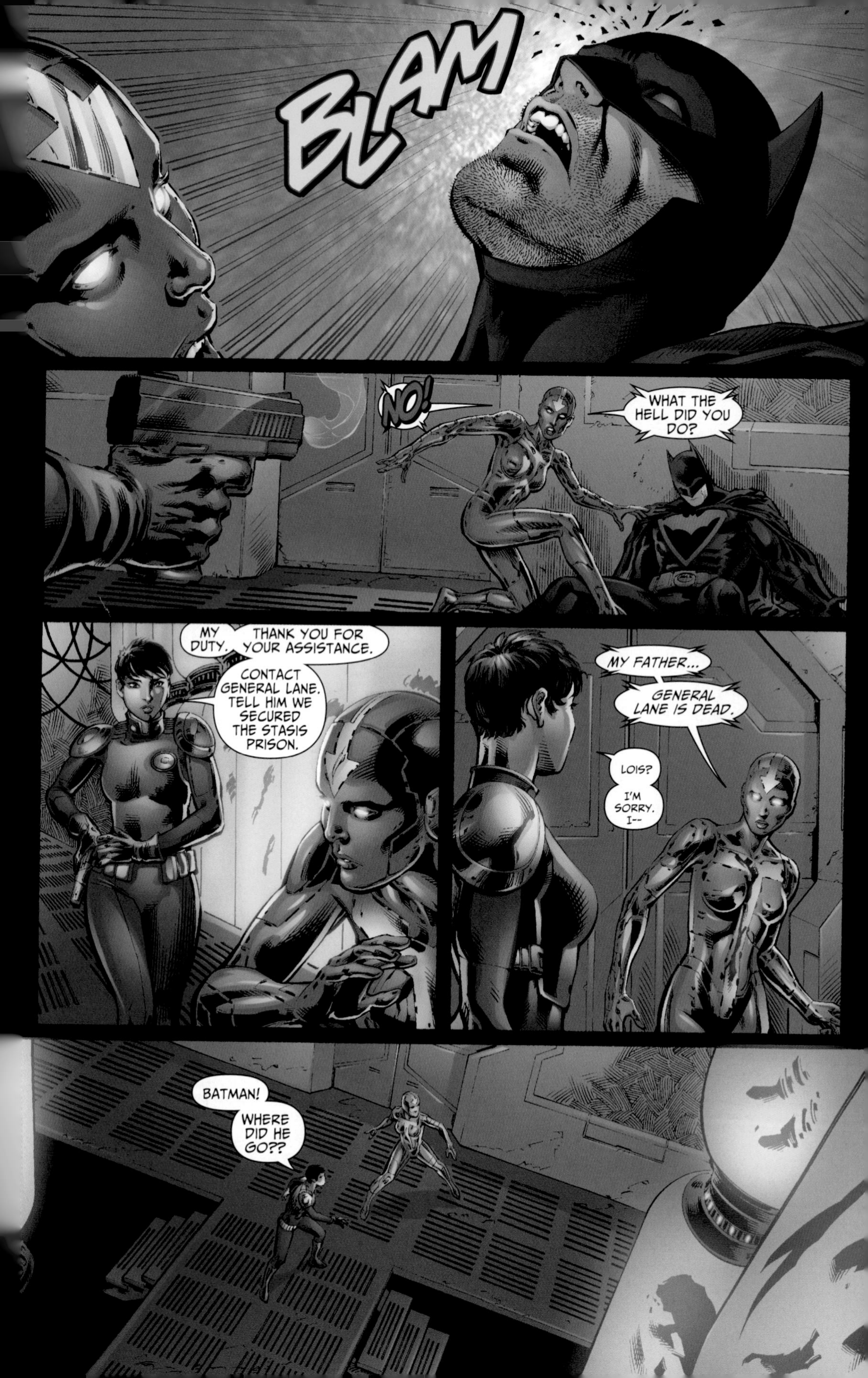
BLAM
NO!
WHAT THE HELL DID YOU DO?
MY DUTY.
THANK YOU FOR YOUR ASSISTANCE.
CONTACT GENERAL LANE. TELL HIM WE SECURED THE STASIS PRISON.
MY FATHER...
GENERAL LANE IS DEAD.
LOIS?
I'M SORRY. I--
BATMAN!
WHERE DID HE GO??

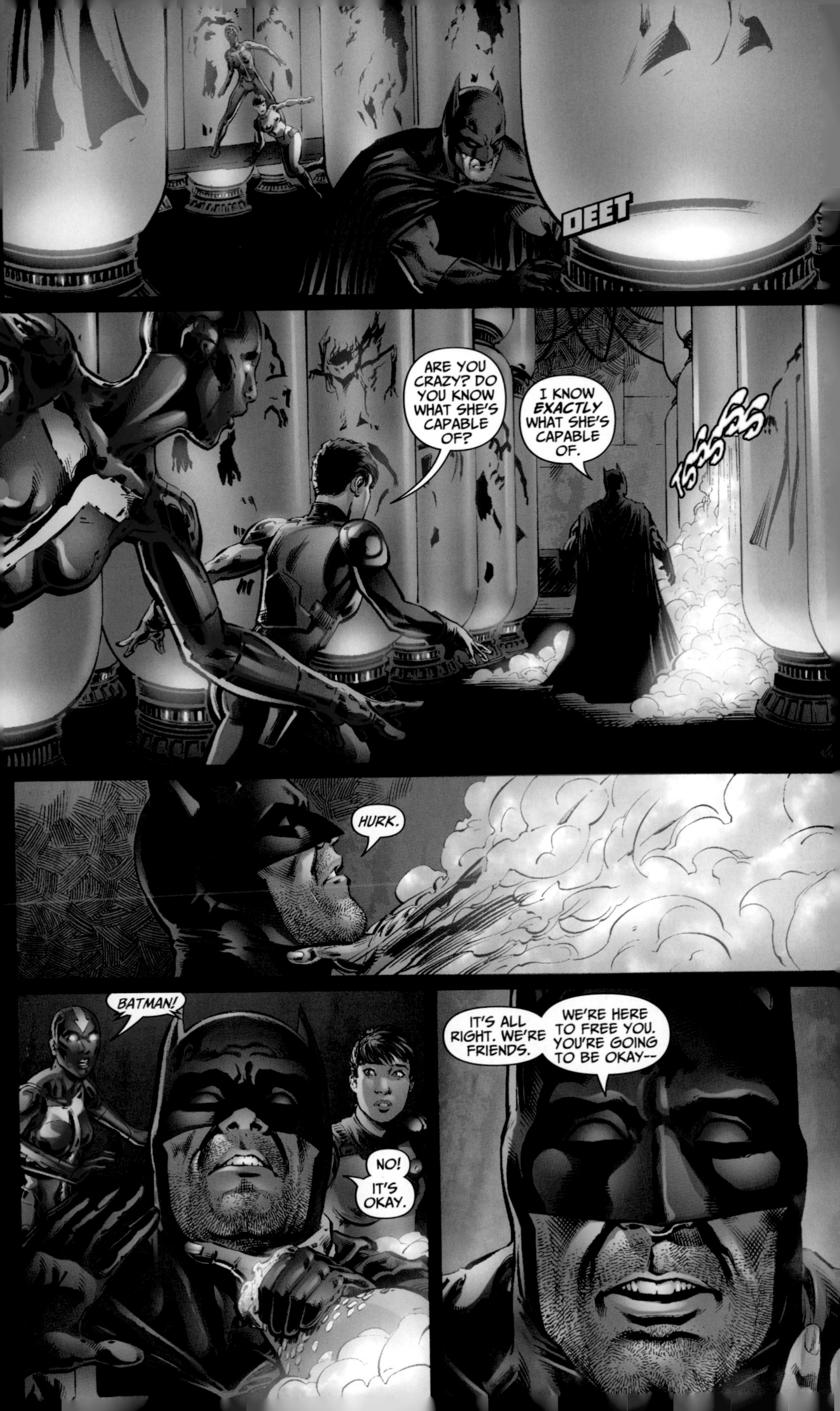
DEET
ARE YOU CRAZY? DO YOU KNOW WHAT SHE'S CAPABLE OF?
I KNOW EXACTLY WHAT SHE'S CAPABLE OF.
TSSSSS
HURK.
BATMAN!
NO! IT'S OKAY.
IT'S ALL RIGHT. WE'RE FRIENDS.
WE'RE HERE TO FREE YOU. YOU'RE GOING TO BE OKAY--

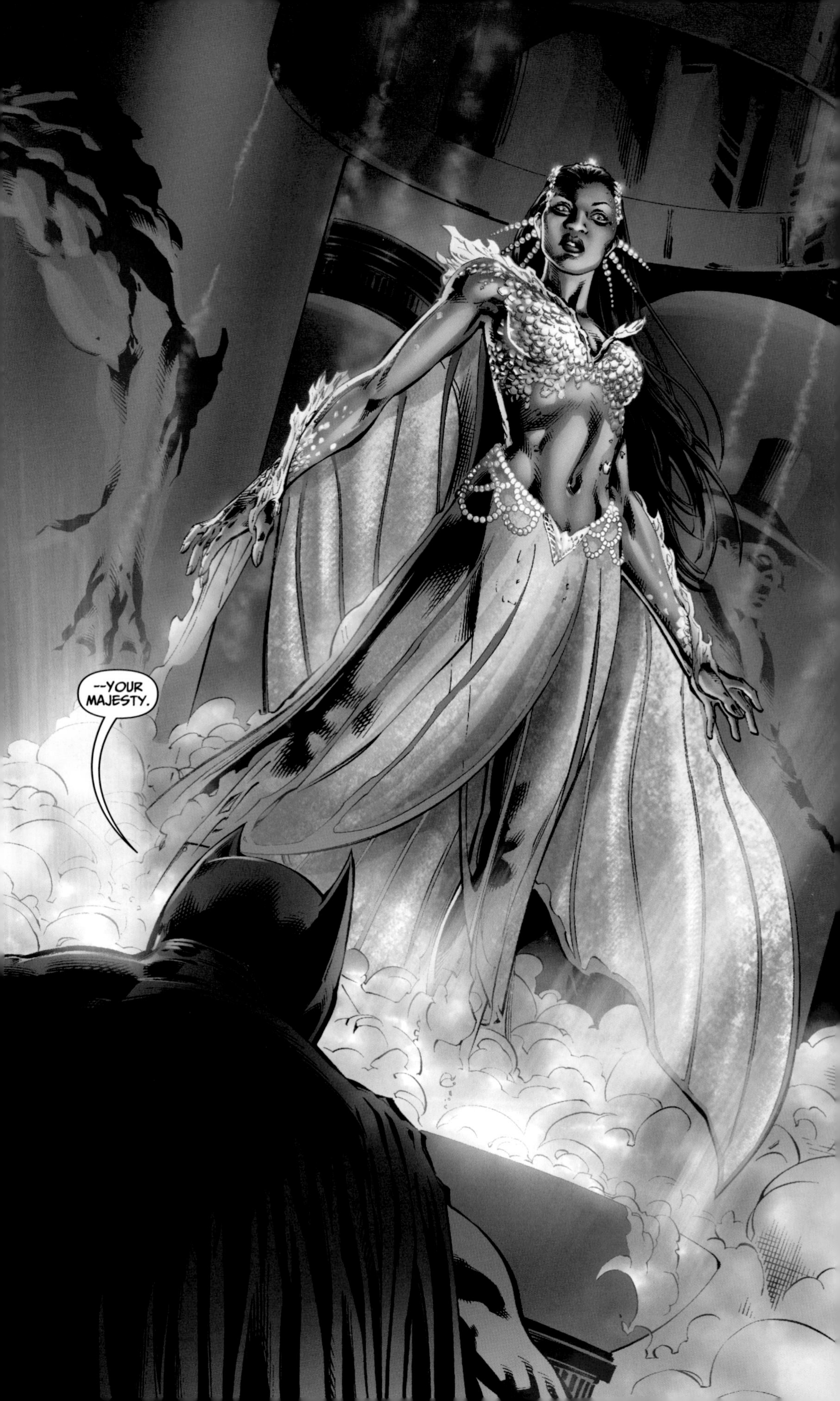
--YOUR MAJESTY.

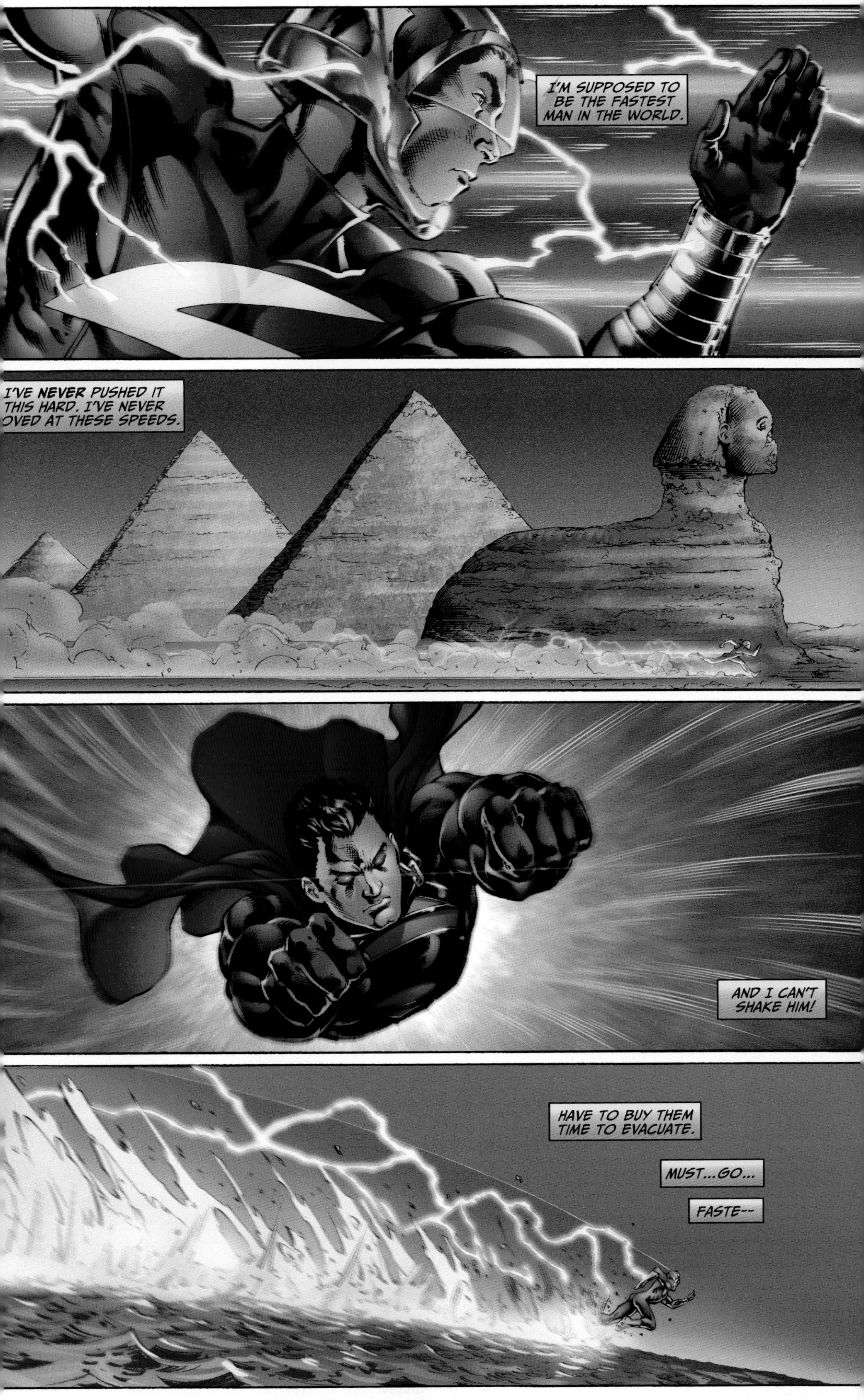

I'M SUPPOSED TO BE THE FASTEST MAN IN THE WORLD.
I'VE **NEVER** PUSHED IT THIS HARD. I'VE NEVER OVED AT THESE SPEEDS.
AND I CAN'T SHAKE HIM!
HAVE TO BUY THEM TIME TO EVACUATE.
MUST...GO...
FASTE--

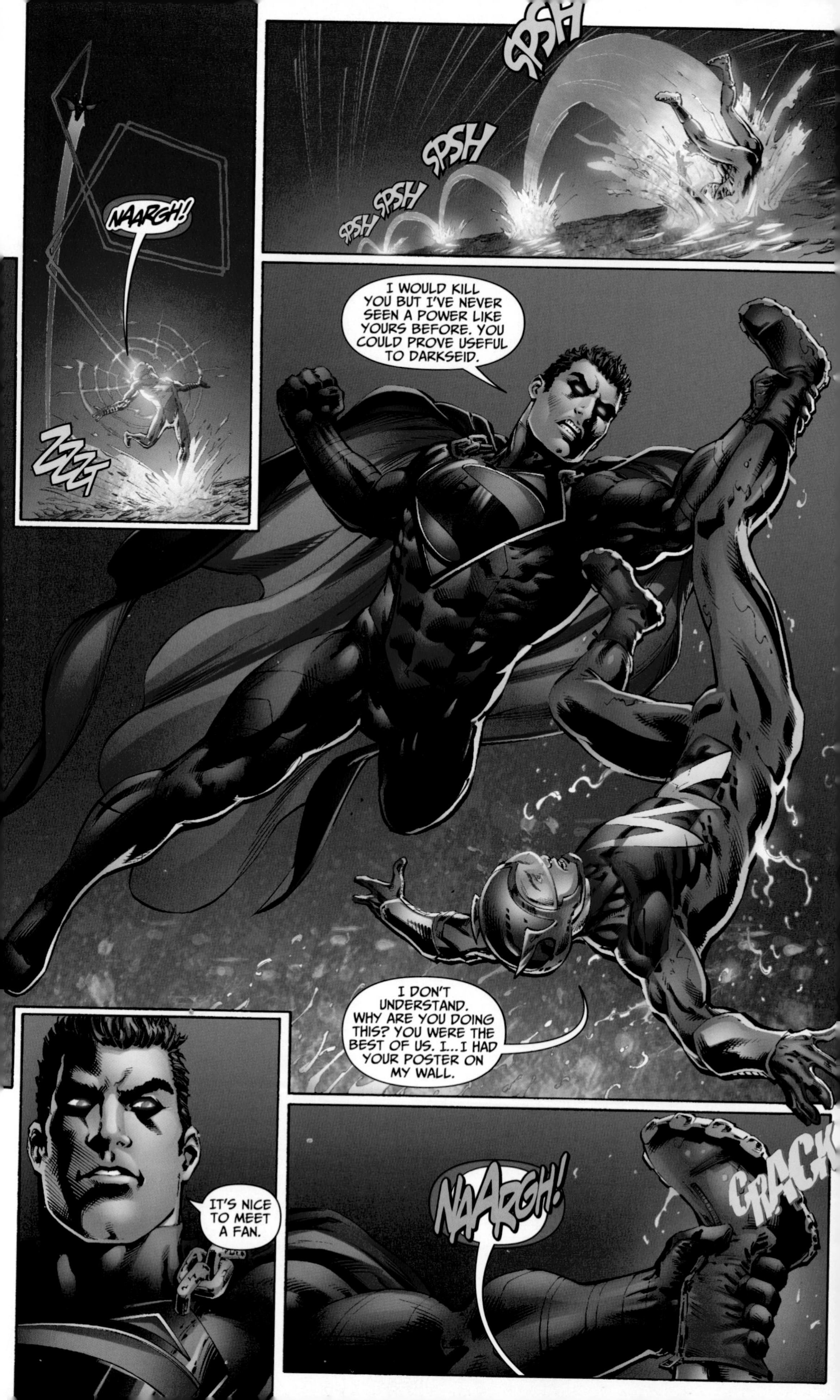
NAARGH!
ZZZZT
SPSH
SPSH
SPSH
SPSH
I WOULD KILL YOU BUT I'VE NEVER SEEN A POWER LIKE YOURS BEFORE. YOU COULD PROVE USEFUL TO DARKSEID.
I DON'T UNDERSTAND. WHY ARE YOU DOING THIS? YOU WERE THE BEST OF US. I...I HAD YOUR POSTER ON MY WALL.
IT'S NICE TO MEET A FAN.
NAARGH!
CRACK

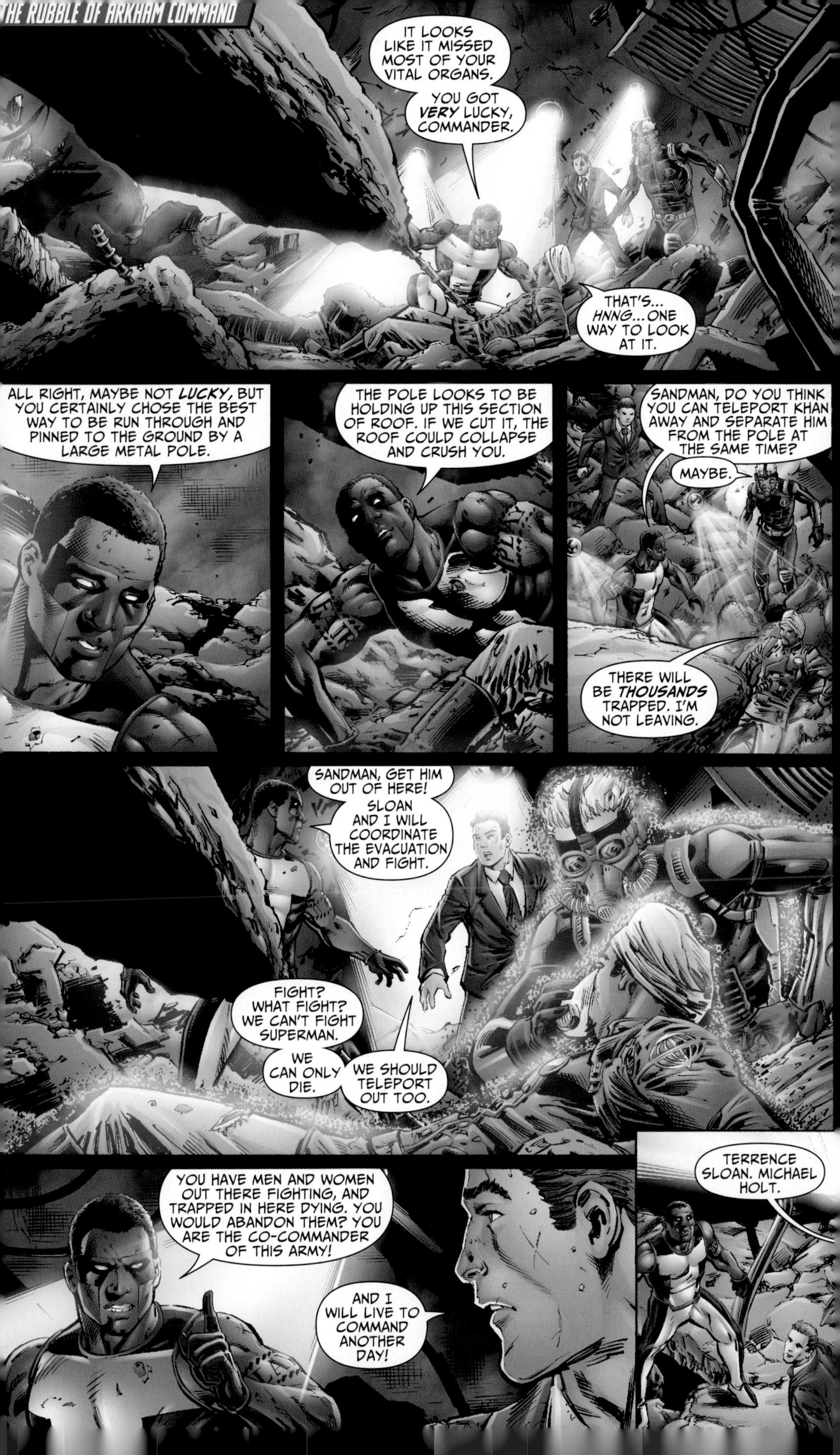
IT LOOKS LIKE IT MISSED MOST OF YOUR VITAL ORGANS.
YOU GOT *VERY* LUCKY, COMMANDER.
THAT'S... *HNNG*... ONE WAY TO LOOK AT IT.
ALL RIGHT, MAYBE NOT *LUCKY*, BUT YOU CERTAINLY CHOSE THE BEST WAY TO BE RUN THROUGH AND PINNED TO THE GROUND BY A LARGE METAL POLE.
THE POLE LOOKS TO BE HOLDING UP THIS SECTION OF ROOF. IF WE CUT IT, THE ROOF COULD COLLAPSE AND CRUSH YOU.
SANDMAN, DO YOU THINK YOU CAN TELEPORT KHAN AWAY AND SEPARATE HIM FROM THE POLE AT THE SAME TIME?
MAYBE.
THERE WILL BE *THOUSANDS* TRAPPED. I'M NOT LEAVING.
SANDMAN, GET HIM OUT OF HERE!
SLOAN AND I WILL COORDINATE THE EVACUATION AND FIGHT.
FIGHT? WHAT FIGHT? WE CAN'T FIGHT SUPERMAN.
WE CAN ONLY DIE.
WE SHOULD TELEPORT OUT TOO.
YOU HAVE MEN AND WOMEN OUT THERE FIGHTING, AND TRAPPED IN HERE DYING. YOU WOULD ABANDON THEM? YOU ARE THE CO-COMMANDER OF THIS ARMY!
AND I WILL LIVE TO COMMAND ANOTHER DAY!
TERRENCE SLOAN. MICHAEL HOLT.

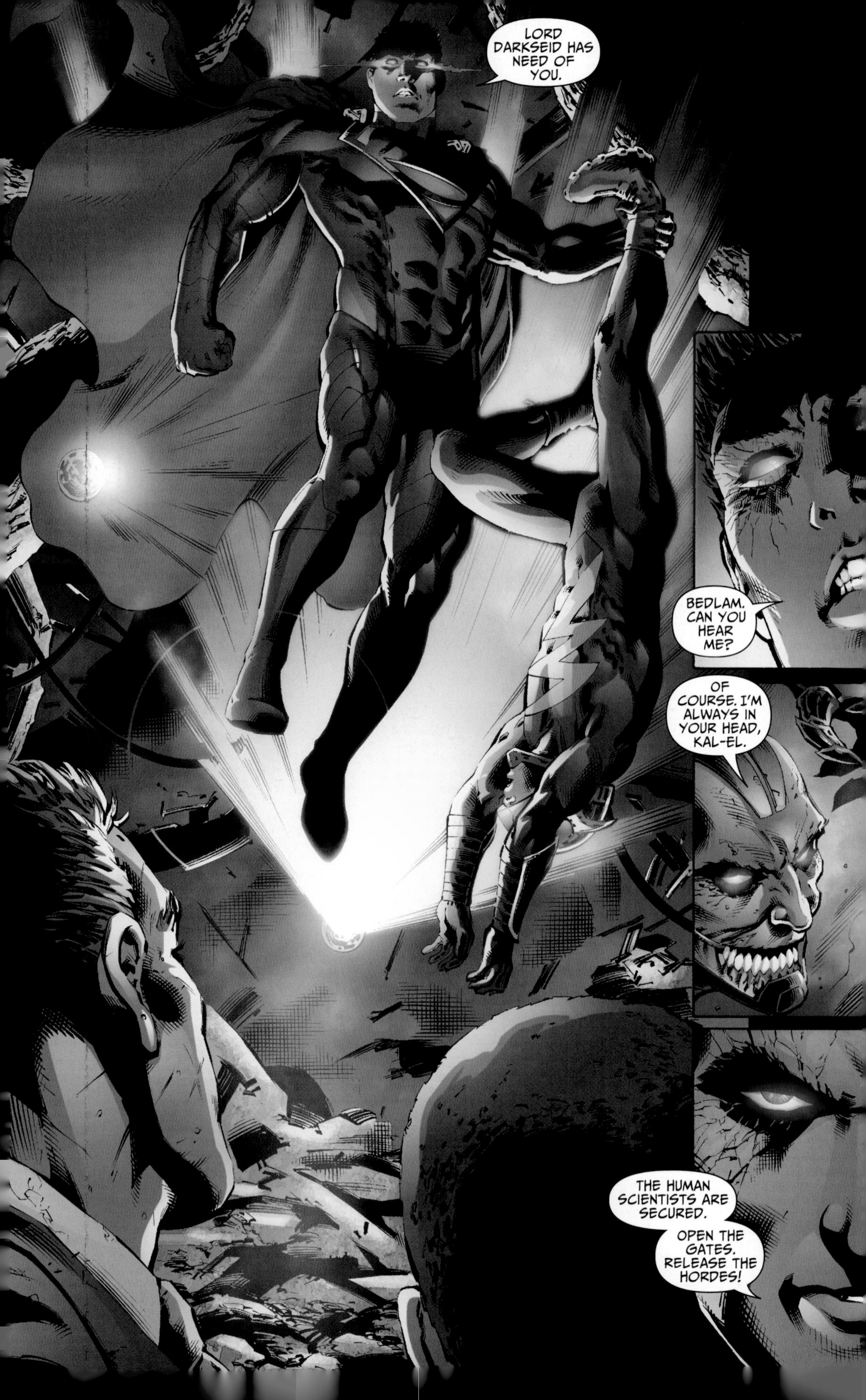
LORD DARKSEID HAS NEED OF YOU.
BEDLAM. CAN YOU HEAR ME?
OF COURSE. I'M ALWAYS IN YOUR HEAD, KAL-EL.
THE HUMAN SCIENTISTS ARE SECURED.
OPEN THE GATES. RELEASE THE HORDES!

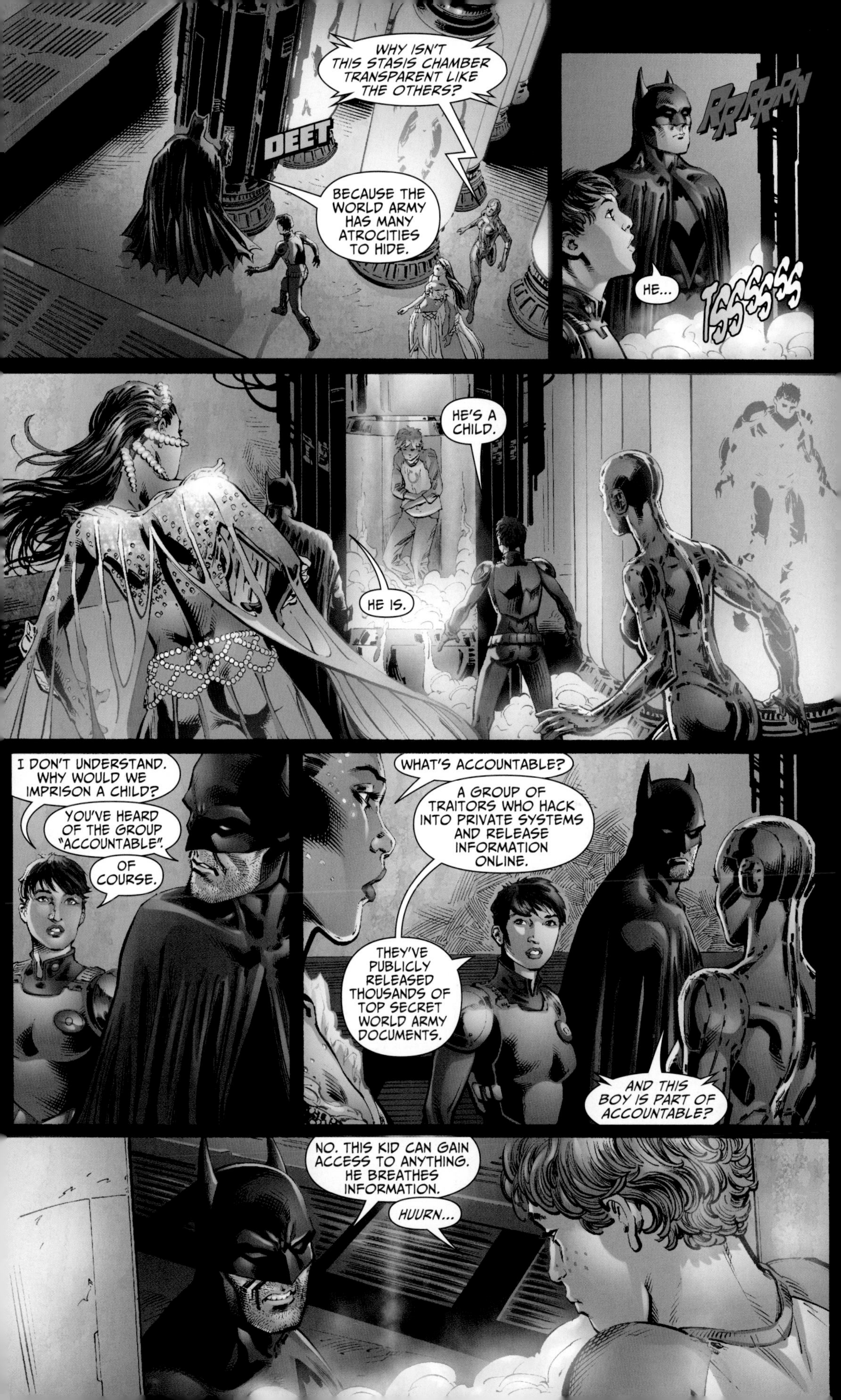
WHY ISN'T THIS STASIS CHAMBER TRANSPARENT LIKE THE OTHERS?
DEET
BECAUSE THE WORLD ARMY HAS MANY ATROCITIES TO HIDE.
RRRRRN
HE...
TSSSSSS
HE'S A CHILD.
HE IS.
I DON'T UNDERSTAND. WHY WOULD WE IMPRISON A CHILD?
YOU'VE HEARD OF THE GROUP "ACCOUNTABLE".
OF COURSE.
WHAT'S ACCOUNTABLE?
A GROUP OF TRAITORS WHO HACK INTO PRIVATE SYSTEMS AND RELEASE INFORMATION ONLINE.
THEY'VE PUBLICLY RELEASED THOUSANDS OF TOP SECRET WORLD ARMY DOCUMENTS.
AND THIS BOY IS PART OF ACCOUNTABLE?
NO. THIS KID CAN GAIN ACCESS TO ANYTHING. HE BREATHES INFORMATION.
HUURN...

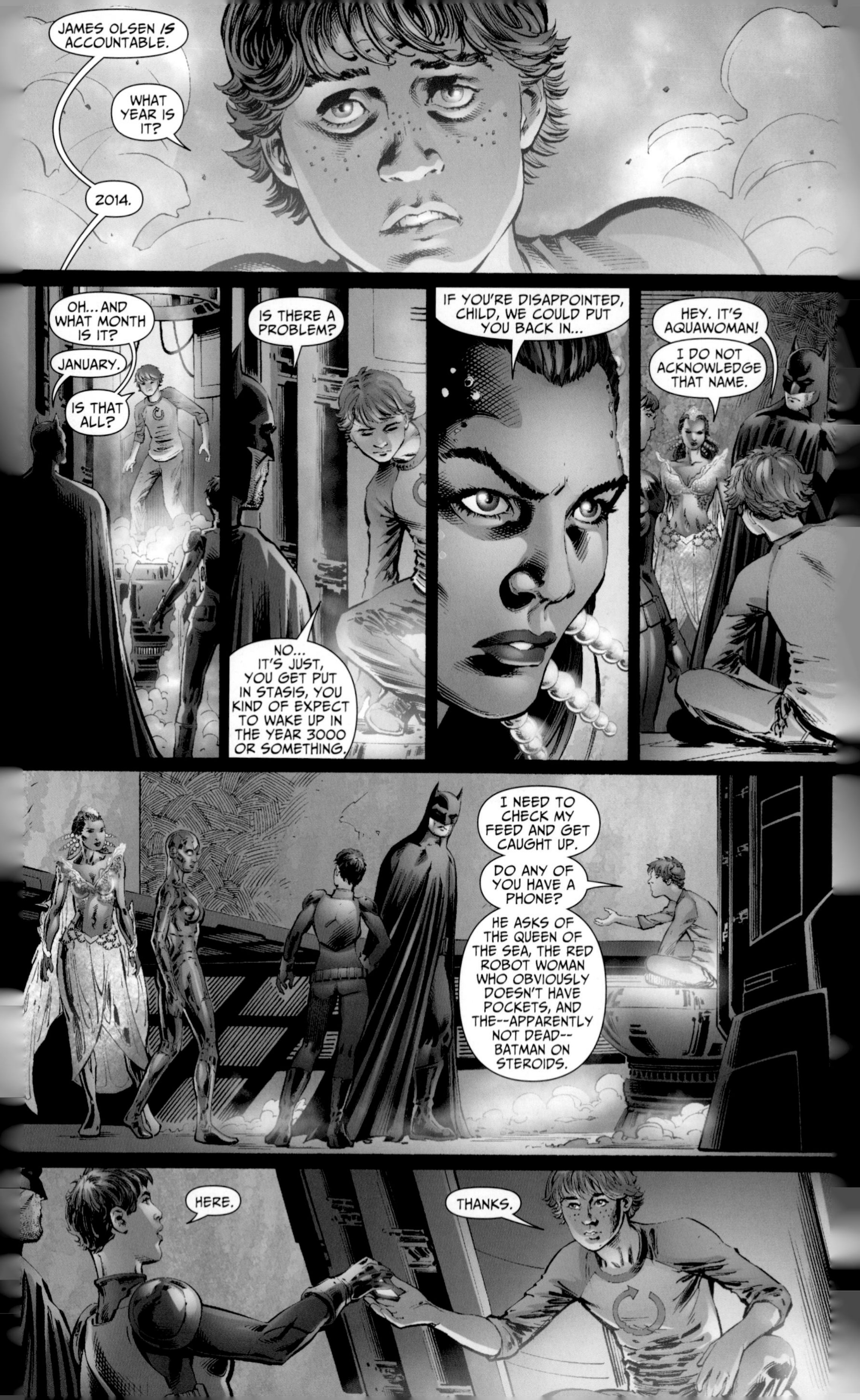
JAMES OLSEN *IS* ACCOUNTABLE.
WHAT YEAR IS IT?
2014.
OH...AND WHAT MONTH IS IT?
JANUARY.
IS THAT ALL?
IS THERE A PROBLEM?
NO... IT'S JUST, YOU GET PUT IN STASIS, YOU KIND OF EXPECT TO WAKE UP IN THE YEAR 3000 OR SOMETHING.
IF YOU'RE DISAPPOINTED, CHILD, WE COULD PUT YOU BACK IN...
HEY. IT'S AQUAWOMAN!
I DO NOT ACKNOWLEDGE THAT NAME.
I NEED TO CHECK MY FEED AND GET CAUGHT UP.
DO ANY OF YOU HAVE A PHONE?
HE ASKS OF THE QUEEN OF THE SEA, THE RED ROBOT WOMAN WHO OBVIOUSLY DOESN'T HAVE POCKETS, AND THE--APPARENTLY NOT DEAD--BATMAN ON STEROIDS.
HERE.
THANKS.

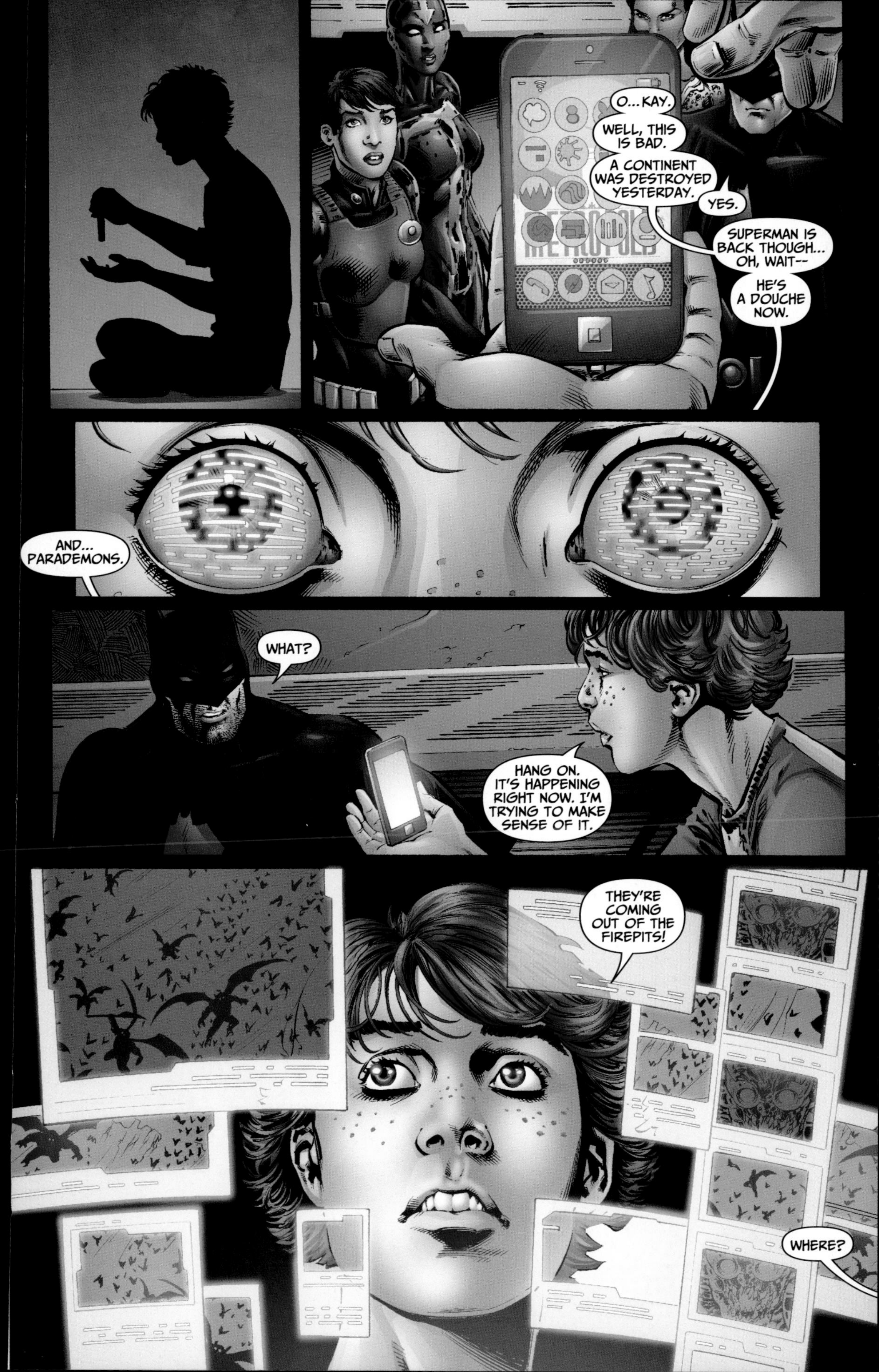
O...KAY.
WELL, THIS IS BAD.
A CONTINENT WAS DESTROYED YESTERDAY.
YES.
SUPERMAN IS BACK THOUGH... OH, WAIT--
HE'S A DOUCHE NOW.
AND... PARADEMONS.
WHAT?
HANG ON. IT'S HAPPENING RIGHT NOW. I'M TRYING TO MAKE SENSE OF IT.
THEY'RE COMING OUT OF THE FIREPITS!
WHERE?

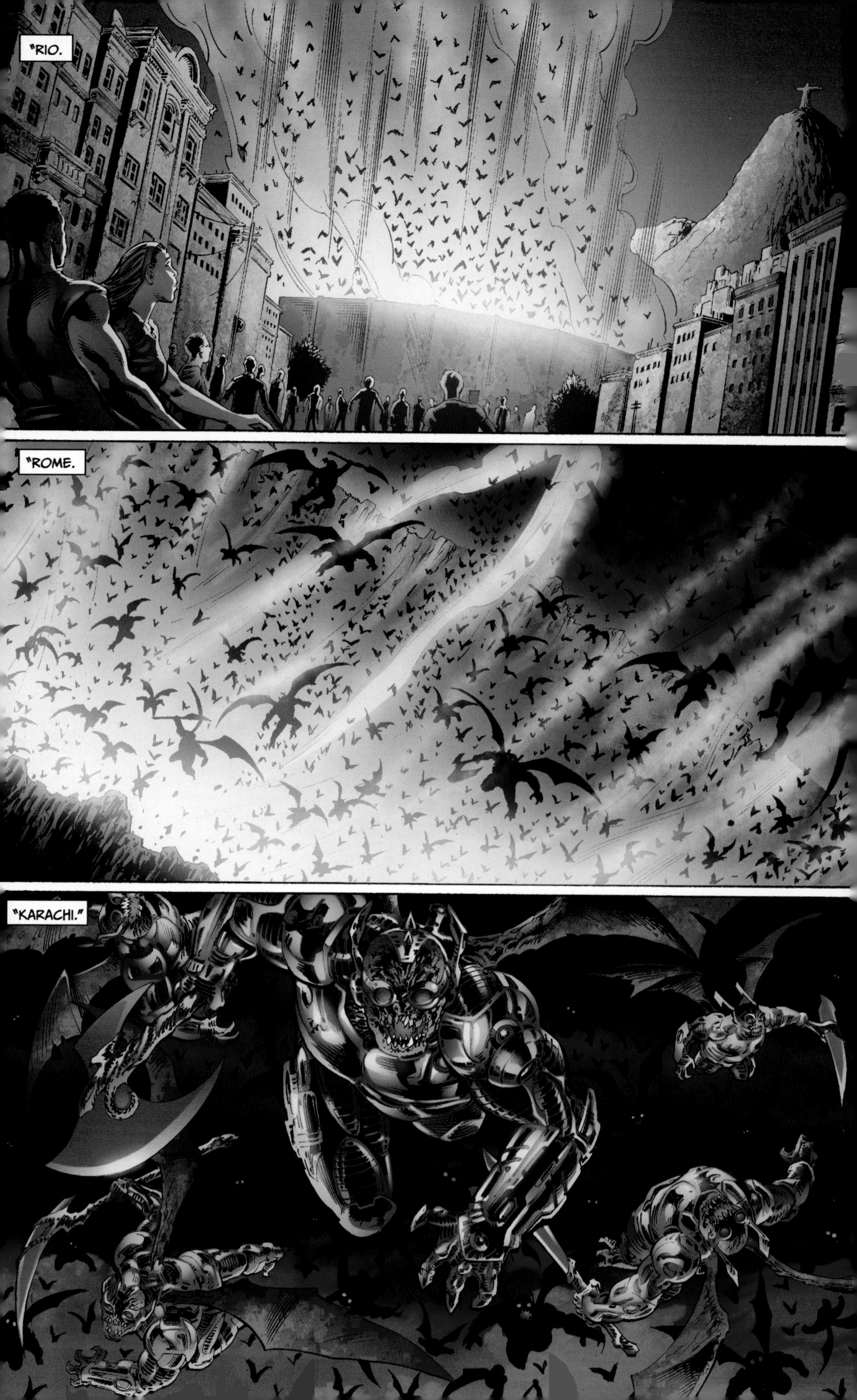
"RIO.
"ROME.
"KARACHI."

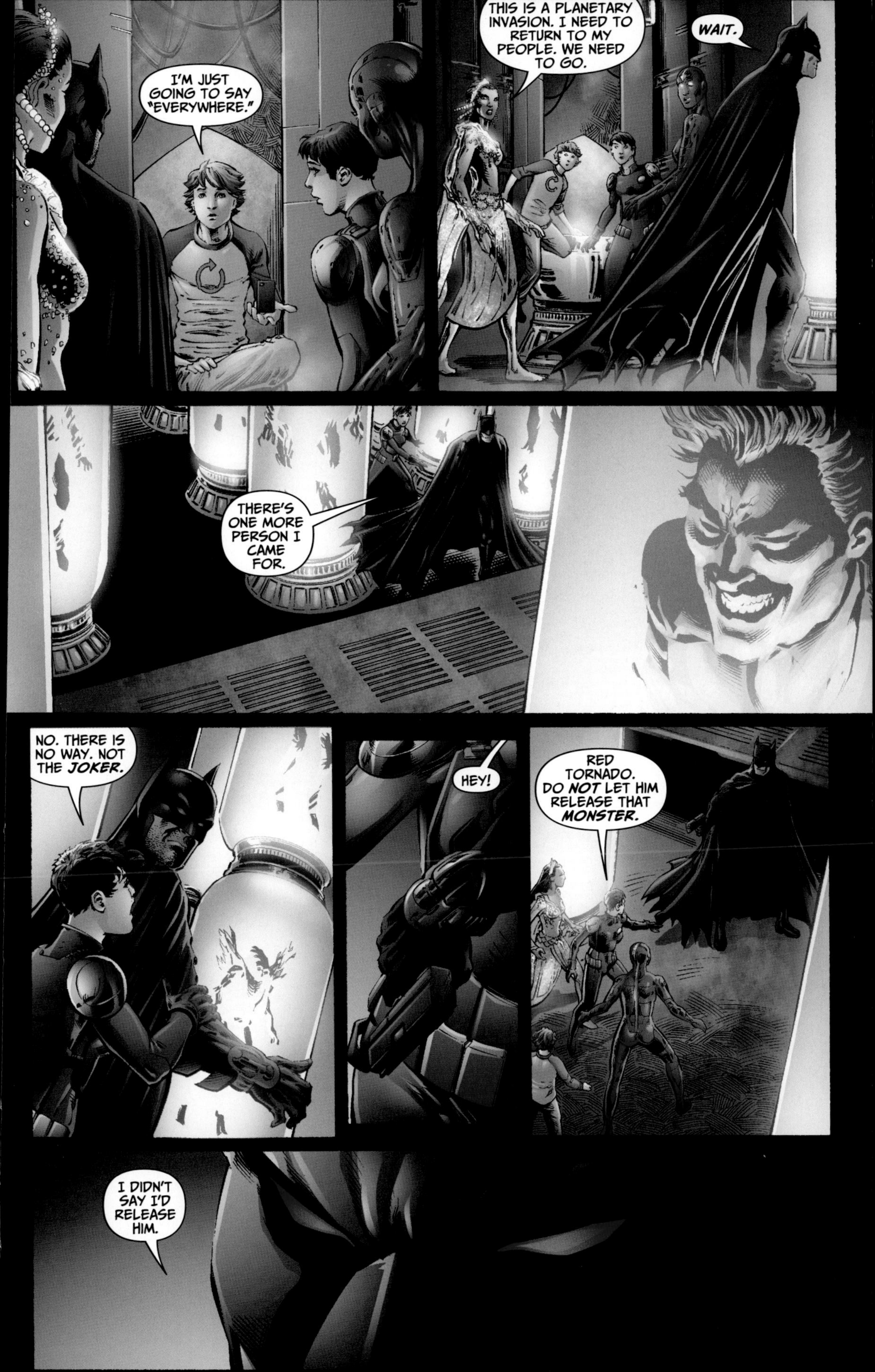
I'M JUST GOING TO SAY "EVERYWHERE."
THIS IS A PLANETARY INVASION. I NEED TO RETURN TO MY PEOPLE. WE NEED TO GO.
WAIT.
THERE'S ONE MORE PERSON I CAME FOR.
NO. THERE IS NO WAY. NOT THE JOKER.
HEY!
RED TORNADO. DO NOT LET HIM RELEASE THAT MONSTER.
I DIDN'T SAY I'D RELEASE HIM.

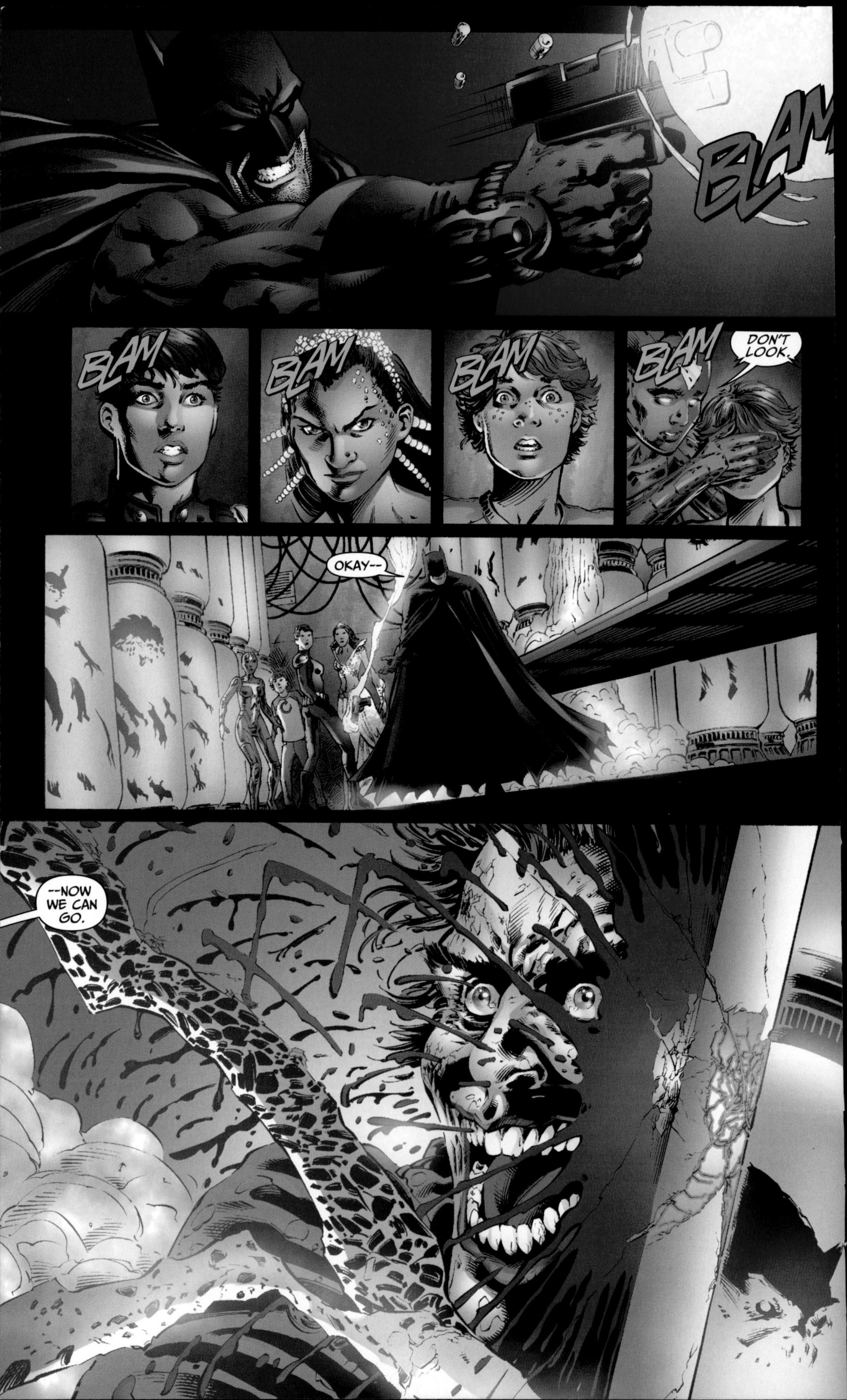
BLAM
BLAM
BLAM
BLAM
BLAM
DON'T LOOK.
OKAY--
--NOW WE CAN GO.

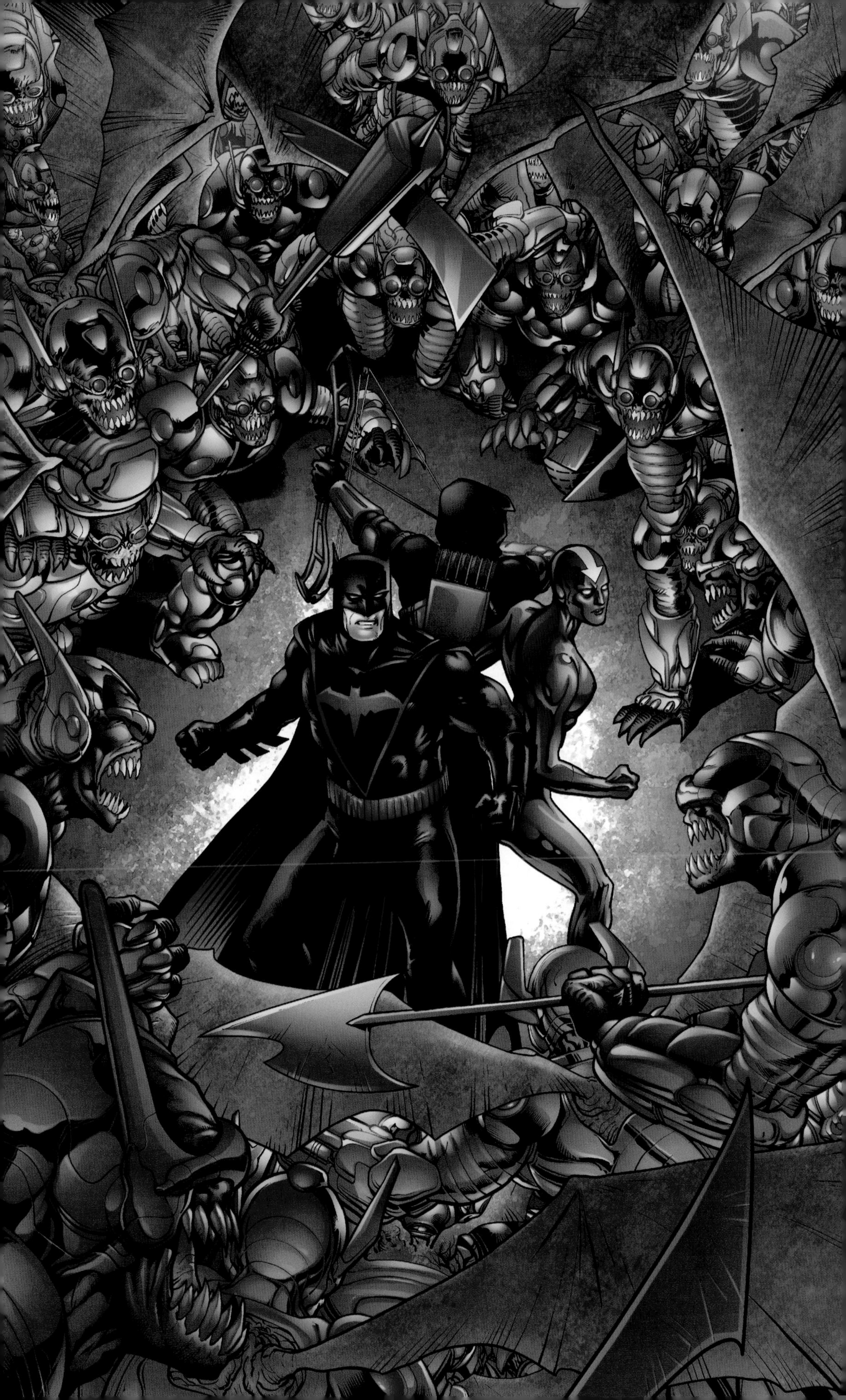

THE DARK AGE
PART 3

TOM TAYLOR
writer

NICOLA SCOTT
ROBSON ROCHA
pencillers

TREVOR SCOTT
OCLAIR ALBERT
inkers

BARRY KITSON & PETE PANTAZIS
cover artists

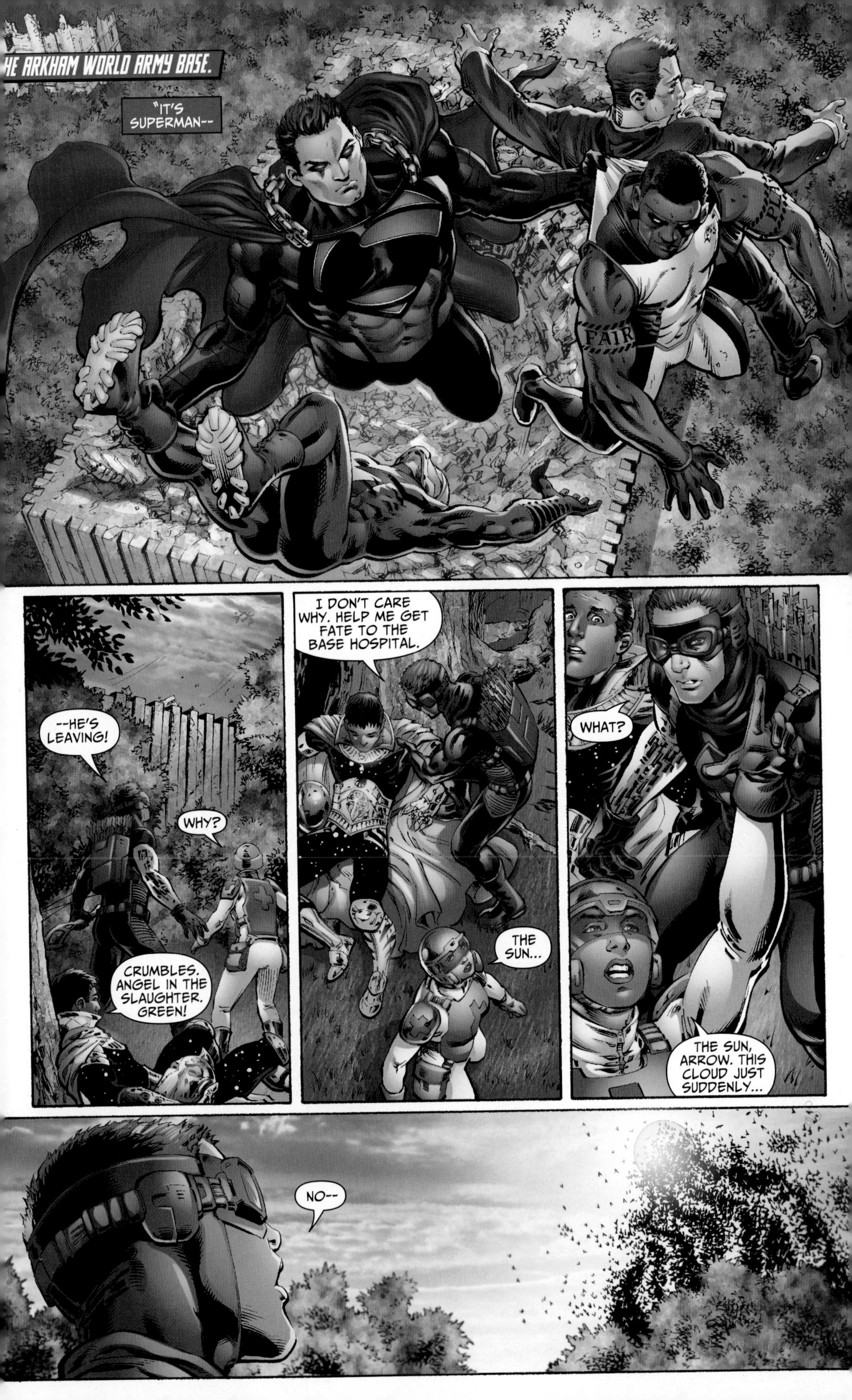

HE ARKHAM WORLD ARMY BASE.
"IT'S SUPERMAN--
FAIR
--HE'S LEAVING!
WHY?
CRUMBLES. ANGEL IN THE SLAUGHTER. GREEN!
I DON'T CARE WHY. HELP ME GET FATE TO THE BASE HOSPITAL.
THE SUN...
WHAT?
THE SUN, ARROW. THIS CLOUD JUST SUDDENLY...
NO--

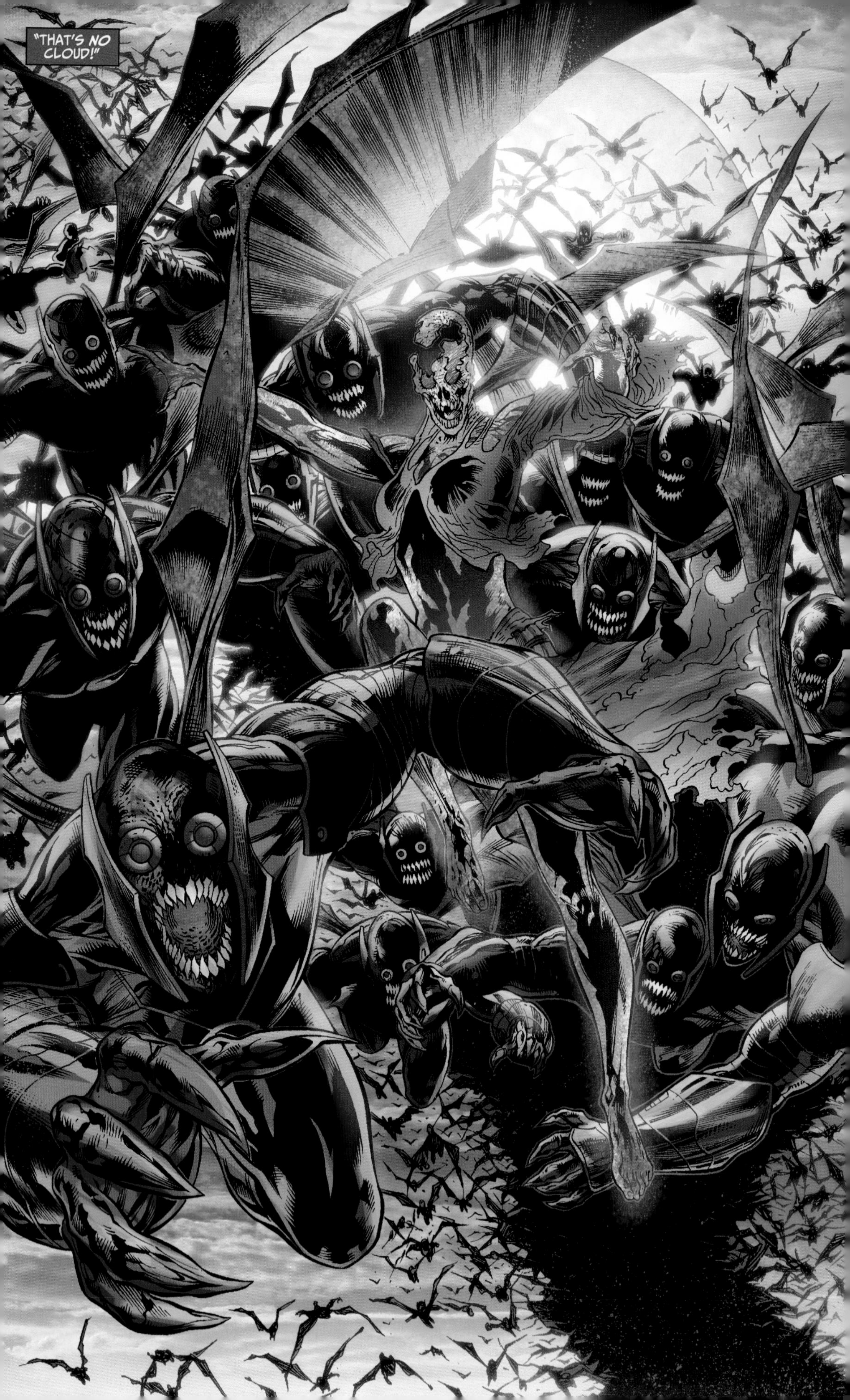
"THAT'S NO CLOUD!"

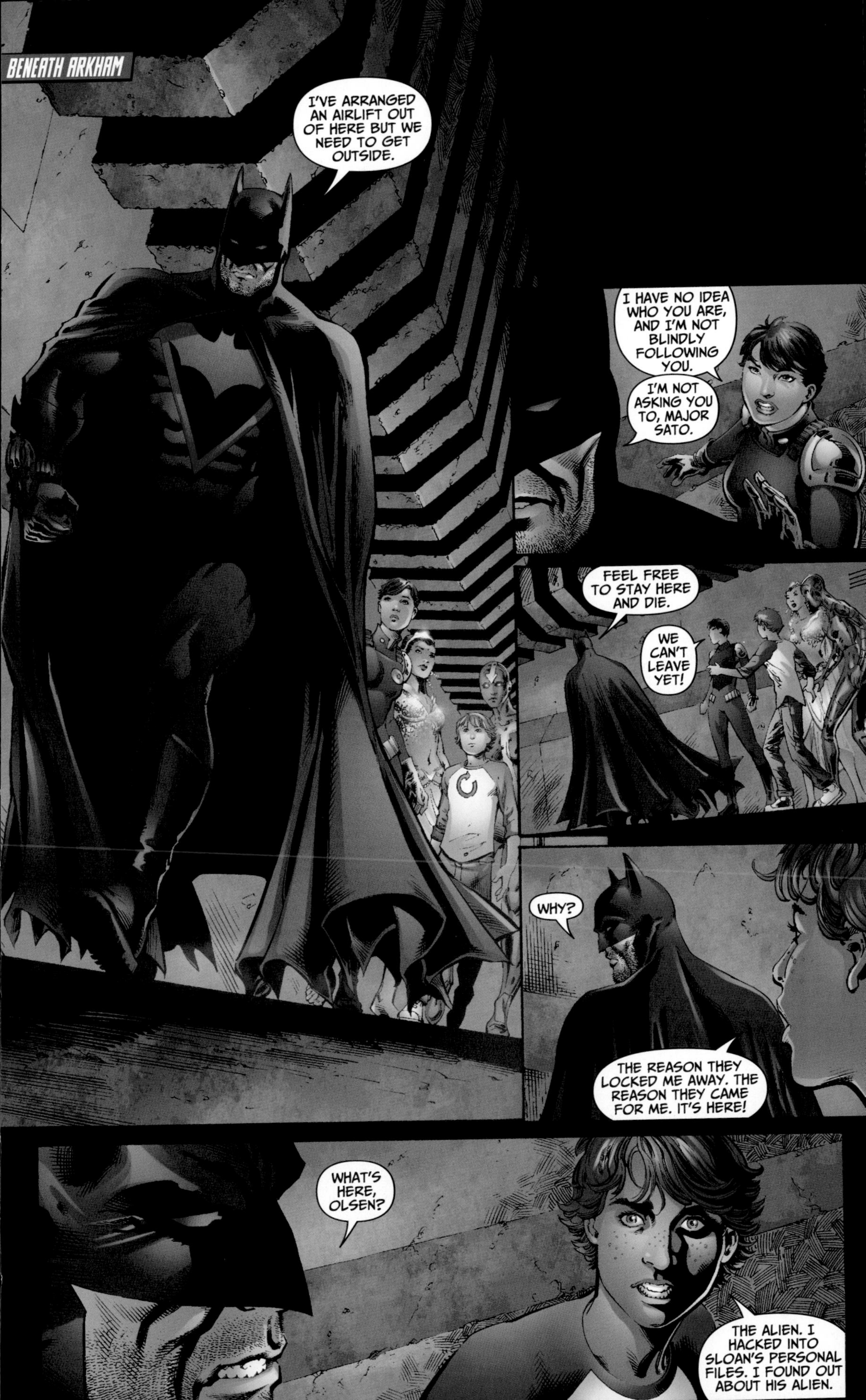

BENEATH ARKHAM
I'VE ARRANGED AN AIRLIFT OUT OF HERE BUT WE NEED TO GET OUTSIDE.
I HAVE NO IDEA WHO YOU ARE, AND I'M NOT BLINDLY FOLLOWING YOU.
I'M NOT ASKING YOU TO, MAJOR SATO.
FEEL FREE TO STAY HERE AND DIE.
WE CAN'T LEAVE YET!
WHY?
THE REASON THEY LOCKED ME AWAY. THE REASON THEY CAME FOR ME. IT'S HERE!
WHAT'S HERE, OLSEN?
THE ALIEN. I HACKED INTO SLOAN'S PERSONAL FILES. I FOUND OUT ABOUT HIS ALIEN.

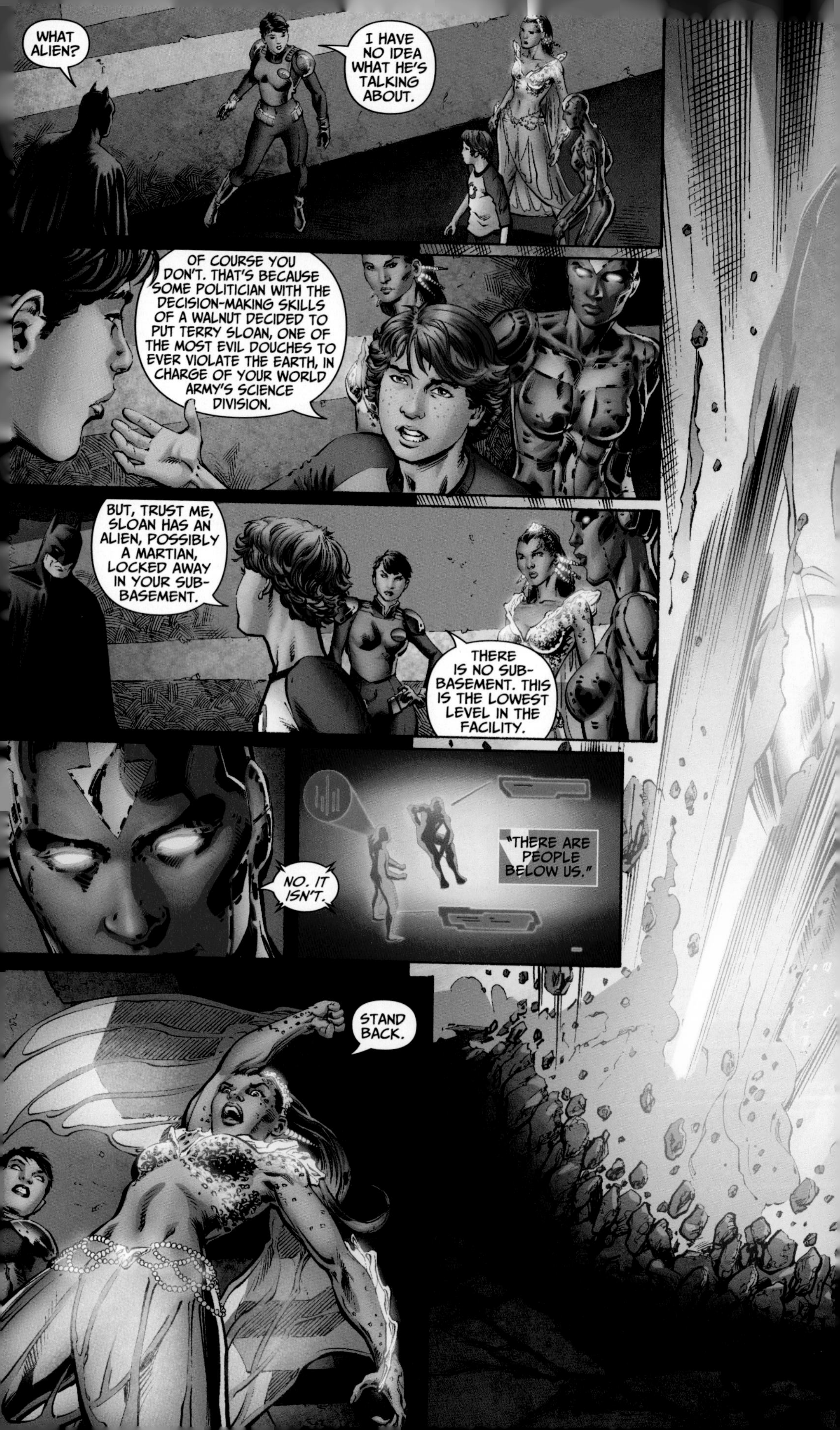
WHAT ALIEN?
I HAVE NO IDEA WHAT HE'S TALKING ABOUT.
OF COURSE YOU DON'T. THAT'S BECAUSE SOME POLITICIAN WITH THE DECISION-MAKING SKILLS OF A WALNUT DECIDED TO PUT TERRY SLOAN, ONE OF THE MOST EVIL DOUCHES TO EVER VIOLATE THE EARTH, IN CHARGE OF YOUR WORLD ARMY'S SCIENCE DIVISION.
BUT, TRUST ME, SLOAN HAS AN ALIEN, POSSIBLY A MARTIAN, LOCKED AWAY IN YOUR SUB-BASEMENT.
THERE IS NO SUB-BASEMENT. THIS IS THE LOWEST LEVEL IN THE FACILITY.
NO. IT ISN'T.
"THERE ARE PEOPLE BELOW US."
STAND BACK.

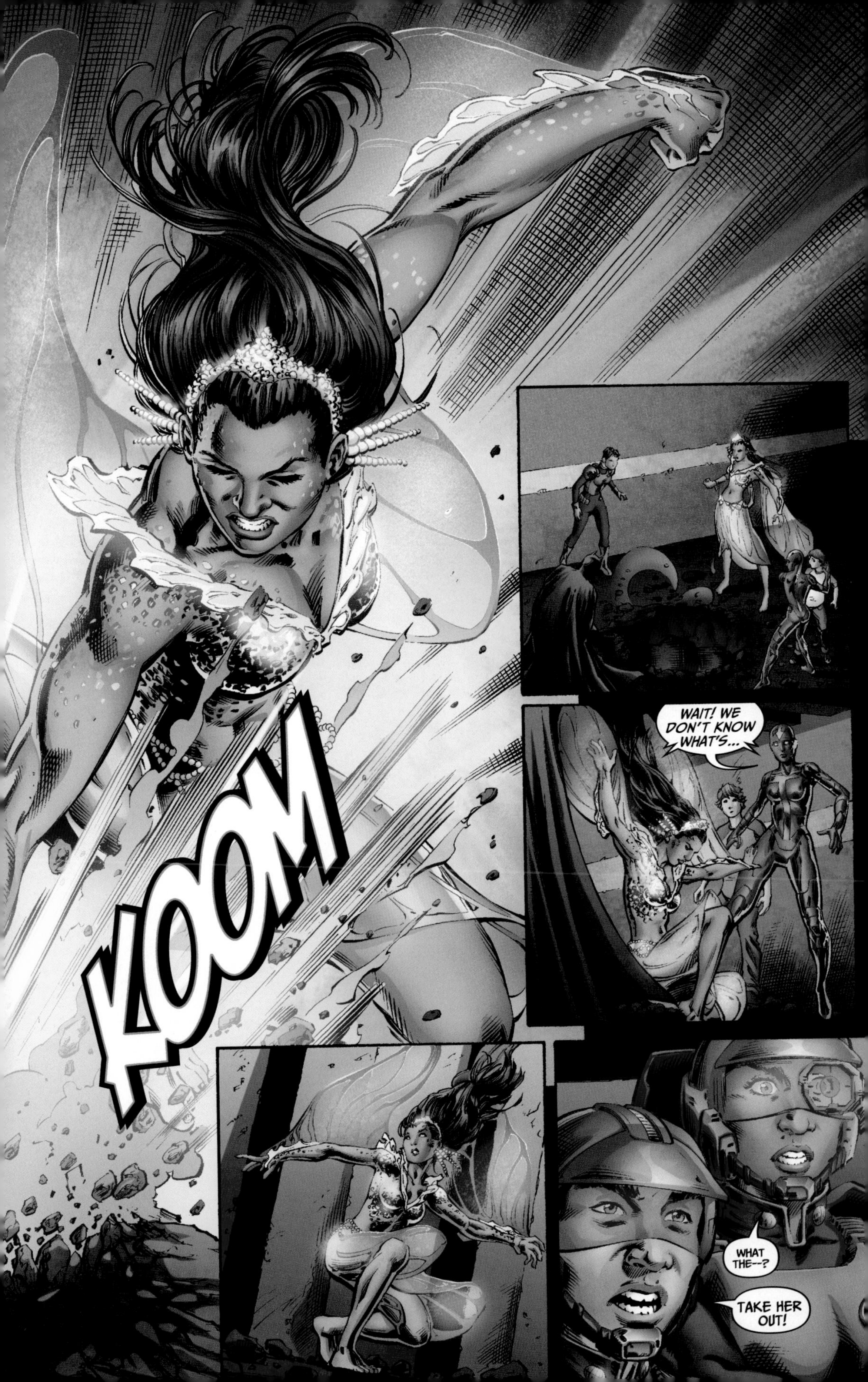
KOOM
WAIT! WE DON'T KNOW WHAT'S...
WHAT THE--?
TAKE HER OUT!

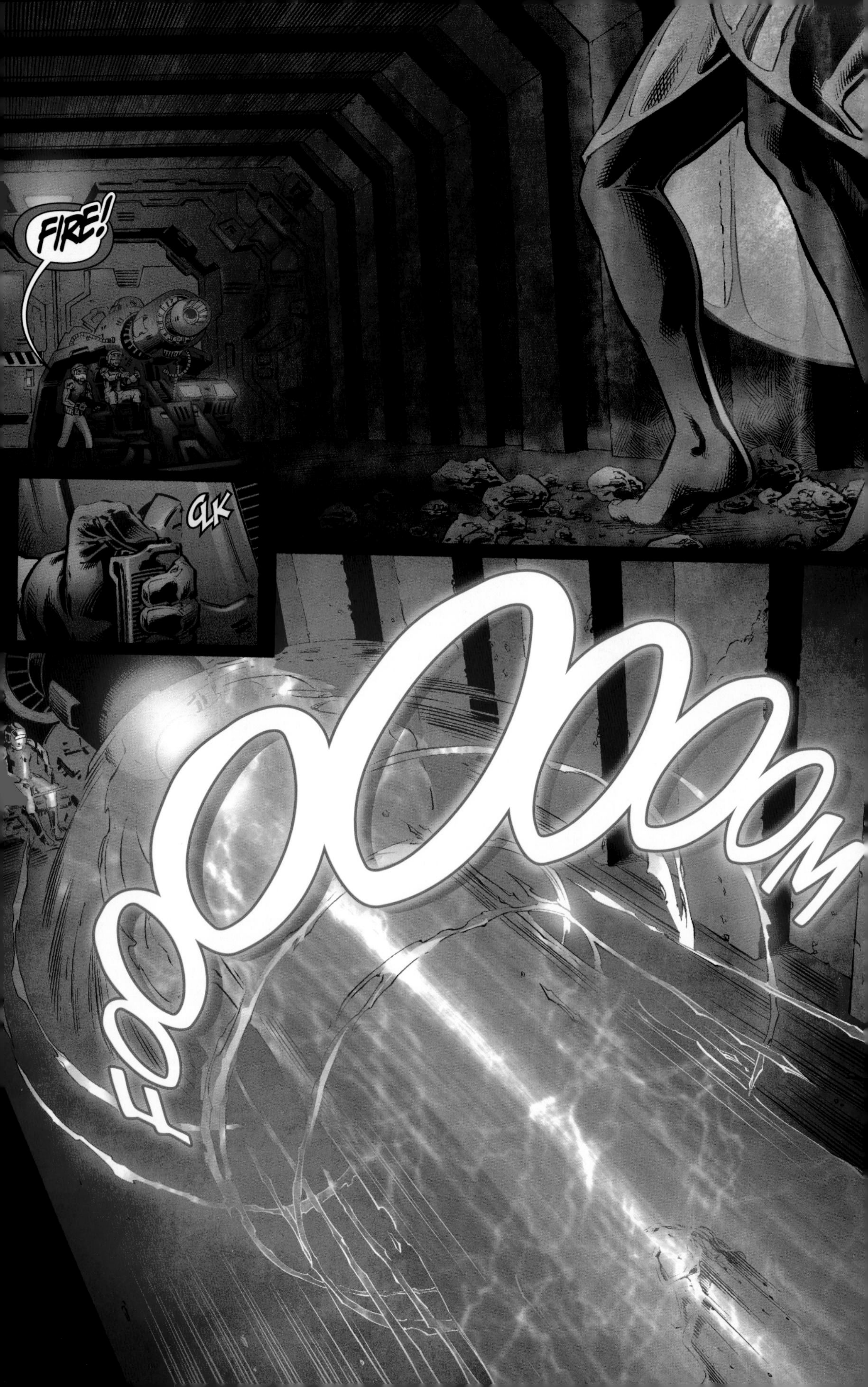
FIRE!
CLK
FOOOOOOM

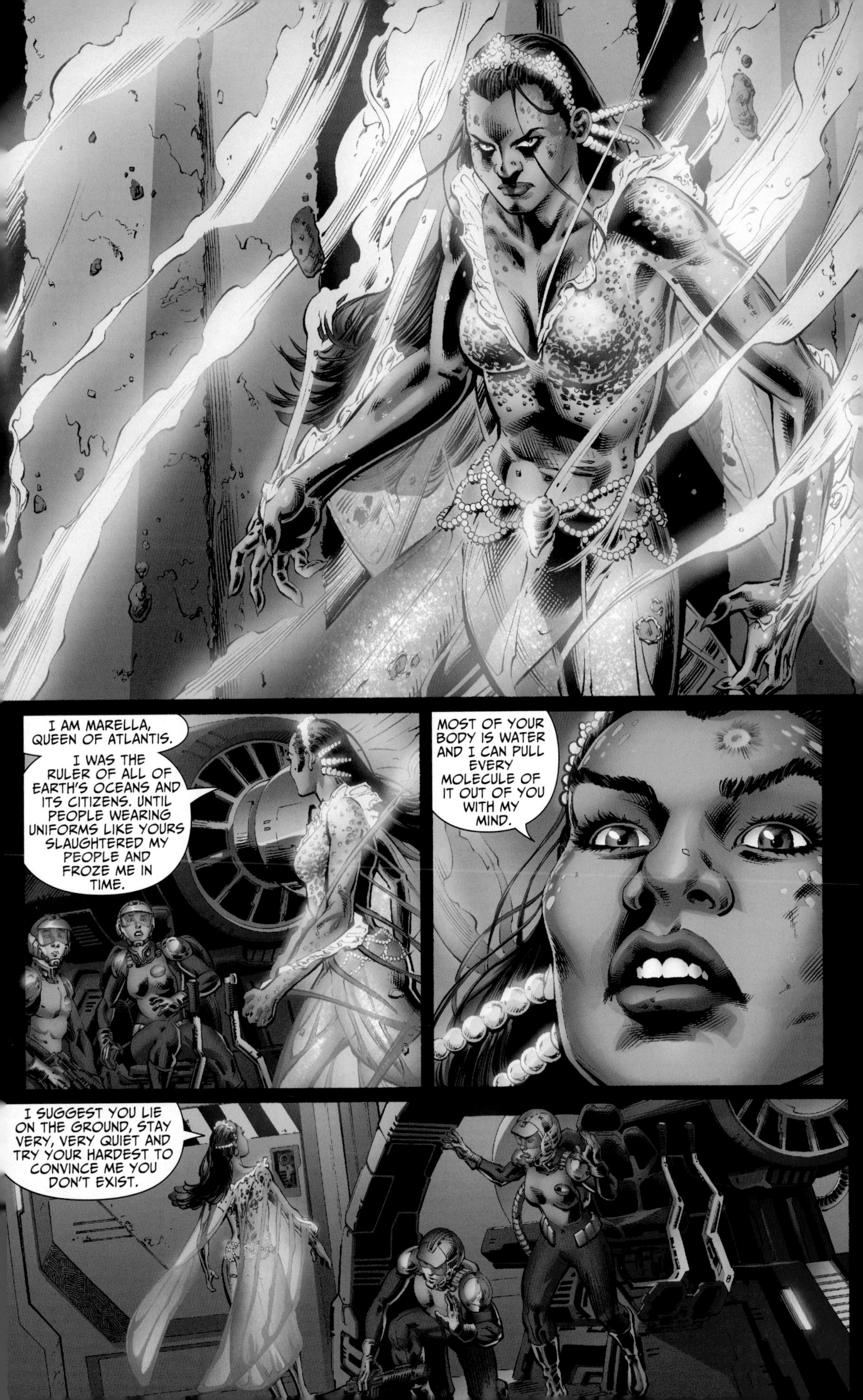
I AM MARELLA, QUEEN OF ATLANTIS.
I WAS THE RULER OF ALL OF EARTH'S OCEANS AND ITS CITIZENS. UNTIL PEOPLE WEARING UNIFORMS LIKE YOURS SLAUGHTERED MY PEOPLE AND FROZE ME IN TIME.
MOST OF YOUR BODY IS WATER AND I CAN PULL EVERY MOLECULE OF IT OUT OF YOU WITH MY MIND.
I SUGGEST YOU LIE ON THE GROUND, STAY VERY, VERY QUIET AND TRY YOUR HARDEST TO CONVINCE ME YOU DON'T EXIST.

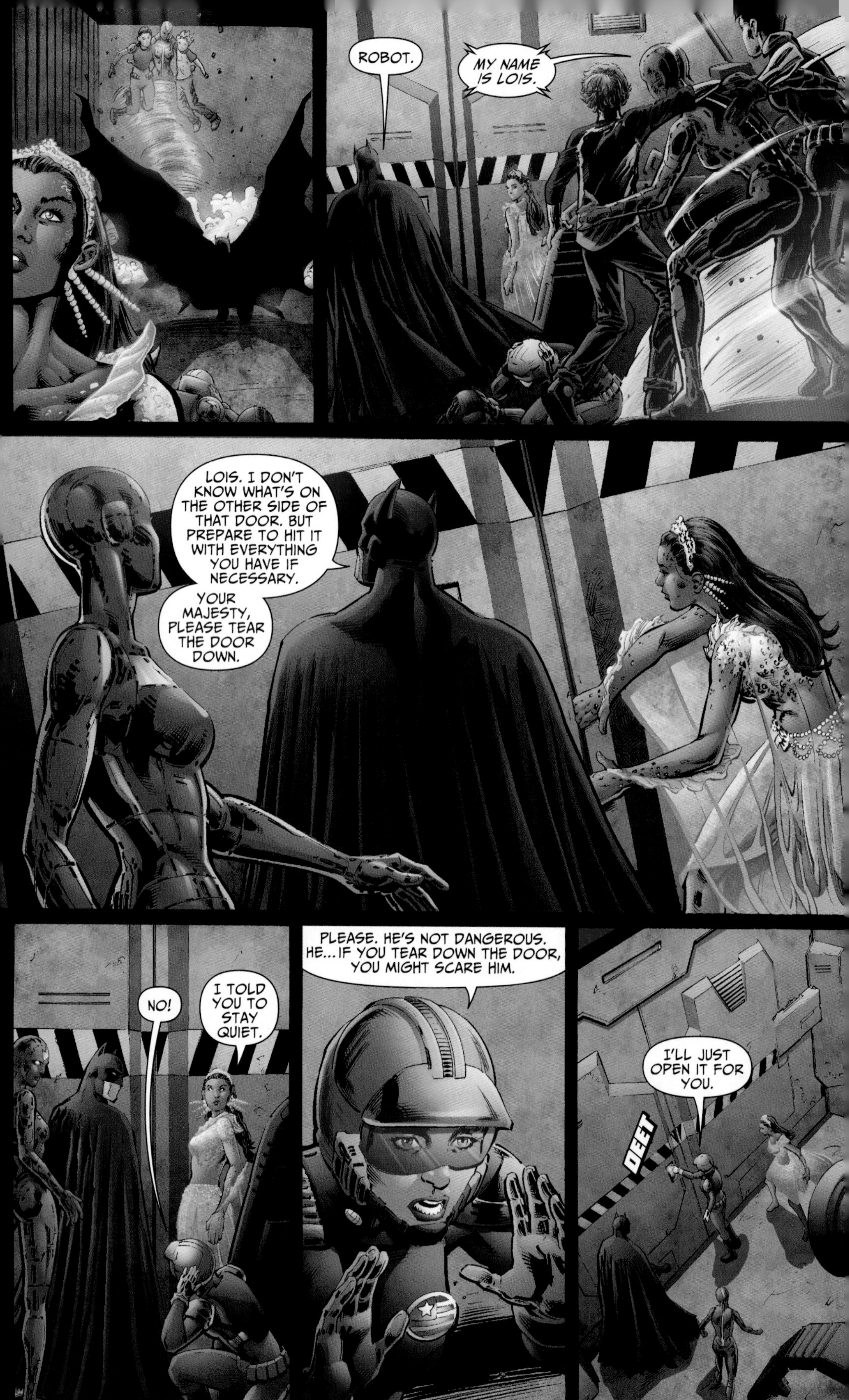
ROBOT.
MY NAME IS LOIS.
LOIS. I DON'T KNOW WHAT'S ON THE OTHER SIDE OF THAT DOOR. BUT PREPARE TO HIT IT WITH EVERYTHING YOU HAVE IF NECESSARY.
YOUR MAJESTY, PLEASE TEAR THE DOOR DOWN.
NO!
I TOLD YOU TO STAY QUIET.
PLEASE. HE'S NOT DANGEROUS. HE... IF YOU TEAR DOWN THE DOOR, YOU MIGHT SCARE HIM.
I'LL JUST OPEN IT FOR YOU.
DEET

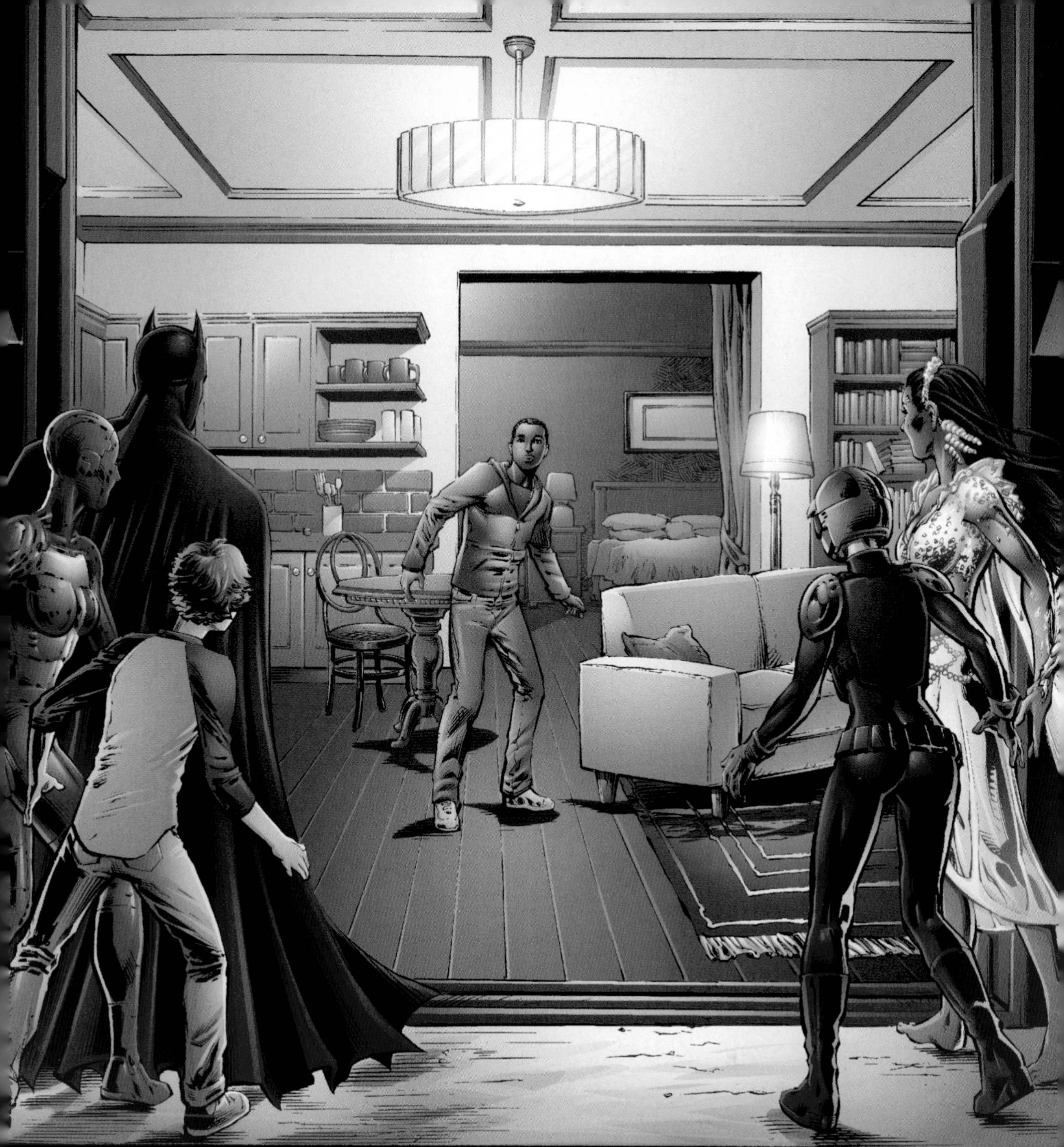

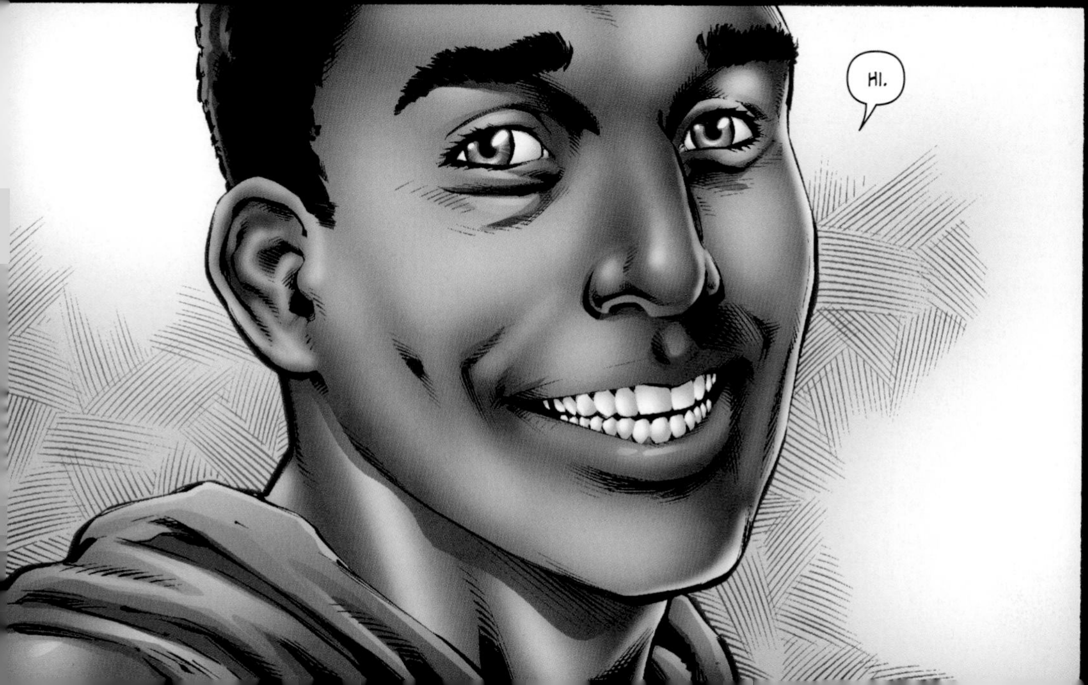
HI.

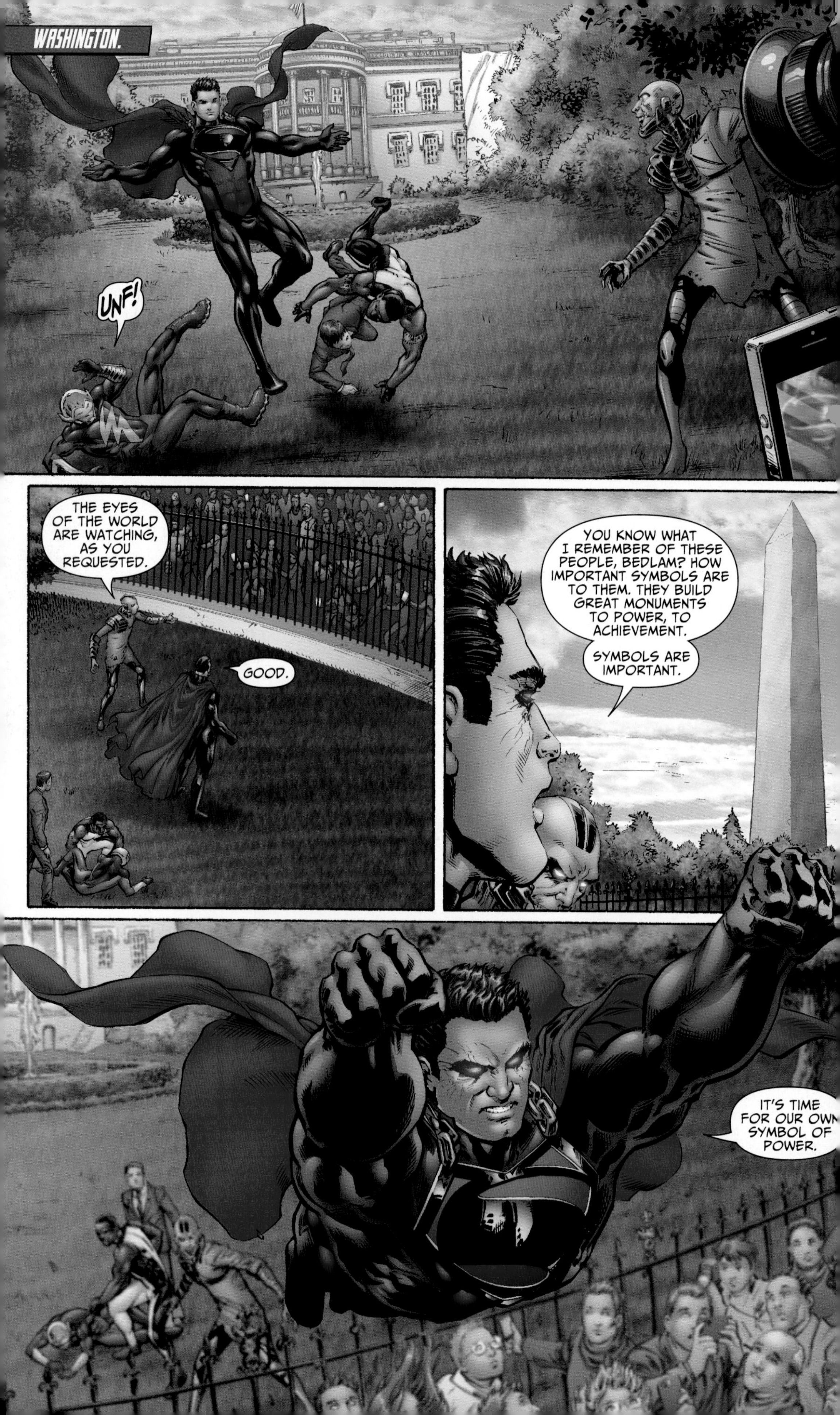
WASHINGTON.
UNF!
THE EYES OF THE WORLD ARE WATCHING, AS YOU REQUESTED.
GOOD.
YOU KNOW WHAT I REMEMBER OF THESE PEOPLE, BEDLAM? HOW IMPORTANT SYMBOLS ARE TO THEM. THEY BUILD GREAT MONUMENTS TO POWER, TO ACHIEVEMENT.
SYMBOLS ARE IMPORTANT.
IT'S TIME FOR OUR OWN SYMBOL OF POWER.

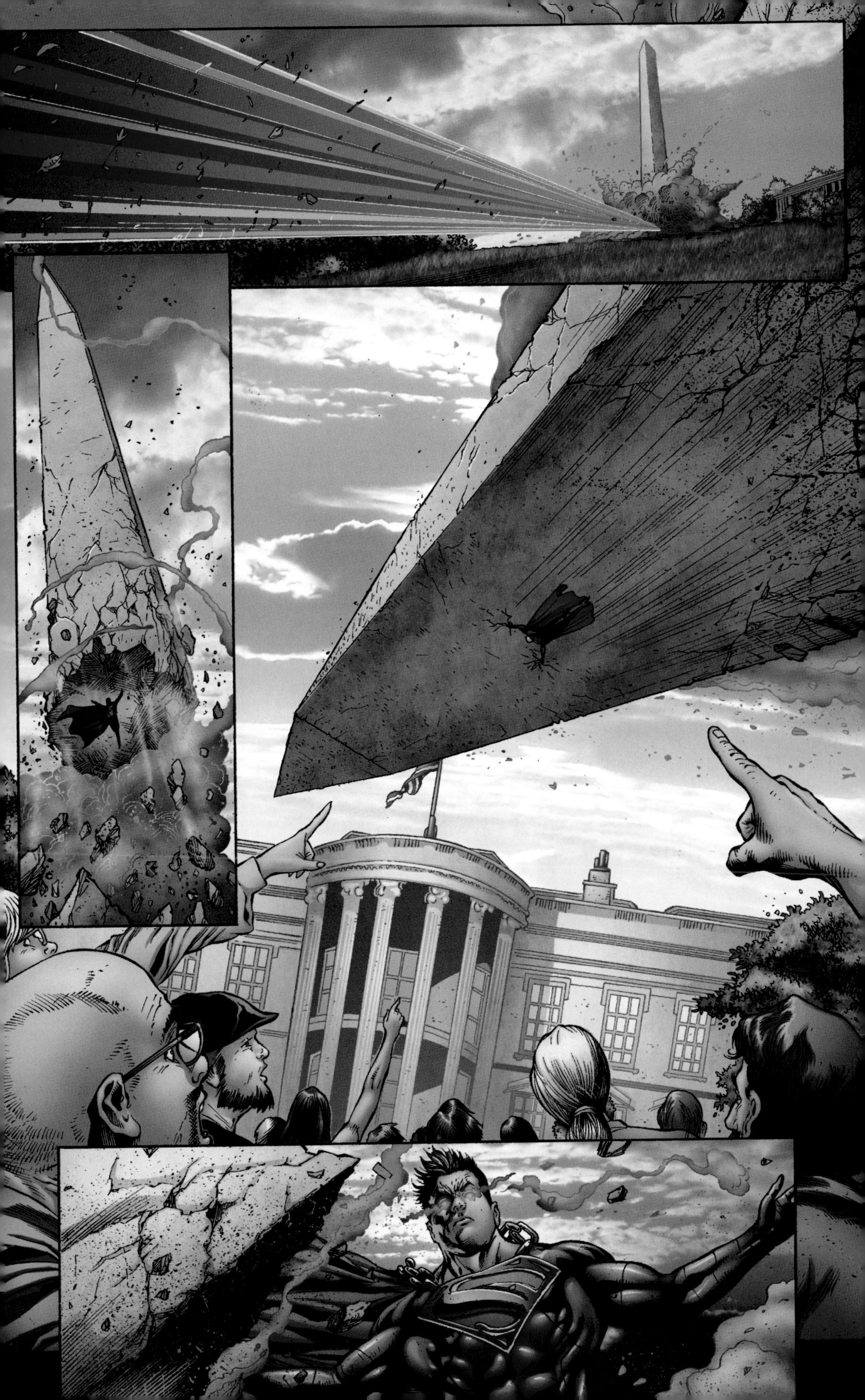

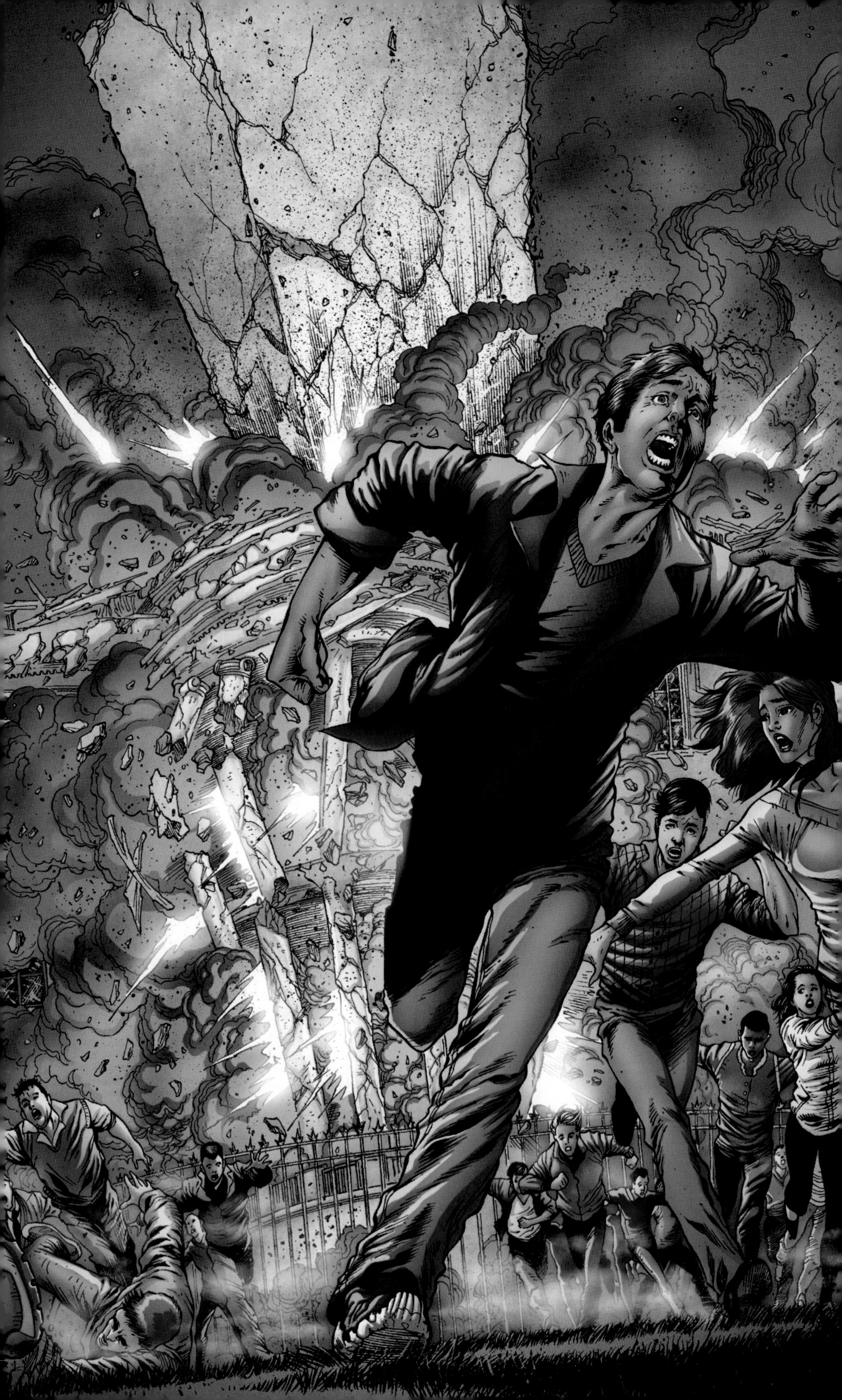

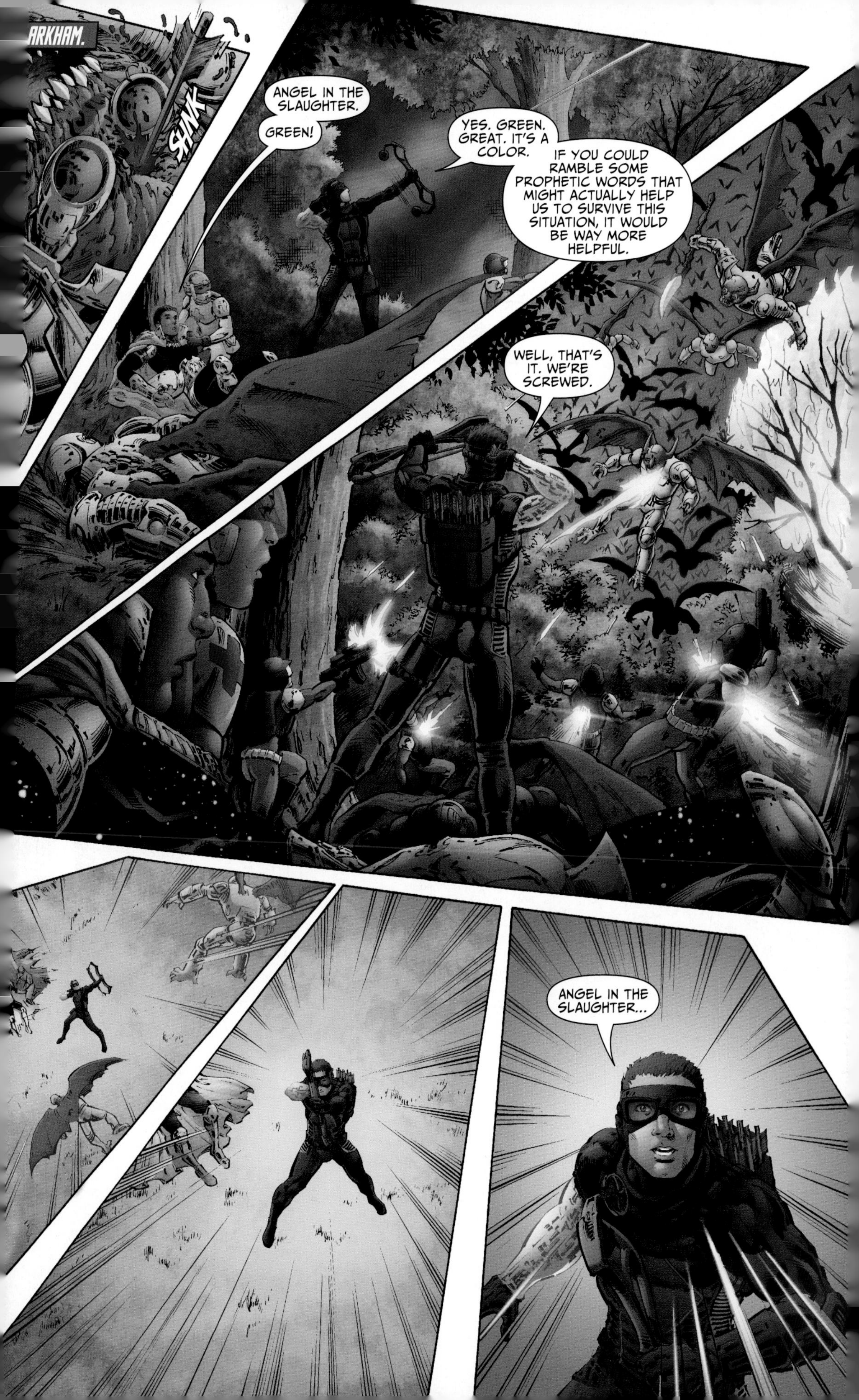
ARKHAM.
SHNK
ANGEL IN THE SLAUGHTER.
GREEN!
YES. GREEN. GREAT. IT'S A COLOR.
IF YOU COULD RAMBLE SOME PROPHETIC WORDS THAT MIGHT ACTUALLY HELP US TO SURVIVE THIS SITUATION, IT WOULD BE WAY MORE HELPFUL.
WELL, THAT'S IT. WE'RE SCREWED.
ANGEL IN THE SLAUGHTER...

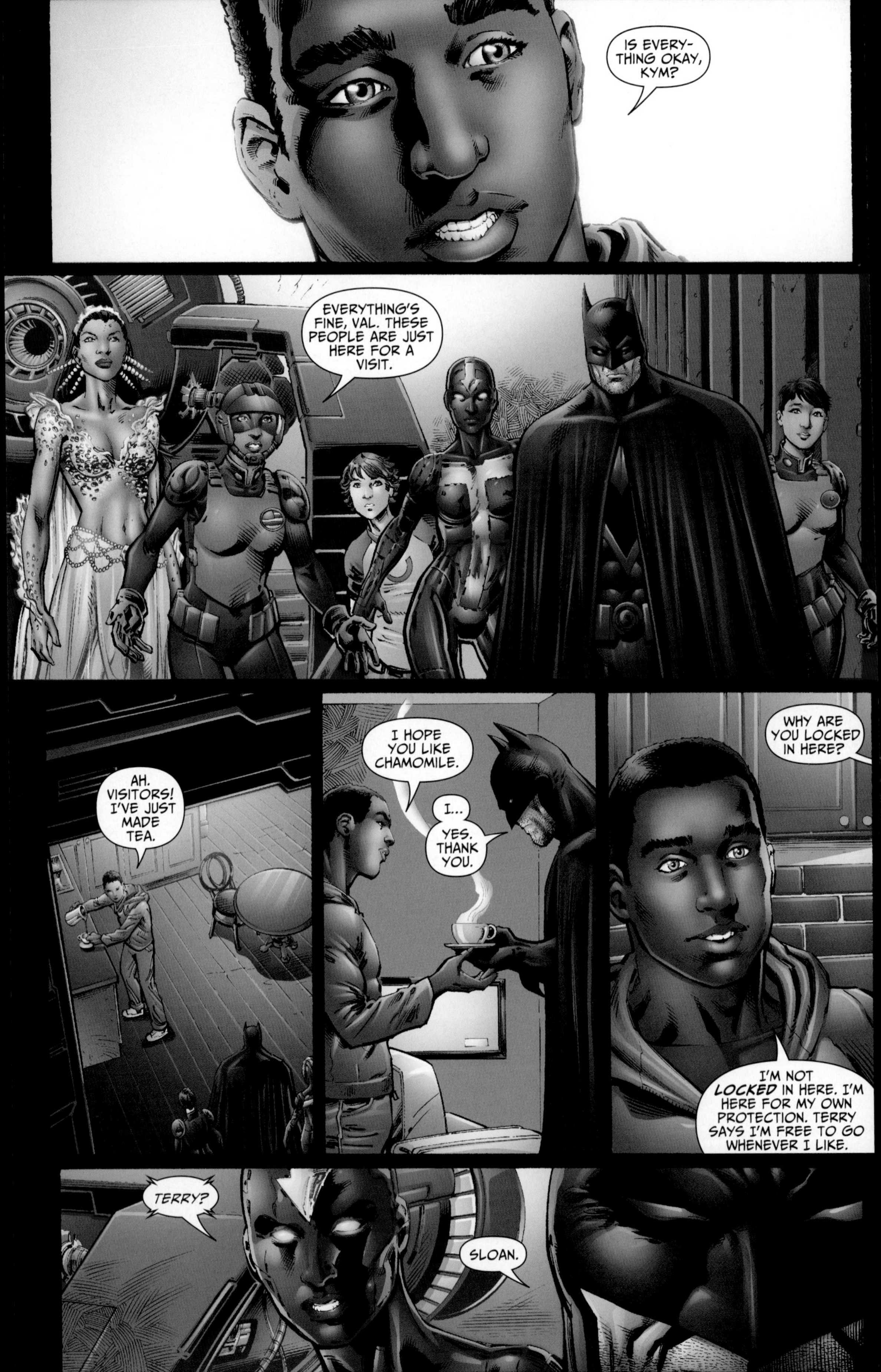
IS EVERY-THING OKAY, KYM?
EVERYTHING'S FINE, VAL. THESE PEOPLE ARE JUST HERE FOR A VISIT.
AH. VISITORS! I'VE JUST MADE TEA.
I HOPE YOU LIKE CHAMOMILE.
I... YES. THANK YOU.
WHY ARE YOU LOCKED IN HERE?
I'M NOT LOCKED IN HERE. I'M HERE FOR MY OWN PROTECTION. TERRY SAYS I'M FREE TO GO WHENEVER I LIKE.
TERRY?
SLOAN.

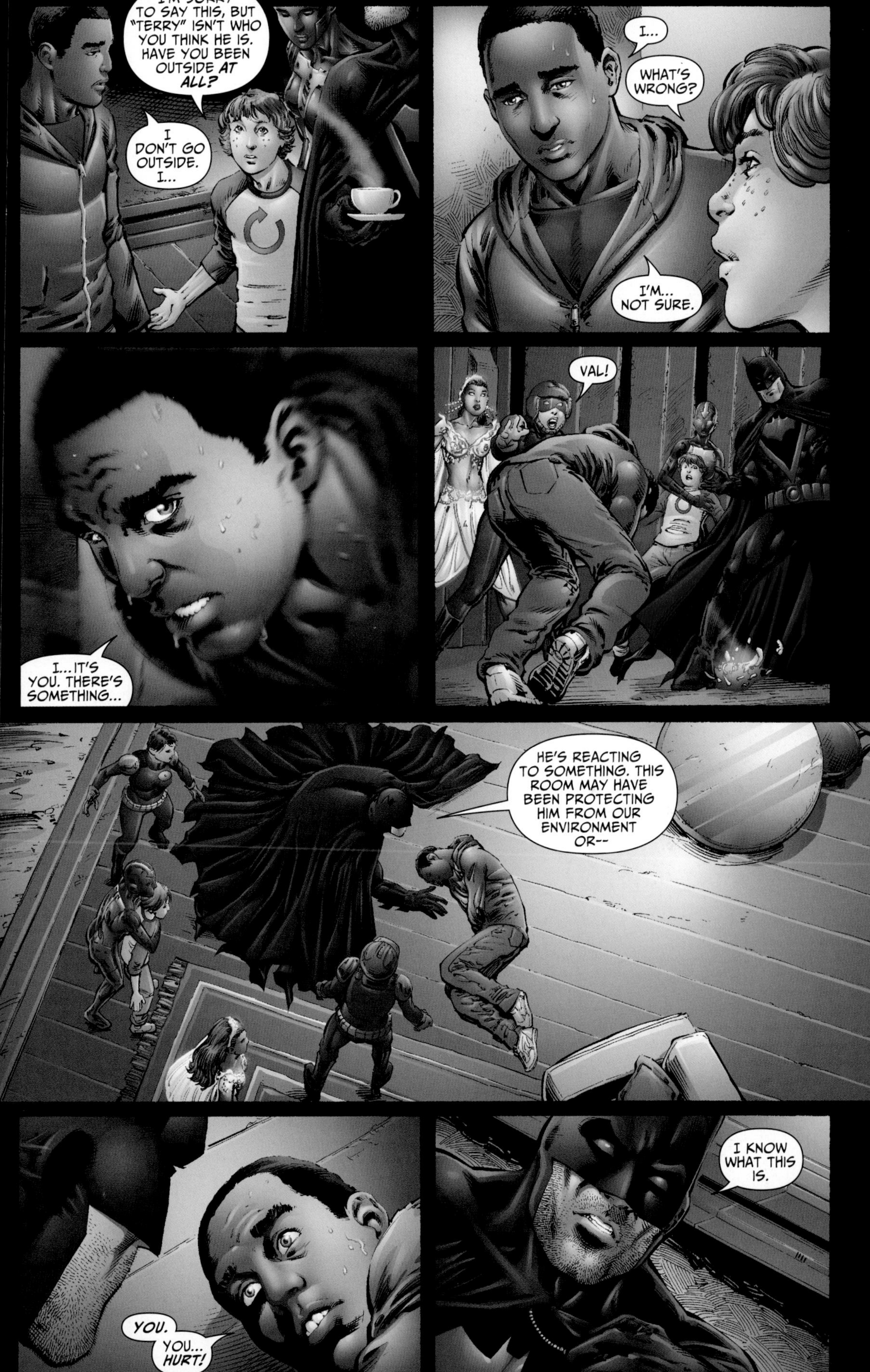
I'M SORRY TO SAY THIS, BUT "TERRY" ISN'T WHO YOU THINK HE IS. HAVE YOU BEEN OUTSIDE AT ALL?
I DON'T GO OUTSIDE. I...
I...
WHAT'S WRONG?
I'M... NOT SURE.
I...IT'S YOU. THERE'S SOMETHING...
VAL!
HE'S REACTING TO SOMETHING. THIS ROOM MAY HAVE BEEN PROTECTING HIM FROM OUR ENVIRONMENT OR--
YOU. YOU... HURT!
I KNOW WHAT THIS IS.

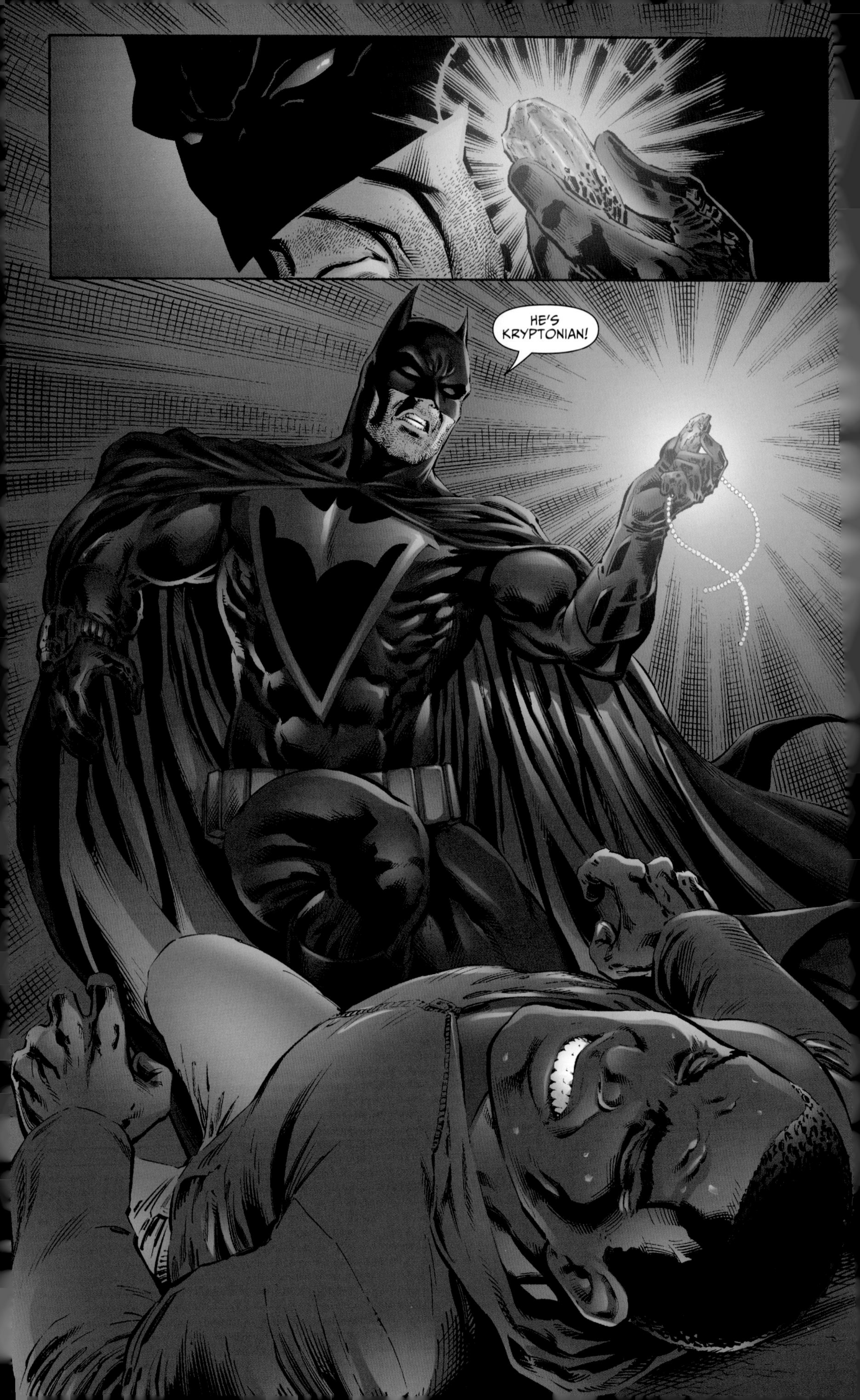
HE'S KRYPTONIAN!

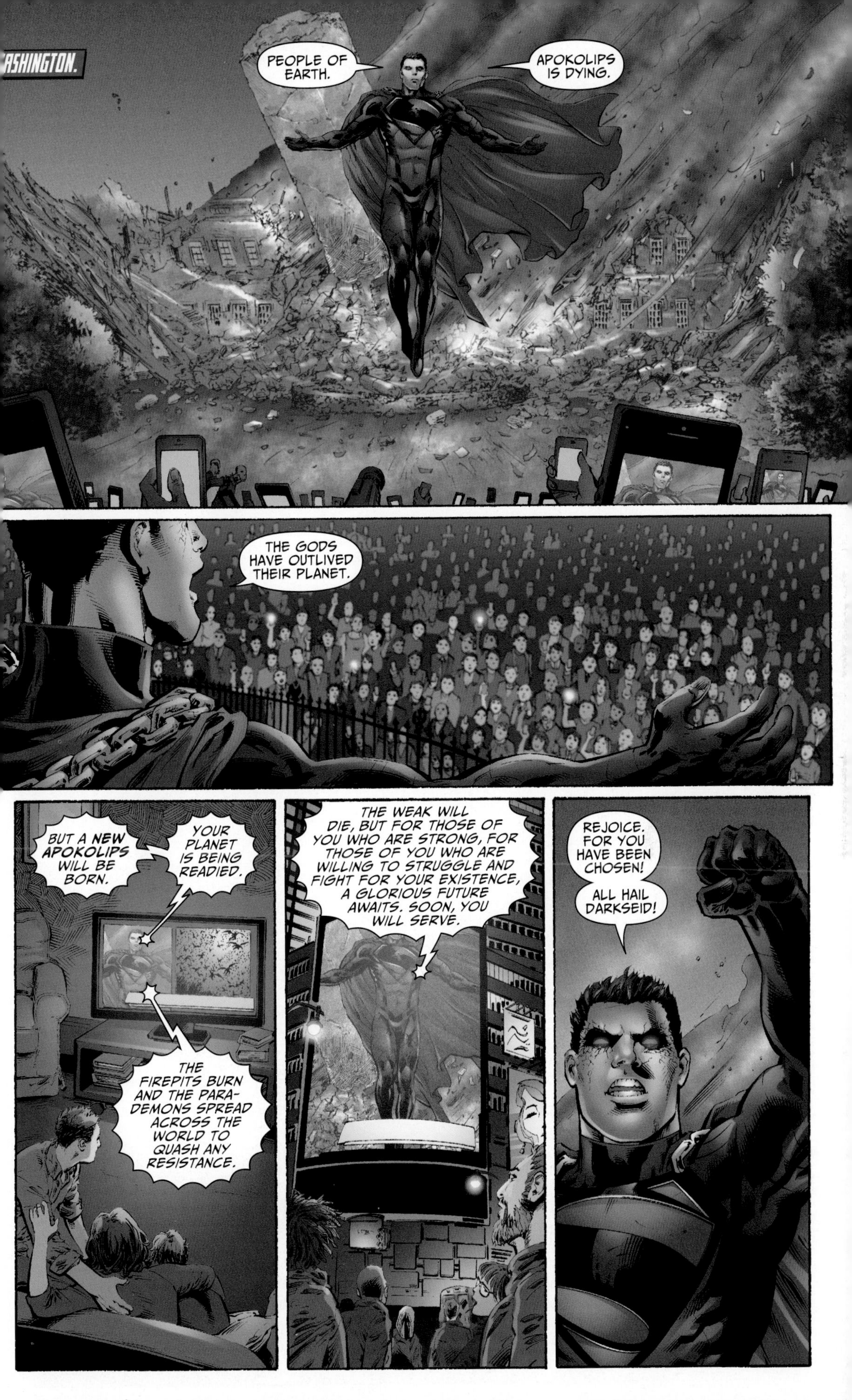

...ASHINGTON.
PEOPLE OF EARTH.
APOKOLIPS IS DYING.
THE GODS HAVE OUTLIVED THEIR PLANET.
BUT A NEW APOKOLIPS WILL BE BORN.
YOUR PLANET IS BEING READIED.
THE FIREPITS BURN AND THE PARA-DEMONS SPREAD ACROSS THE WORLD TO QUASH ANY RESISTANCE.
THE WEAK WILL DIE, BUT FOR THOSE OF YOU WHO ARE STRONG, FOR THOSE OF YOU WHO ARE WILLING TO STRUGGLE AND FIGHT FOR YOUR EXISTENCE, A GLORIOUS FUTURE AWAITS. SOON, YOU WILL SERVE.
REJOICE. FOR YOU HAVE BEEN CHOSEN!
ALL HAIL DARKSEID!

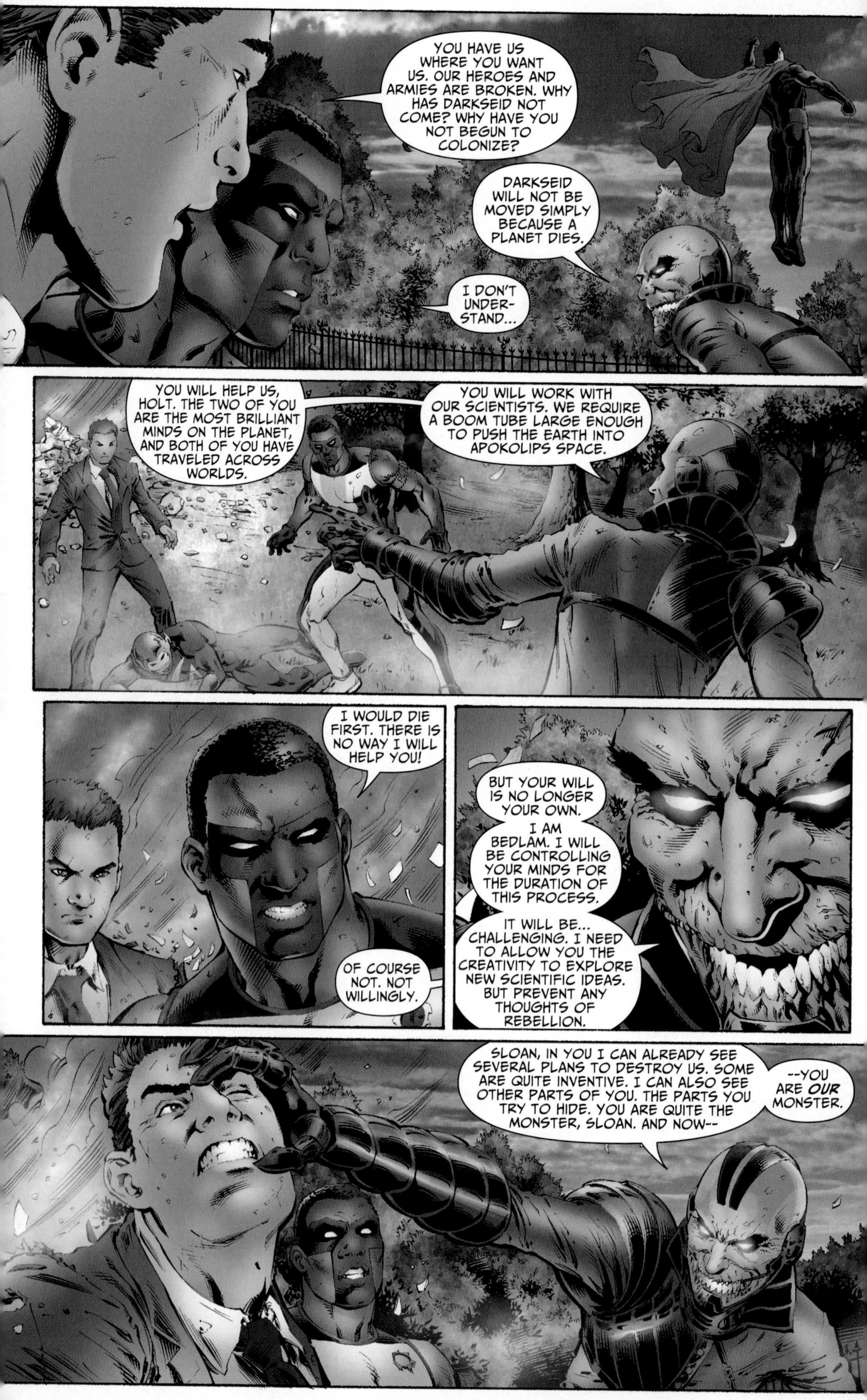
YOU HAVE US WHERE YOU WANT US. OUR HEROES AND ARMIES ARE BROKEN. WHY HAS DARKSEID NOT COME? WHY HAVE YOU NOT BEGUN TO COLONIZE?
DARKSEID WILL NOT BE MOVED SIMPLY BECAUSE A PLANET DIES.
I DON'T UNDER-STAND...
YOU WILL HELP US, HOLT. THE TWO OF YOU ARE THE MOST BRILLIANT MINDS ON THE PLANET, AND BOTH OF YOU HAVE TRAVELED ACROSS WORLDS.
YOU WILL WORK WITH OUR SCIENTISTS. WE REQUIRE A BOOM TUBE LARGE ENOUGH TO PUSH THE EARTH INTO APOKOLIPS SPACE.
I WOULD DIE FIRST. THERE IS NO WAY I WILL HELP YOU!
OF COURSE NOT. NOT WILLINGLY.
BUT YOUR WILL IS NO LONGER YOUR OWN.
I AM BEDLAM. I WILL BE CONTROLLING YOUR MINDS FOR THE DURATION OF THIS PROCESS.
IT WILL BE... CHALLENGING. I NEED TO ALLOW YOU THE CREATIVITY TO EXPLORE NEW SCIENTIFIC IDEAS. BUT PREVENT ANY THOUGHTS OF REBELLION.
SLOAN, IN YOU I CAN ALREADY SEE SEVERAL PLANS TO DESTROY US. SOME ARE QUITE INVENTIVE. I CAN ALSO SEE OTHER PARTS OF YOU. THE PARTS YOU TRY TO HIDE. YOU ARE QUITE THE MONSTER, SLOAN. AND NOW--
--YOU ARE *OUR* MONSTER.

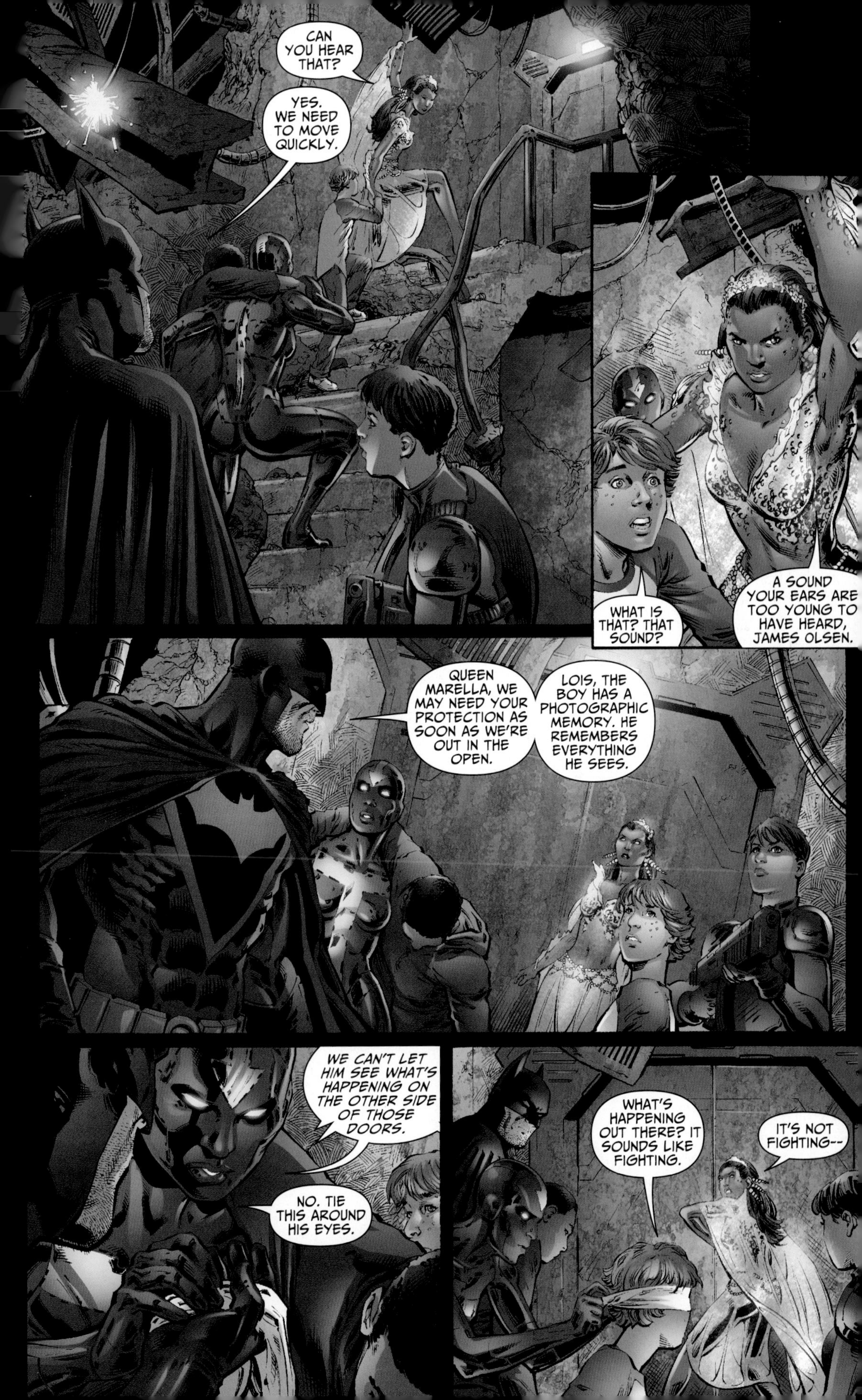
CAN YOU HEAR THAT?
YES. WE NEED TO MOVE QUICKLY.
WHAT IS THAT? THAT SOUND?
A SOUND YOUR EARS ARE TOO YOUNG TO HAVE HEARD, JAMES OLSEN.
QUEEN MARELLA, WE MAY NEED YOUR PROTECTION AS SOON AS WE'RE OUT IN THE OPEN.
LOIS, THE BOY HAS A PHOTOGRAPHIC MEMORY. HE REMEMBERS EVERYTHING HE SEES.
WE CAN'T LET HIM SEE WHAT'S HAPPENING ON THE OTHER SIDE OF THOSE DOORS.
NO. TIE THIS AROUND HIS EYES.
WHAT'S HAPPENING OUT THERE? IT SOUNDS LIKE FIGHTING.
IT'S NOT FIGHTING--

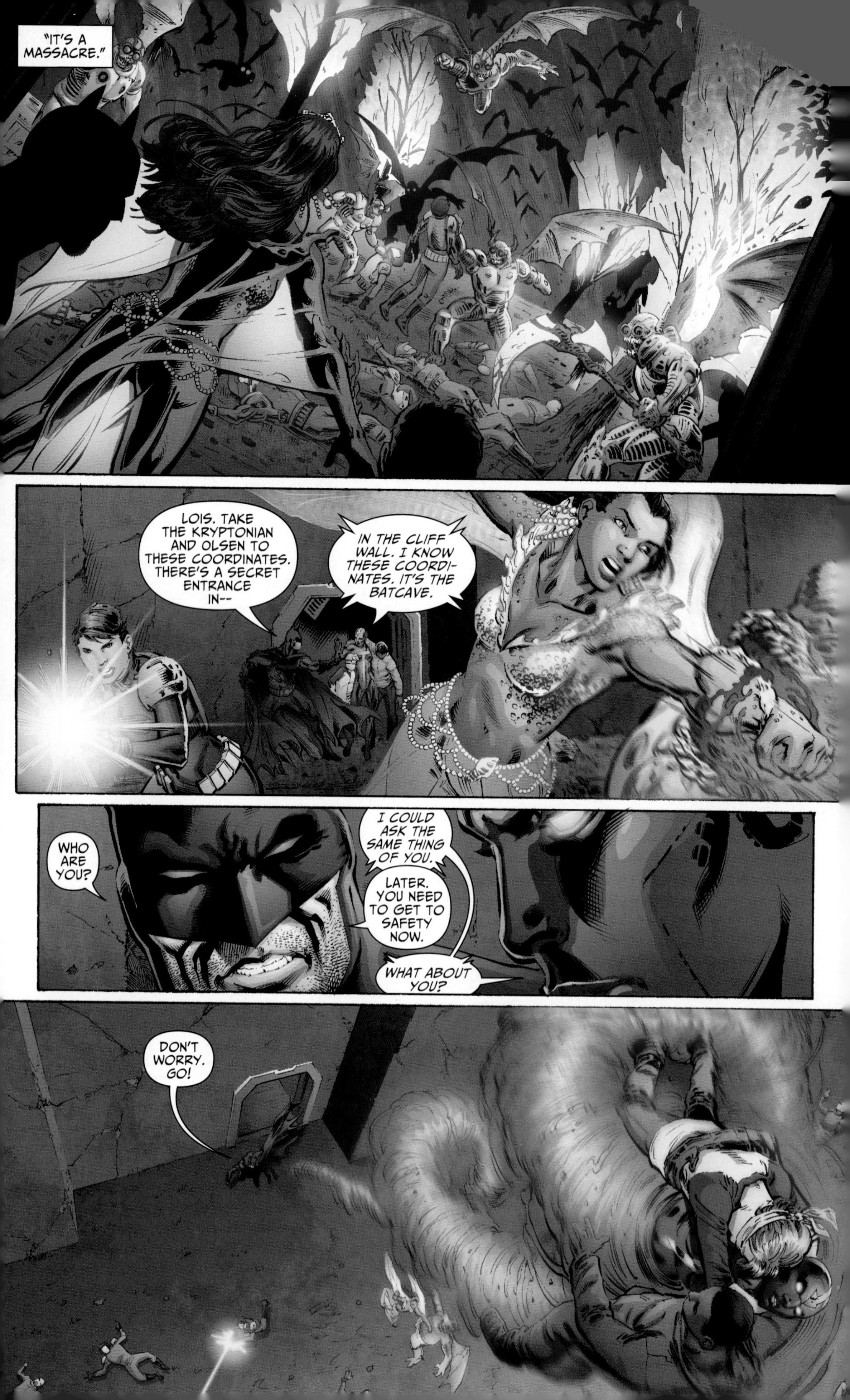
"IT'S A MASSACRE."
LOIS. TAKE THE KRYPTONIAN AND OLSEN TO THESE COORDINATES. THERE'S A SECRET ENTRANCE IN--
IN THE CLIFF WALL. I KNOW THESE COORDI-NATES. IT'S THE BATCAVE.
WHO ARE YOU?
I COULD ASK THE SAME THING OF YOU.
LATER. YOU NEED TO GET TO SAFETY NOW.
WHAT ABOUT YOU?
DON'T WORRY. GO!

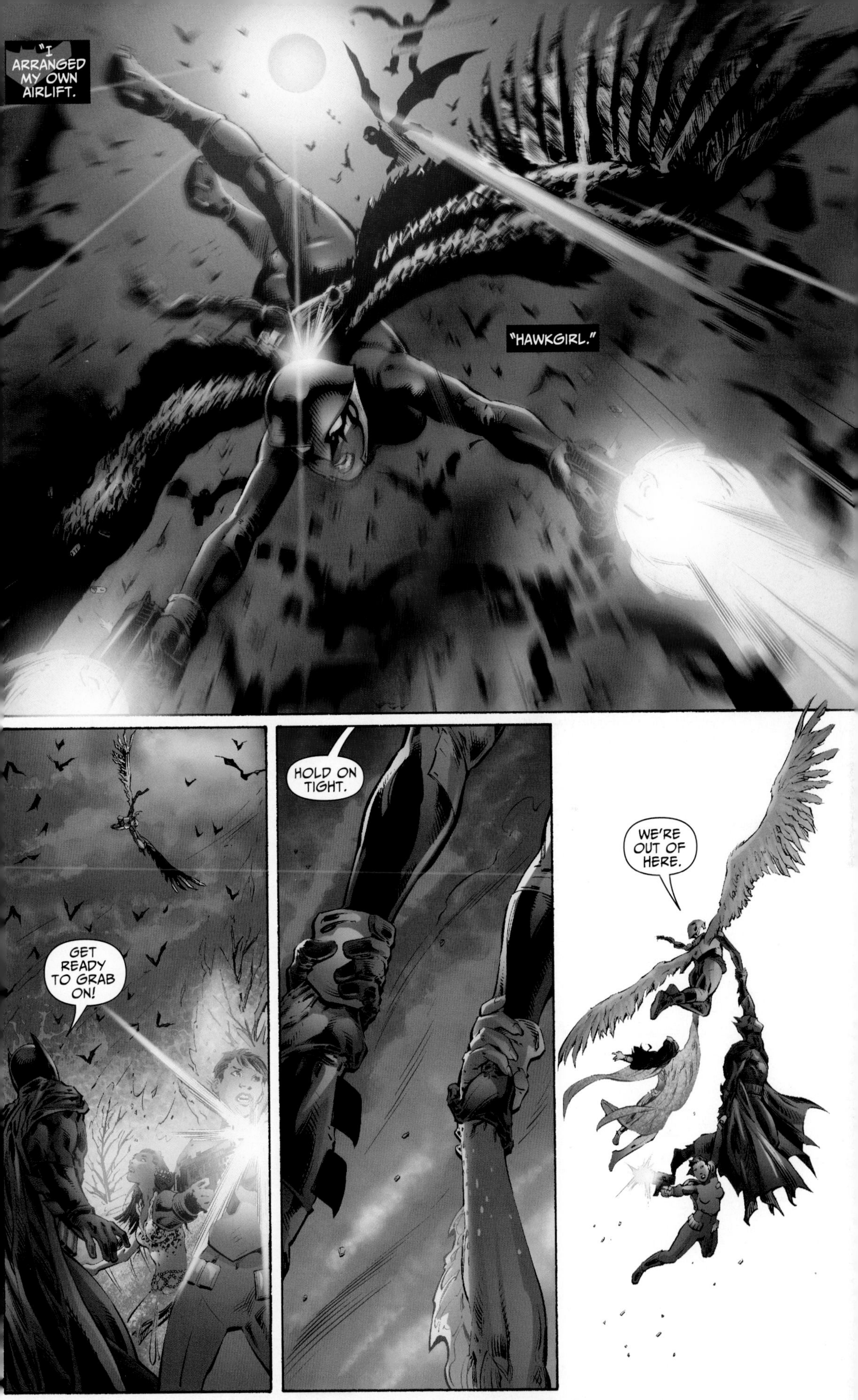
"I ARRANGED MY OWN AIRLIFT.
"HAWKGIRL."
GET READY TO GRAB ON!
HOLD ON TIGHT.
WE'RE OUT OF HERE.

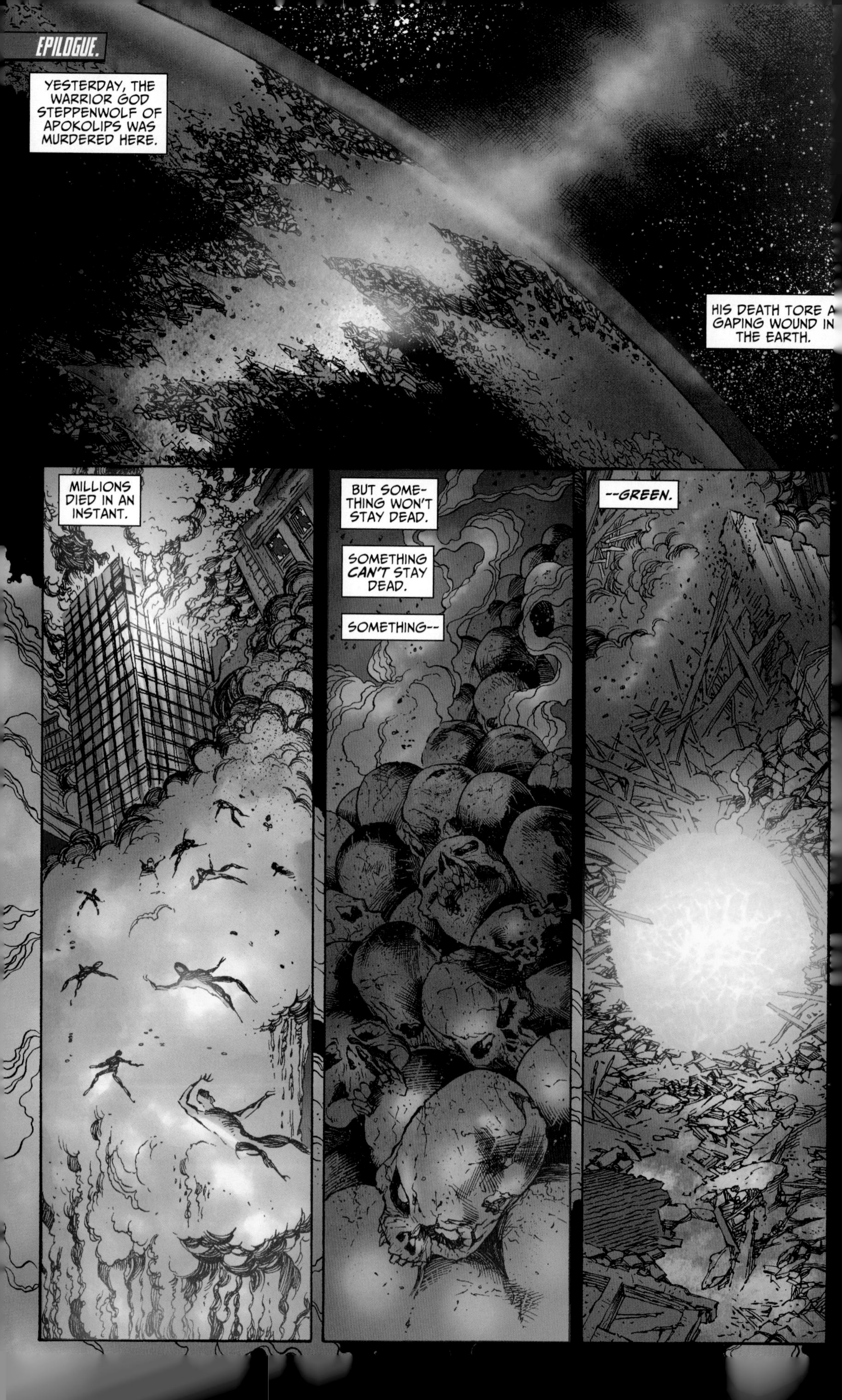
EPILOGUE.
YESTERDAY, THE WARRIOR GOD STEPPENWOLF OF APOKOLIPS WAS MURDERED HERE.
HIS DEATH TORE A GAPING WOUND IN THE EARTH.
MILLIONS DIED IN AN INSTANT.
BUT SOMETHING WON'T STAY DEAD.
SOMETHING CAN'T STAY DEAD.
SOMETHING--
--GREEN.

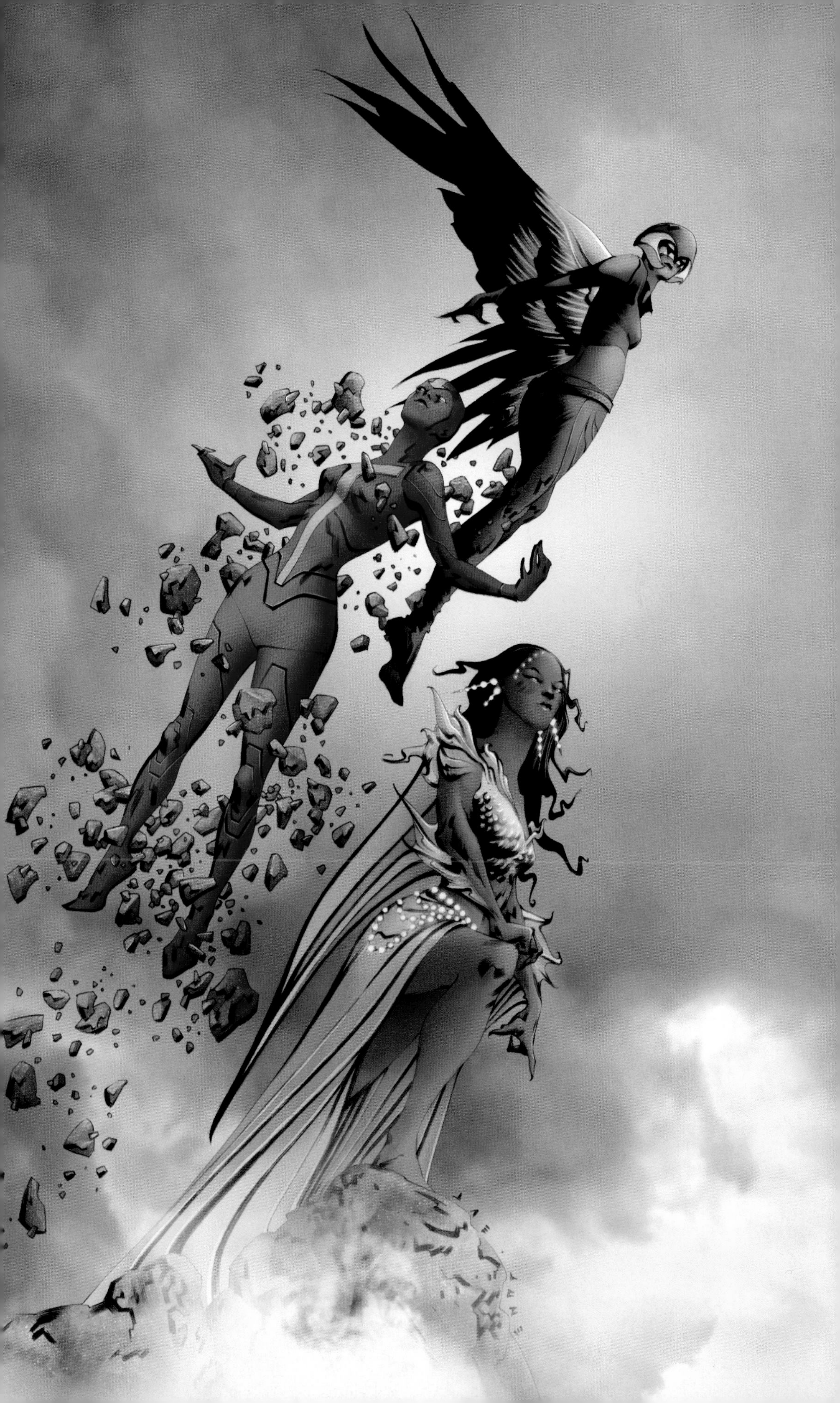

THE DARK AGE
PART 4

TOM TAYLOR
writer

BARRY KITSON
ROBSON ROCHA
pencillers

BARRY KITSON
OCLAIR ALBERT
inkers

JAE LEE & JUNE CHUNG
cover artists

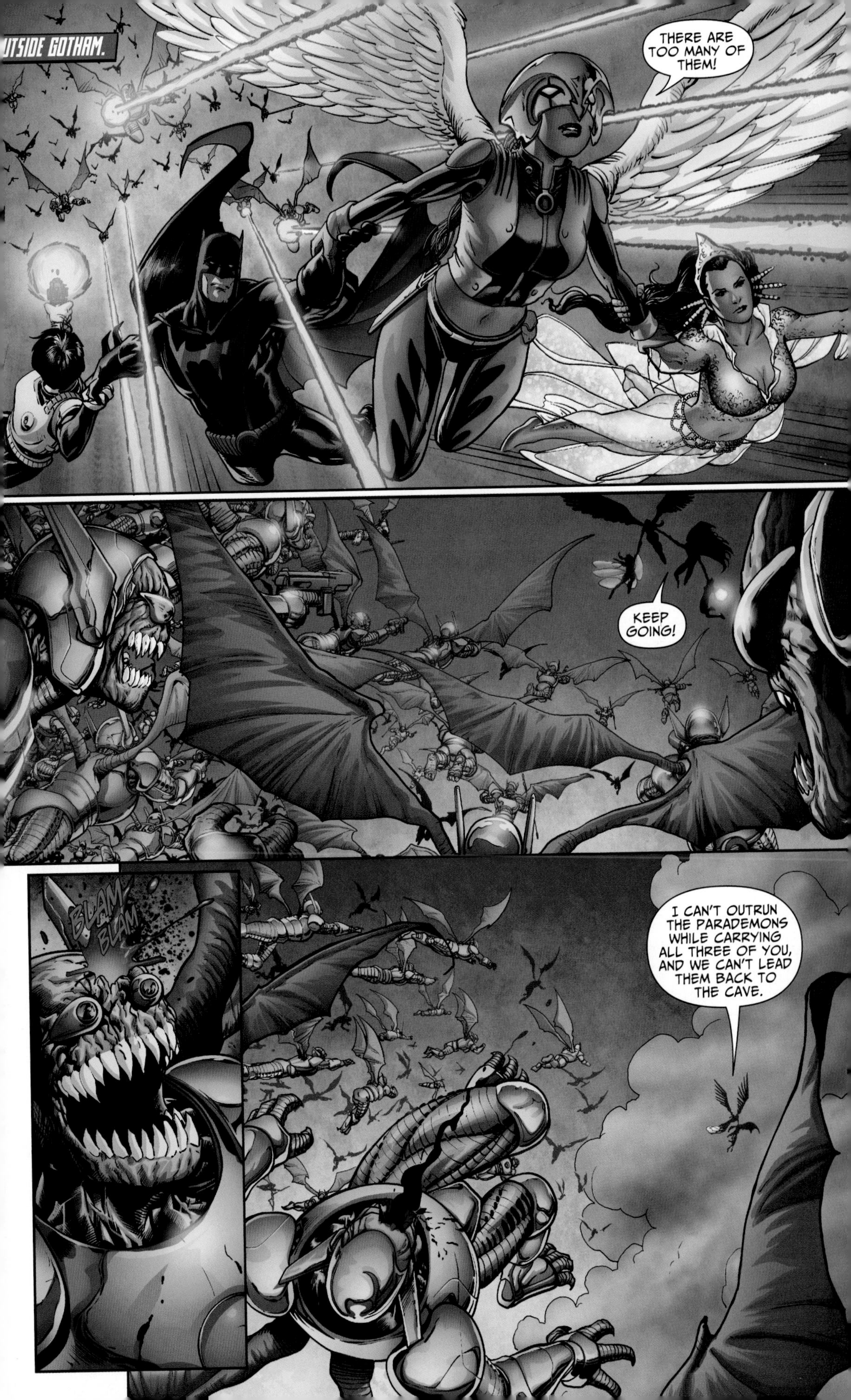
UTSIDE GOTHAM.
THERE ARE TOO MANY OF THEM!
KEEP GOING!
BLAM BLAM
I CAN'T OUTRUN THE PARADEMONS WHILE CARRYING ALL THREE OF YOU, AND WE CAN'T LEAD THEM BACK TO THE CAVE.

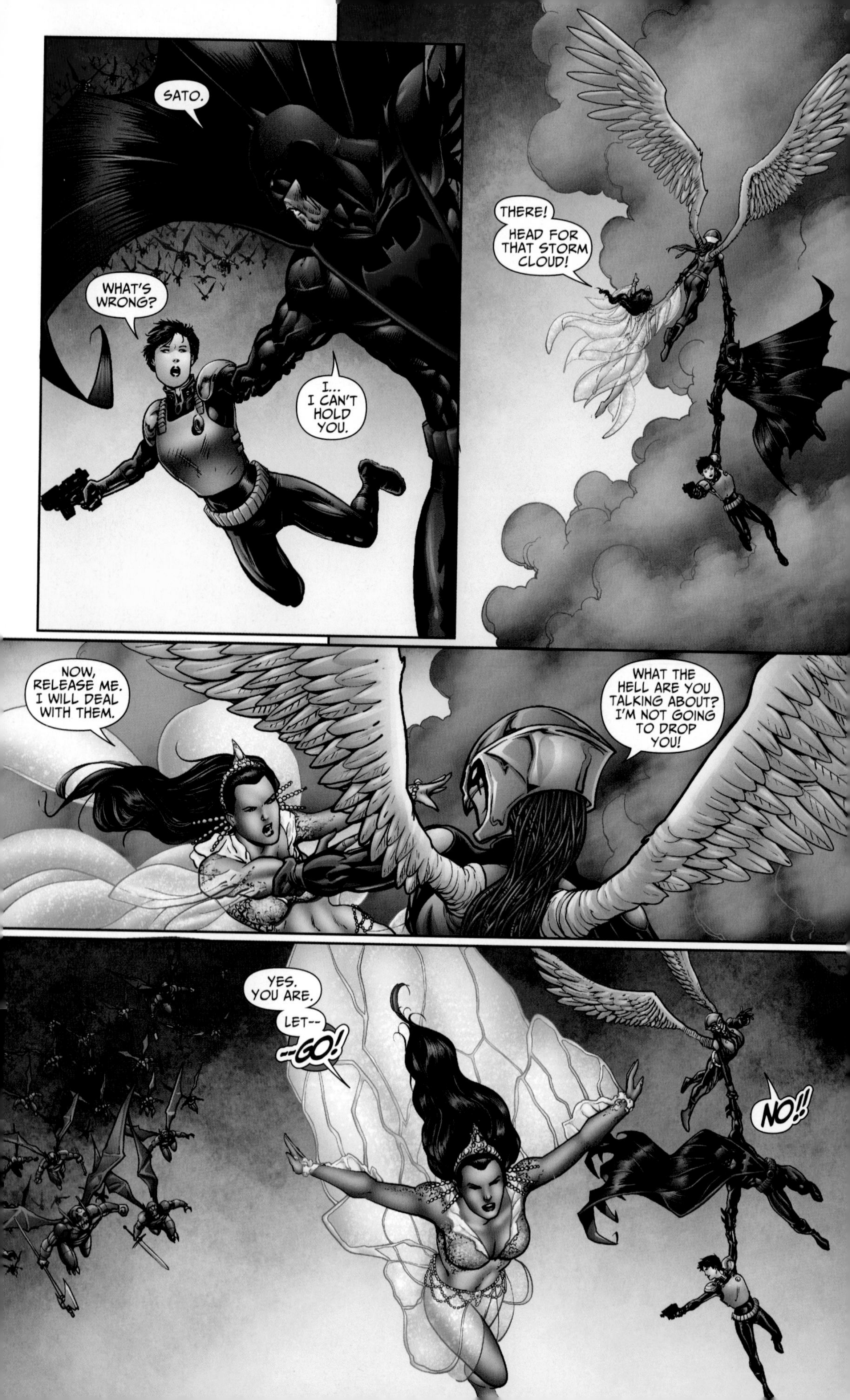

SATO.
WHAT'S WRONG?
I... I CAN'T HOLD YOU.
THERE! HEAD FOR THAT STORM CLOUD!
NOW, RELEASE ME. I WILL DEAL WITH THEM.
WHAT THE HELL ARE YOU TALKING ABOUT? I'M NOT GOING TO DROP YOU!
YES. YOU ARE.
LET--
--GO!
NO!!

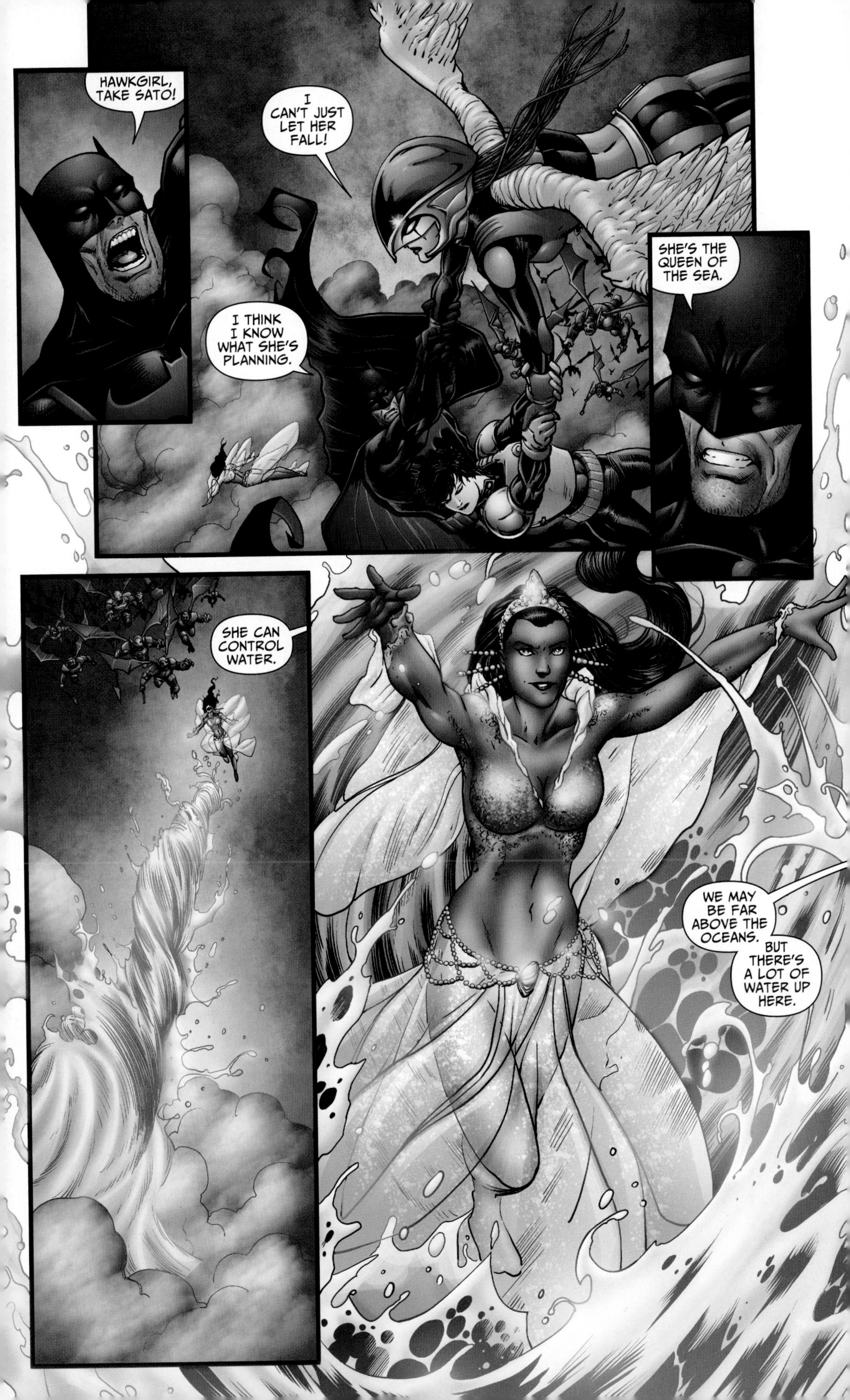
HAWKGIRL, TAKE SATO!
I CAN'T JUST LET HER FALL!
I THINK I KNOW WHAT SHE'S PLANNING.
SHE'S THE QUEEN OF THE SEA.
SHE CAN CONTROL WATER.
WE MAY BE FAR ABOVE THE OCEANS.
BUT THERE'S A LOT OF WATER UP HERE.

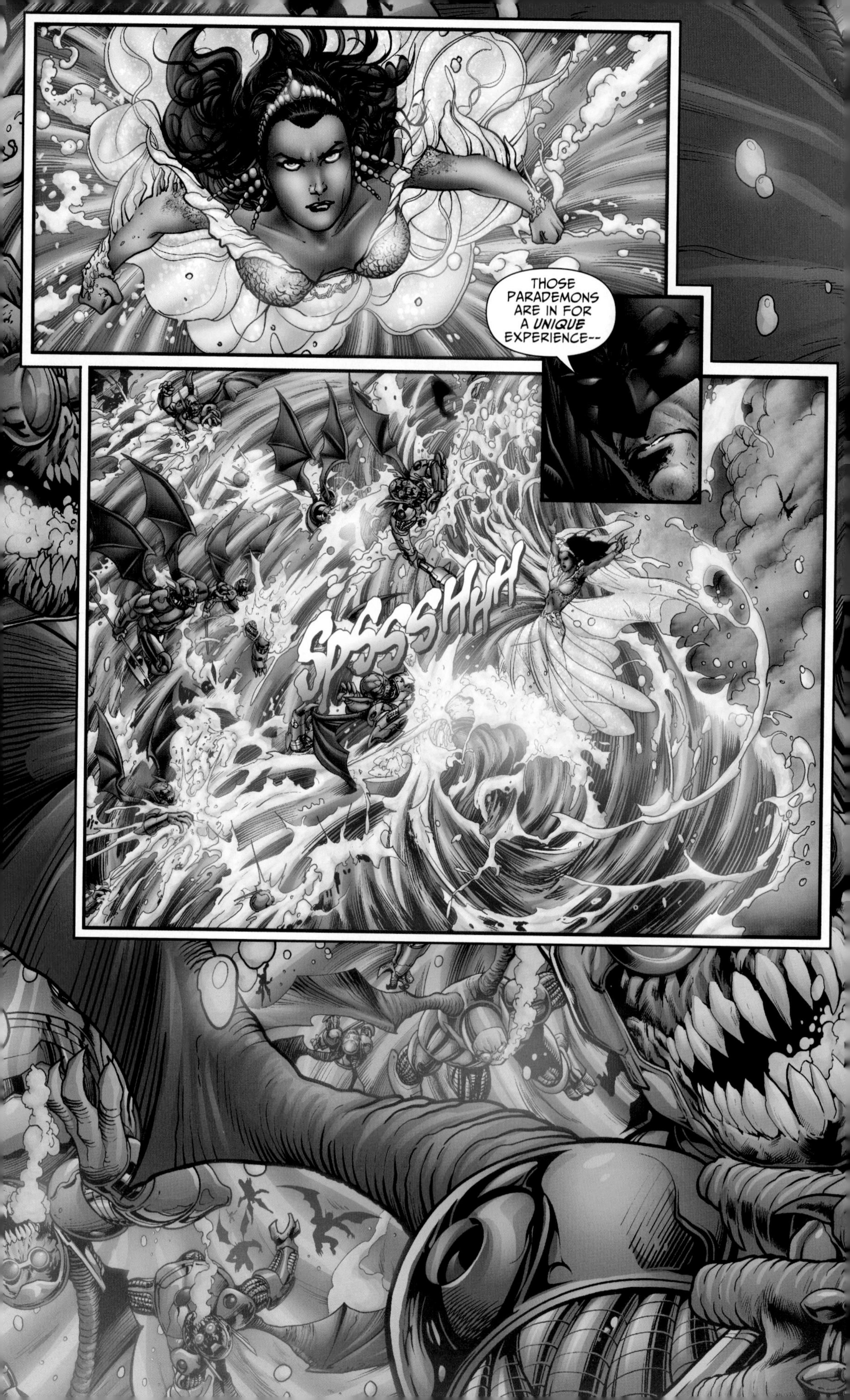
THOSE PARADEMONS ARE IN FOR A *UNIQUE* EXPERIENCE--
SPSSSHHH

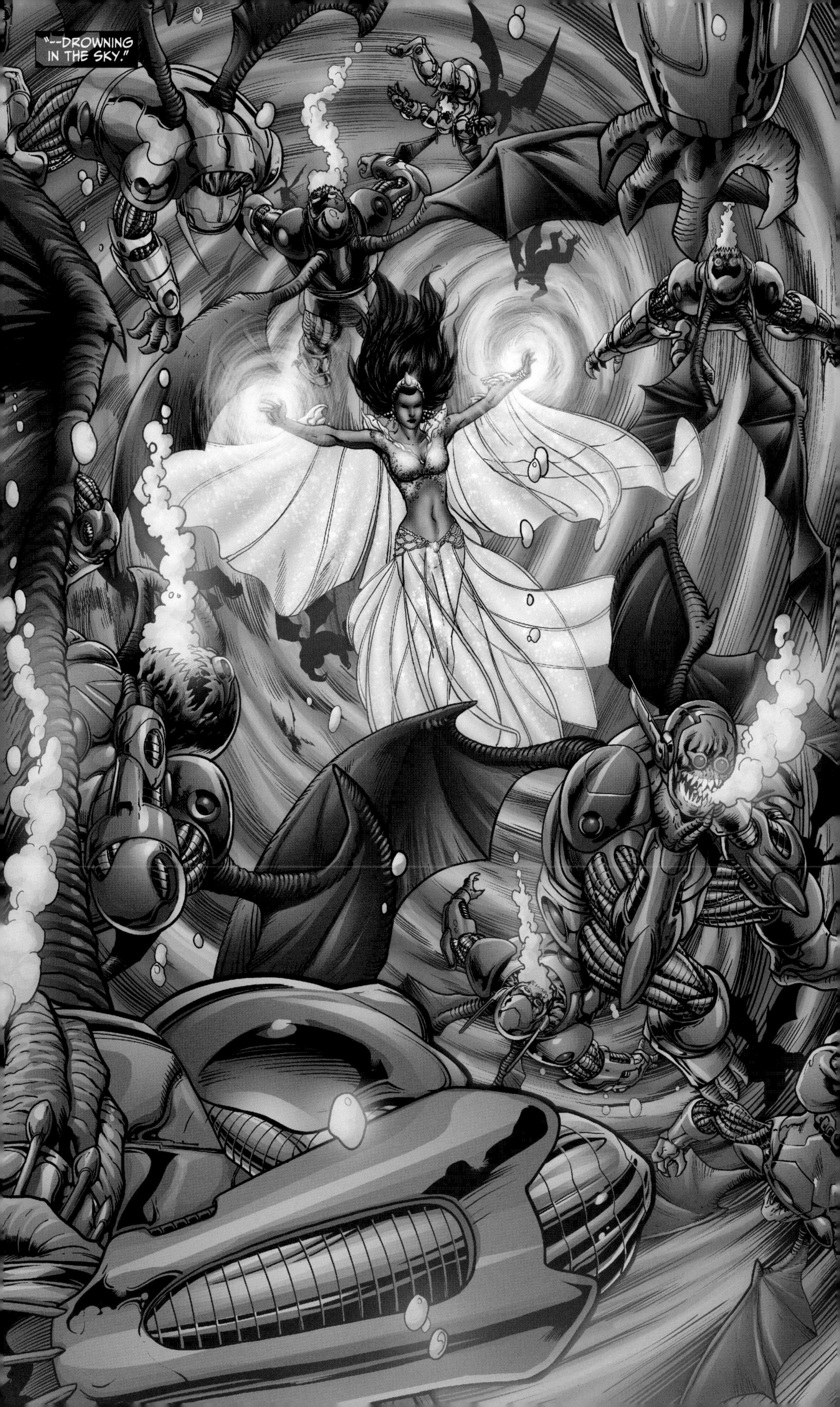
"--DROWNING IN THE SKY."

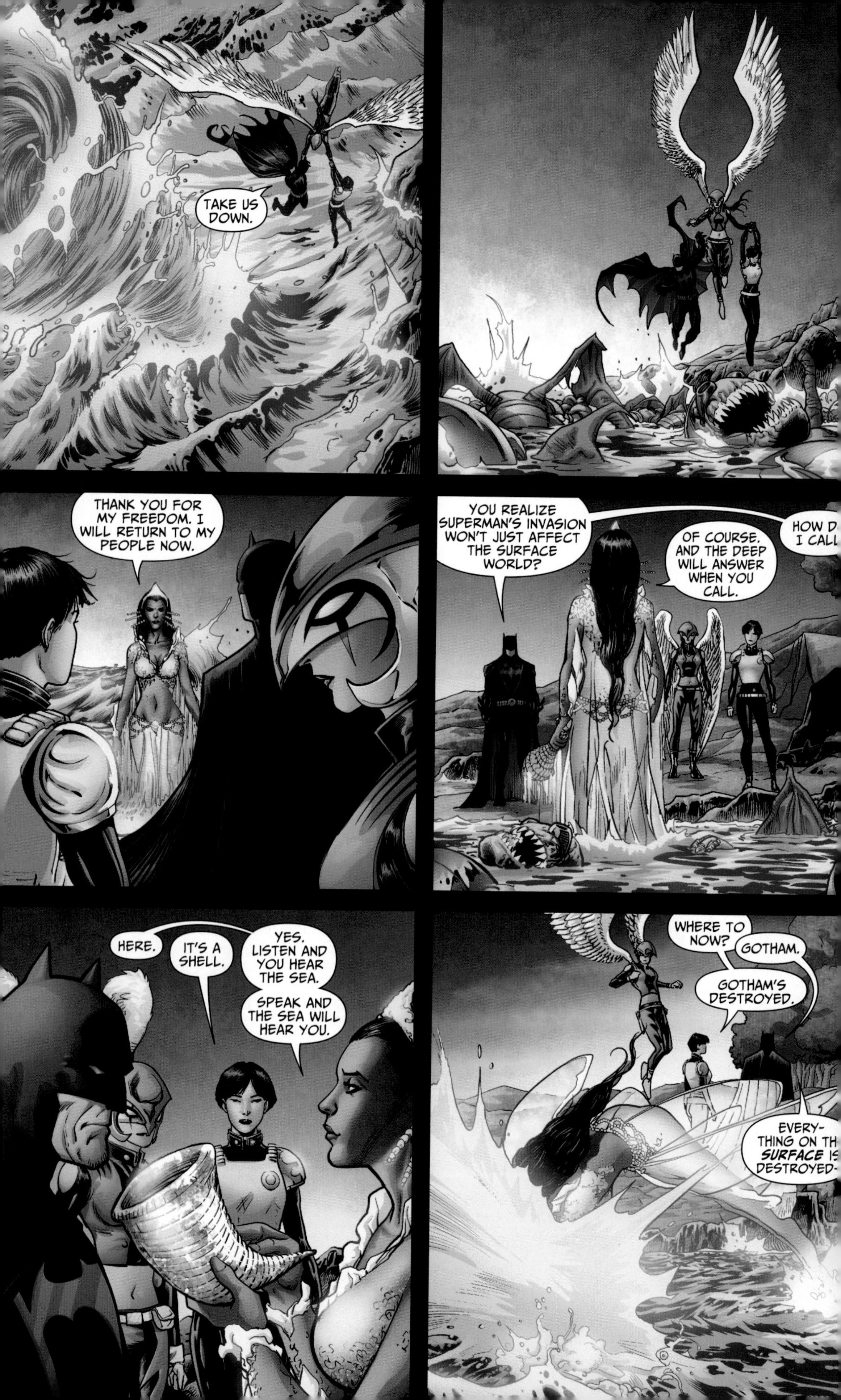
TAKE US DOWN.
THANK YOU FOR MY FREEDOM. I WILL RETURN TO MY PEOPLE NOW.
YOU REALIZE SUPERMAN'S INVASION WON'T JUST AFFECT THE SURFACE WORLD?
OF COURSE. AND THE DEEP WILL ANSWER WHEN YOU CALL.
HOW D I CALL
HERE.
IT'S A SHELL.
YES. LISTEN AND YOU HEAR THE SEA.
SPEAK AND THE SEA WILL HEAR YOU.
WHERE TO NOW?
GOTHAM.
GOTHAM'S DESTROYED.
EVERY-THING ON TH SURFACE IS DESTROYED-

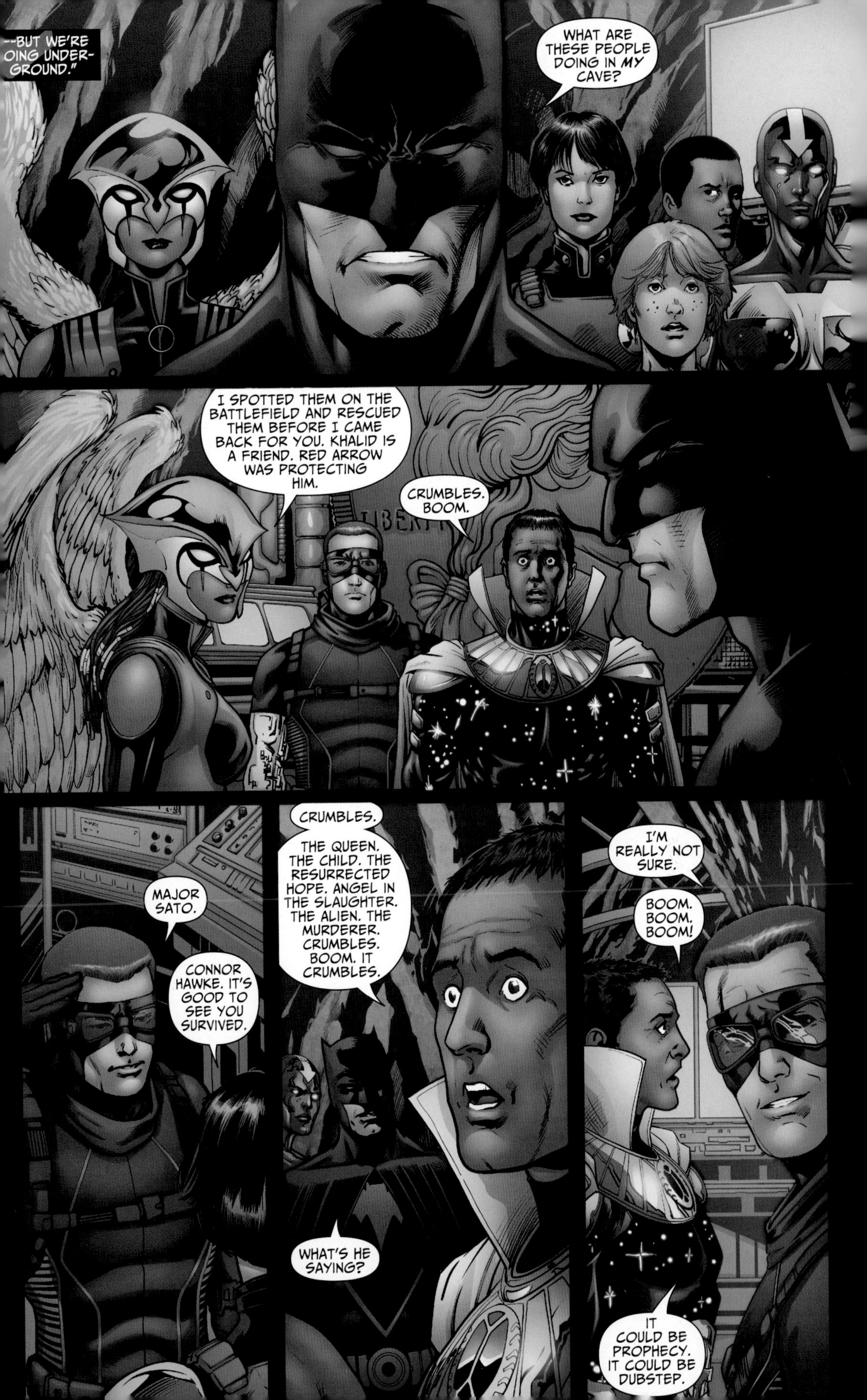
--BUT WE'RE
OING UNDER-
GROUND."
WHAT ARE THESE PEOPLE DOING IN MY CAVE?
I SPOTTED THEM ON THE BATTLEFIELD AND RESCUED THEM BEFORE I CAME BACK FOR YOU. KHALID IS A FRIEND. RED ARROW WAS PROTECTING HIM.
CRUMBLES. BOOM.
MAJOR SATO.
CONNOR HAWKE. IT'S GOOD TO SEE YOU SURVIVED.
CRUMBLES.
THE QUEEN. THE CHILD. THE RESURRECTED HOPE. ANGEL IN THE SLAUGHTER. THE ALIEN. THE MURDERER. CRUMBLES. BOOM. IT CRUMBLES.
WHAT'S HE SAYING?
I'M REALLY NOT SURE.
BOOM. BOOM. BOOM!
IT COULD BE PROPHECY. IT COULD BE DUBSTEP.

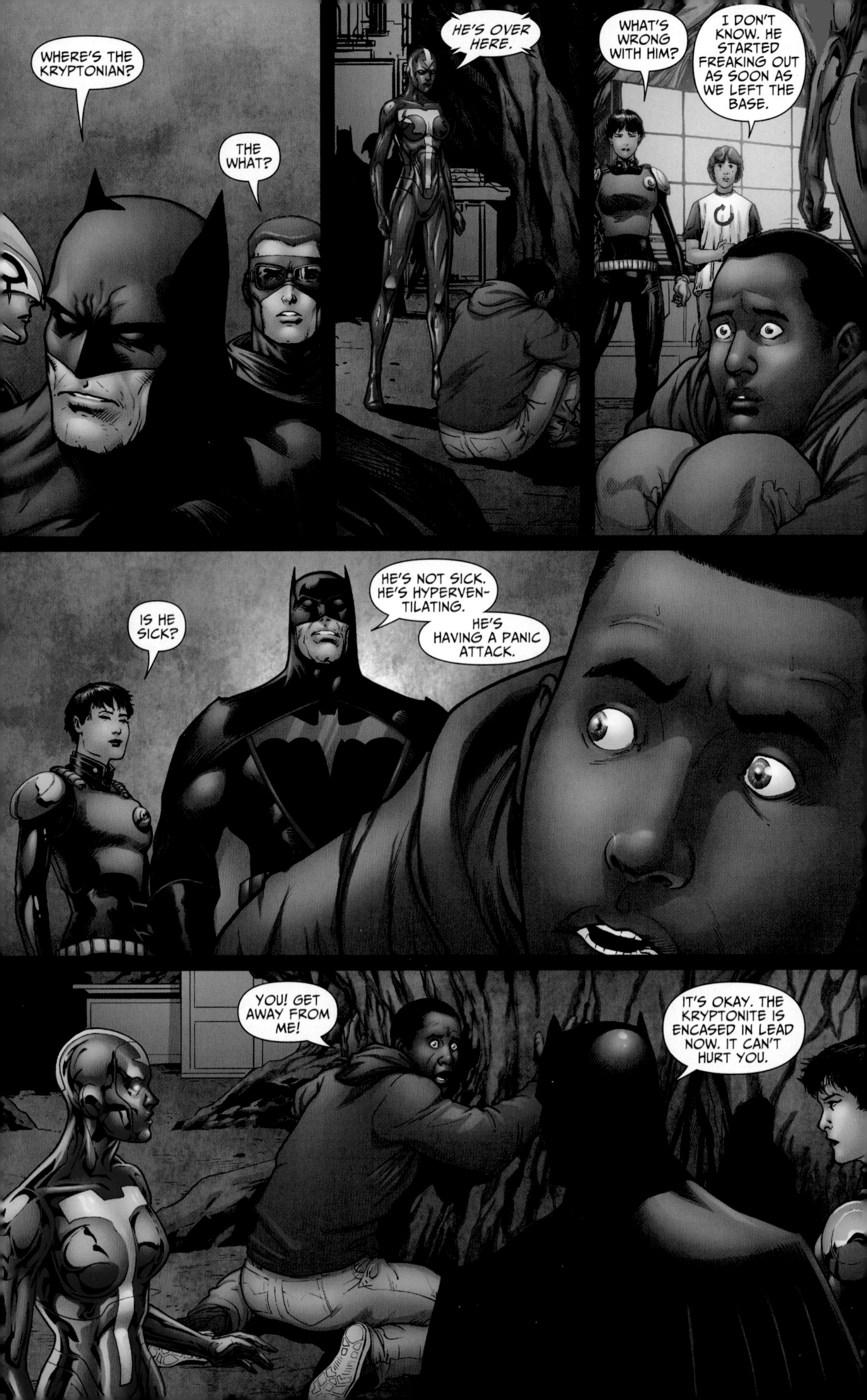

WHERE'S THE KRYPTONIAN?
THE WHAT?
HE'S OVER HERE.
WHAT'S WRONG WITH HIM?
I DON'T KNOW. HE STARTED FREAKING OUT AS SOON AS WE LEFT THE BASE.
IS HE SICK?
HE'S NOT SICK. HE'S HYPERVEN-TILATING.
HE'S HAVING A PANIC ATTACK.
YOU! GET AWAY FROM ME!
IT'S OKAY. THE KRYPTONITE IS ENCASED IN LEAD NOW. IT CAN'T HURT YOU.

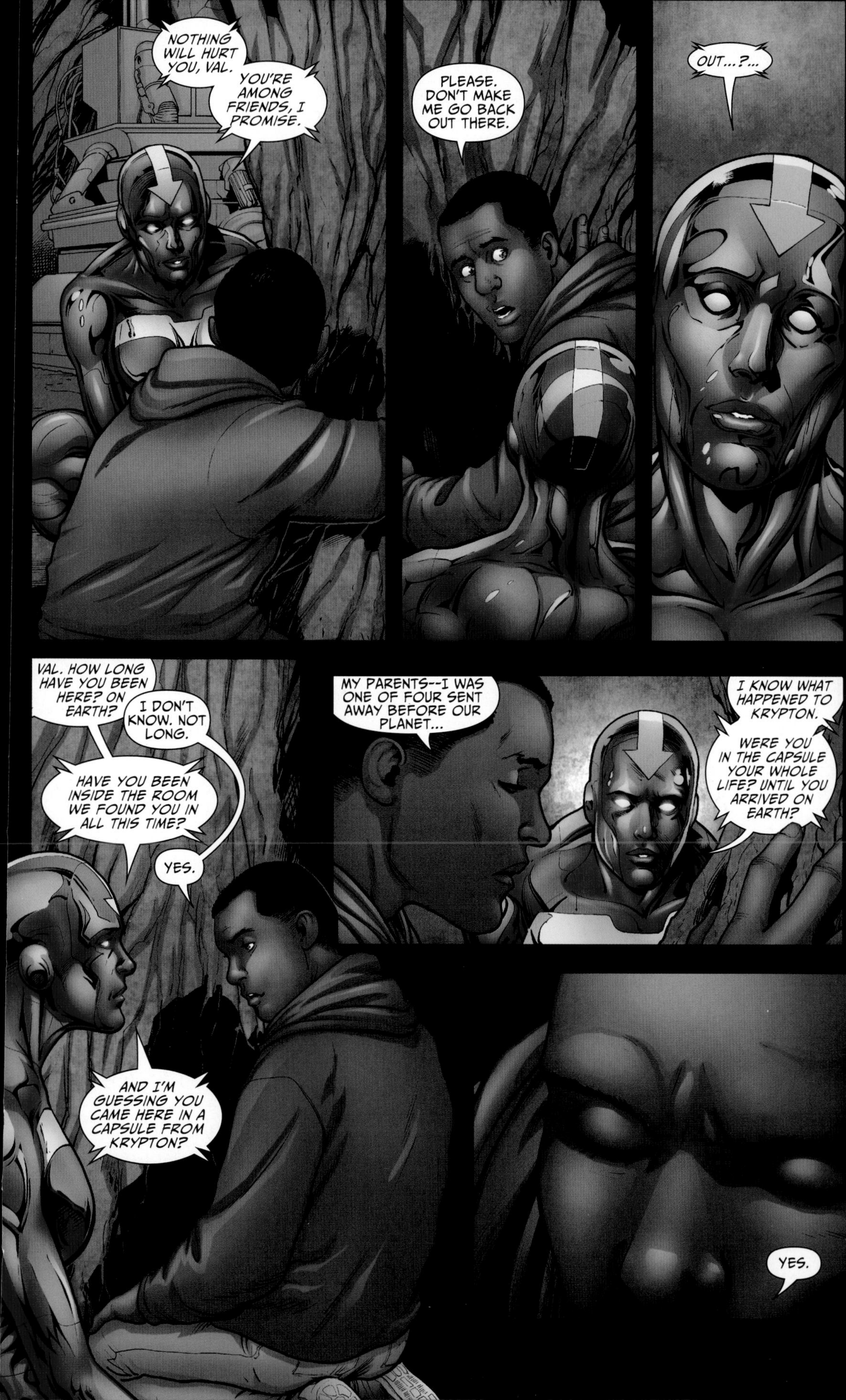
NOTHING WILL HURT YOU, VAL.
YOU'RE AMONG FRIENDS, I PROMISE.
PLEASE. DON'T MAKE ME GO BACK OUT THERE.
OUT...?...
VAL. HOW LONG HAVE YOU BEEN HERE? ON EARTH?
I DON'T KNOW. NOT LONG.
HAVE YOU BEEN INSIDE THE ROOM WE FOUND YOU IN ALL THIS TIME?
YES.
AND I'M GUESSING YOU CAME HERE IN A CAPSULE FROM KRYPTON?
MY PARENTS--I WAS ONE OF FOUR SENT AWAY BEFORE OUR PLANET...
I KNOW WHAT HAPPENED TO KRYPTON.
WERE YOU IN THE CAPSULE YOUR WHOLE LIFE? UNTIL YOU ARRIVED ON EARTH?
YES.

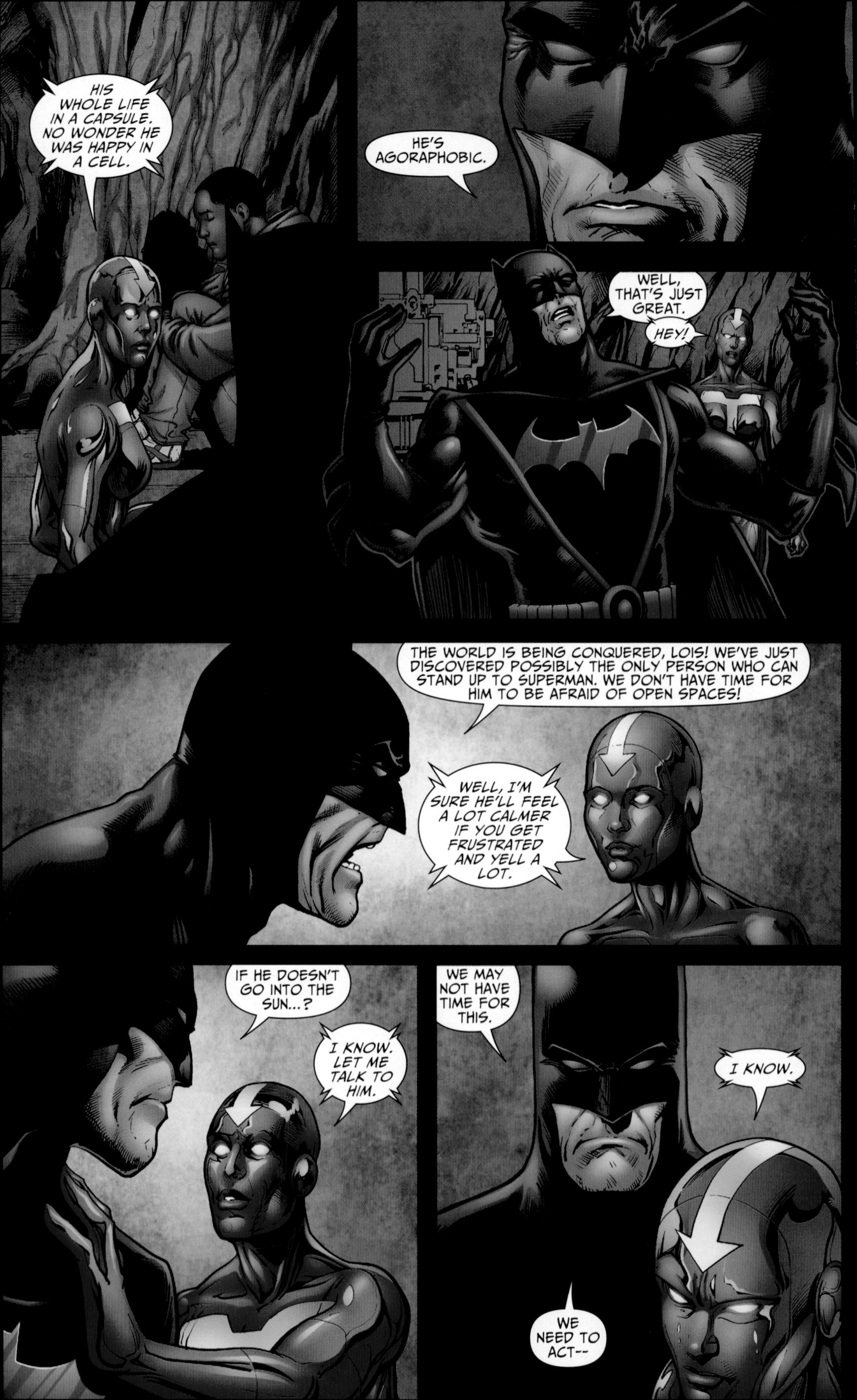
HIS WHOLE LIFE IN A CAPSULE. NO WONDER HE WAS HAPPY IN A CELL.
HE'S AGORAPHOBIC.
WELL, THAT'S JUST GREAT.
HEY!
THE WORLD IS BEING CONQUERED, LOIS! WE'VE JUST DISCOVERED POSSIBLY THE ONLY PERSON WHO CAN STAND UP TO SUPERMAN. WE DON'T HAVE TIME FOR HIM TO BE AFRAID OF OPEN SPACES!
WELL, I'M SURE HE'LL FEEL A LOT CALMER IF YOU GET FRUSTRATED AND YELL A LOT.
IF HE DOESN'T GO INTO THE SUN...?
I KNOW. LET ME TALK TO HIM.
WE MAY NOT HAVE TIME FOR THIS.
I KNOW.
WE NEED TO ACT--

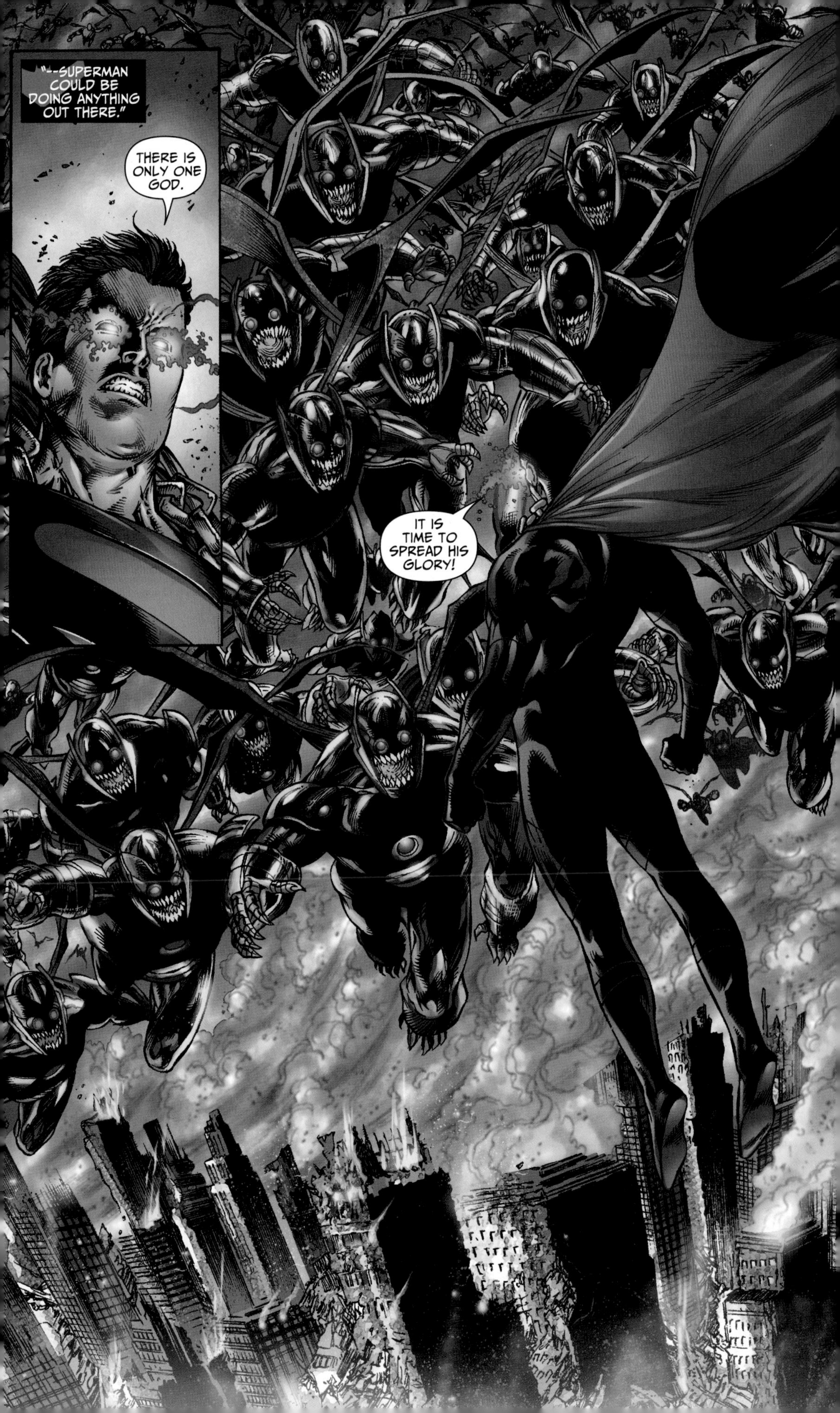
"--SUPERMAN COULD BE DOING ANYTHING OUT THERE."
THERE IS ONLY ONE GOD.
IT IS TIME TO SPREAD HIS GLORY!

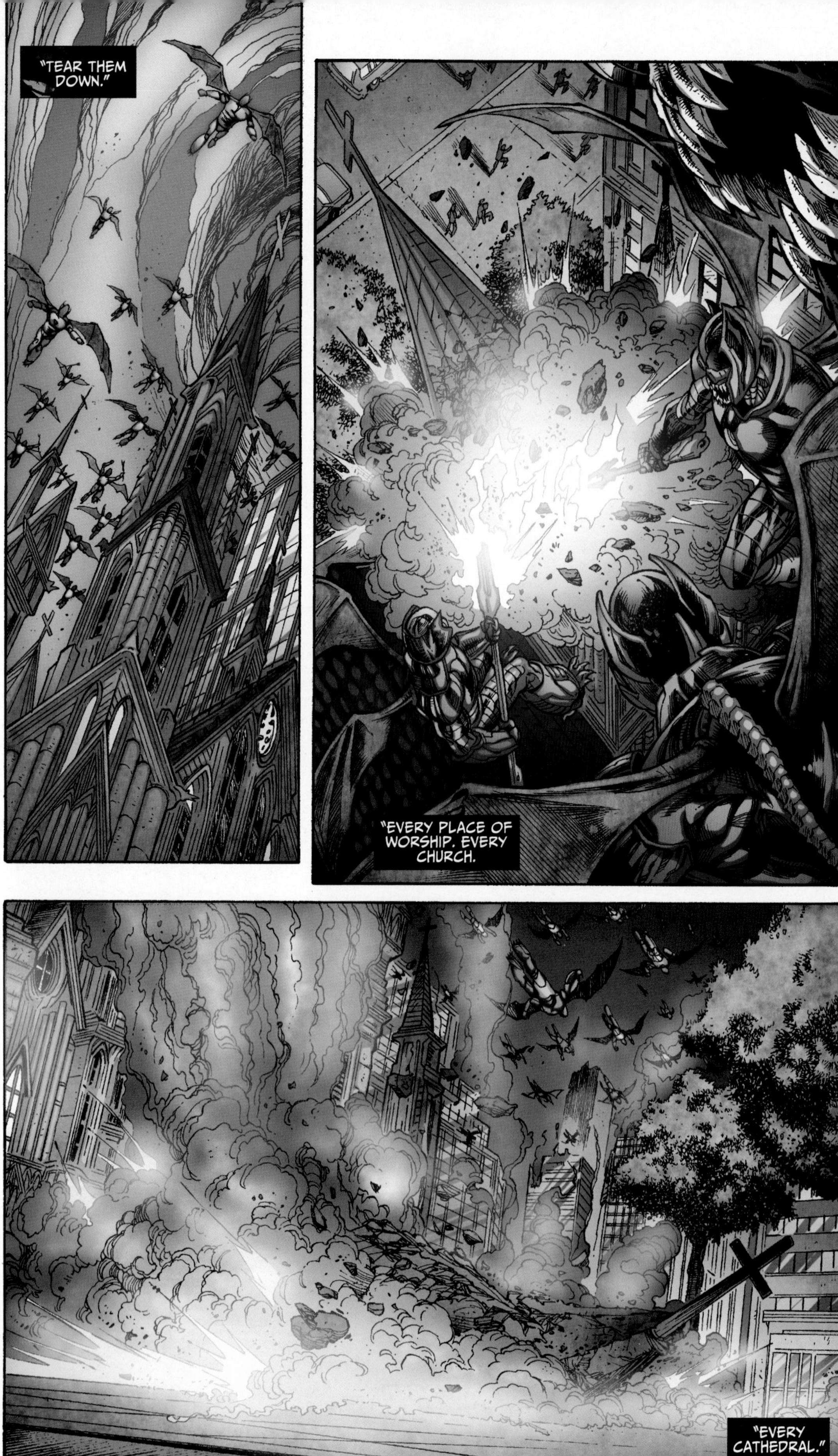
"TEAR THEM DOWN."
"EVERY PLACE OF WORSHIP. EVERY CHURCH.
"EVERY CATHEDRAL."

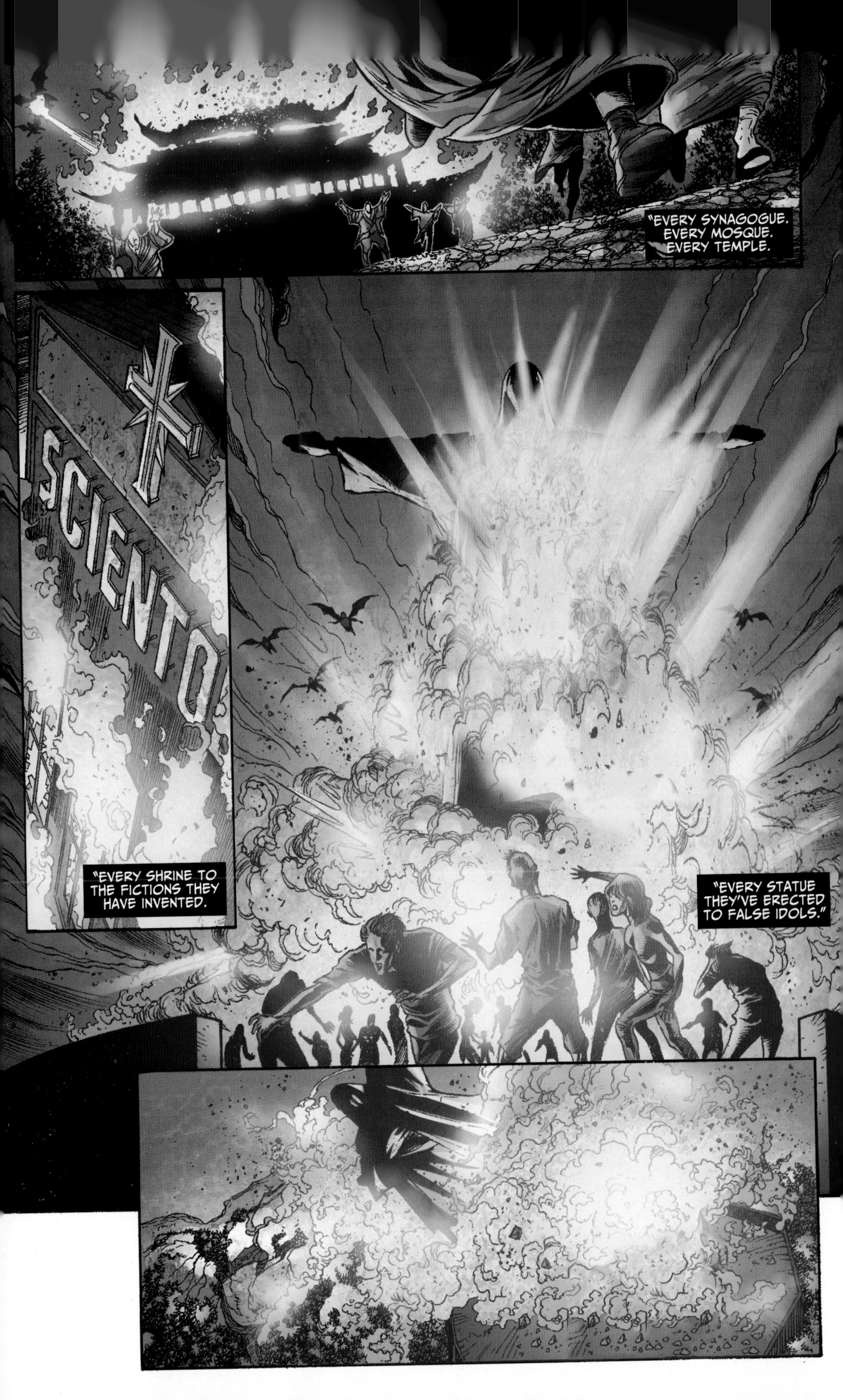
"EVERY SYNAGOGUE. EVERY MOSQUE. EVERY TEMPLE.
SCIENTO
"EVERY SHRINE TO THE FICTIONS THEY HAVE INVENTED.
"EVERY STATUE THEY'VE ERECTED TO FALSE IDOLS."

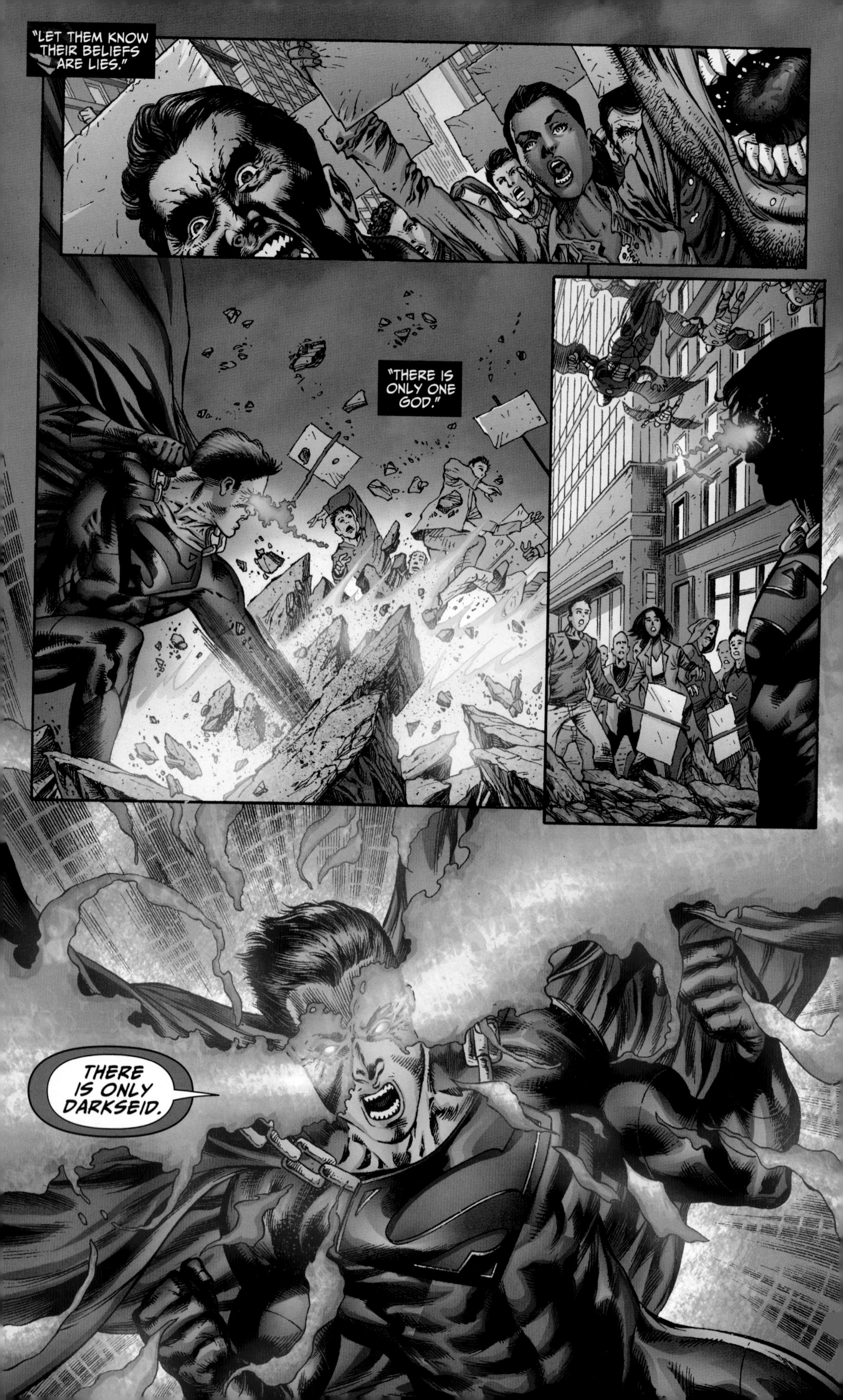
"LET THEM KNOW THEIR BELIEFS ARE LIES."
"THERE IS ONLY ONE GOD."
THERE IS ONLY DARKSEID.

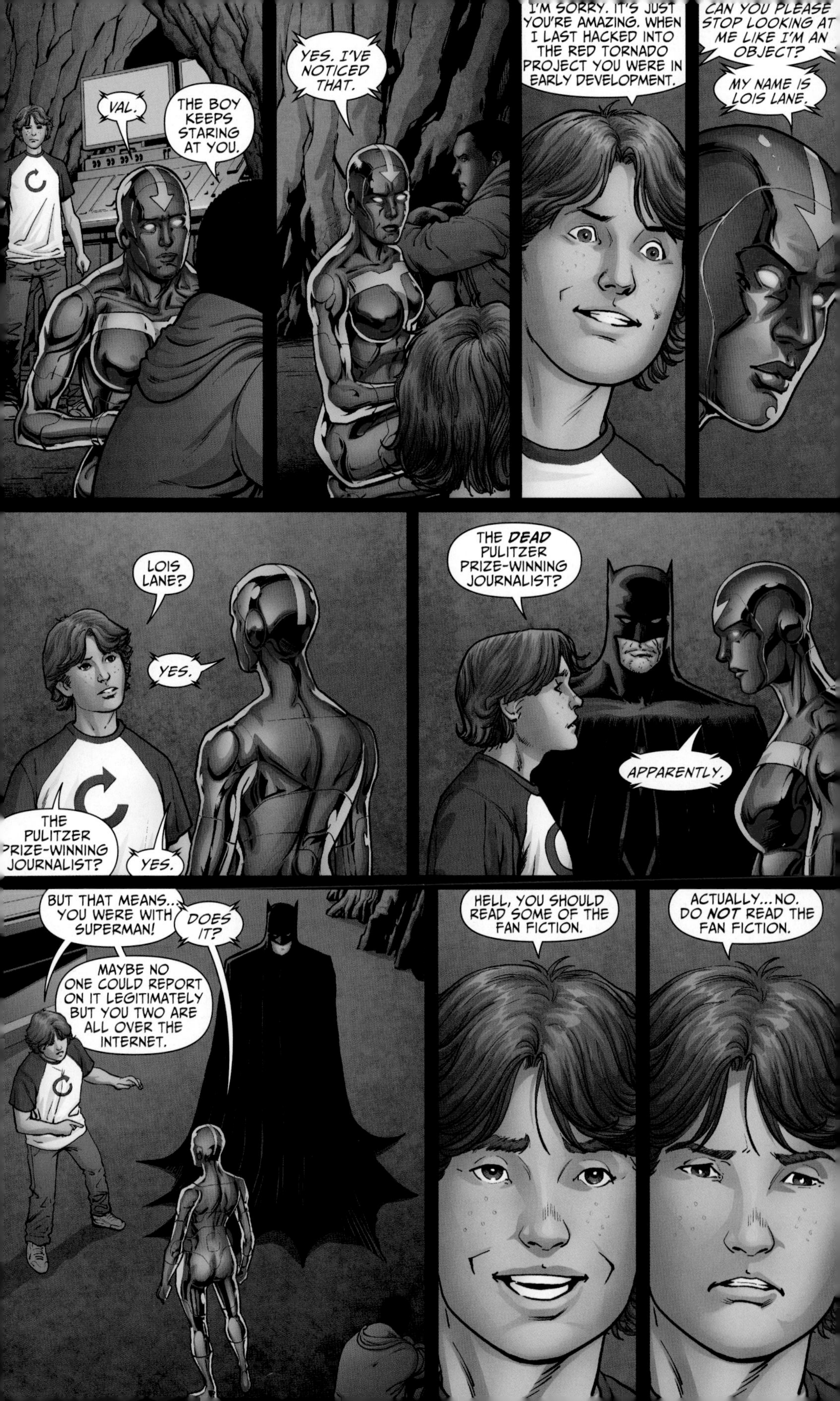
VAL.
THE BOY KEEPS STARING AT YOU.
YES. I'VE NOTICED THAT.
I'M SORRY. IT'S JUST YOU'RE AMAZING. WHEN I LAST HACKED INTO THE RED TORNADO PROJECT YOU WERE IN EARLY DEVELOPMENT.
CAN YOU PLEASE STOP LOOKING AT ME LIKE I'M AN OBJECT?
MY NAME IS LOIS LANE.
LOIS LANE?
YES.
THE PULITZER PRIZE-WINNING JOURNALIST?
YES.
THE DEAD PULITZER PRIZE-WINNING JOURNALIST?
APPARENTLY.
BUT THAT MEANS... YOU WERE WITH SUPERMAN!
DOES IT?
MAYBE NO ONE COULD REPORT ON IT LEGITIMATELY BUT YOU TWO ARE ALL OVER THE INTERNET.
HELL, YOU SHOULD READ SOME OF THE FAN FICTION.
ACTUALLY...NO. DO NOT READ THE FAN FICTION.

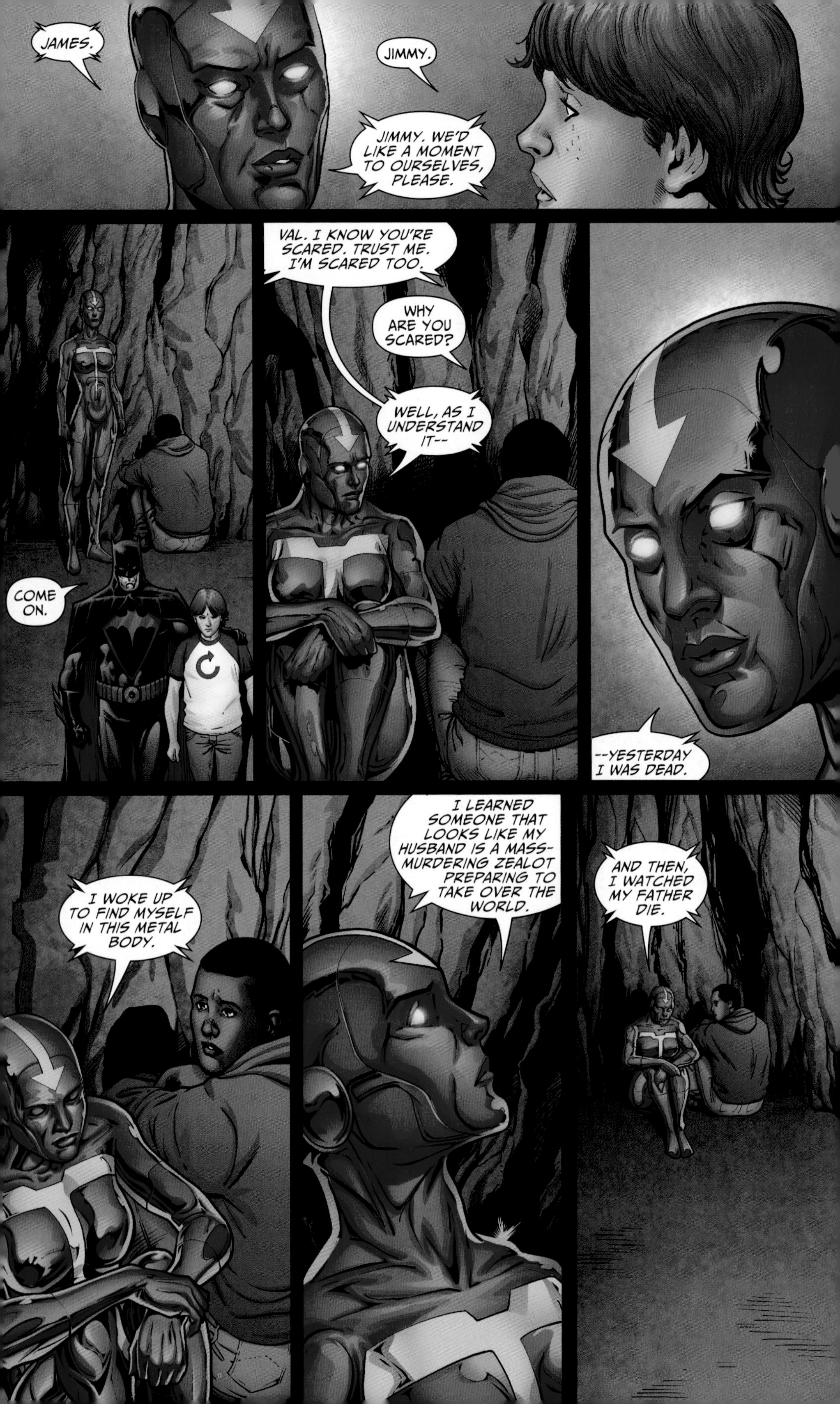

JAMES.
JIMMY.
JIMMY. WE'D LIKE A MOMENT TO OURSELVES, PLEASE.
COME ON.
VAL. I KNOW YOU'RE SCARED. TRUST ME. I'M SCARED TOO.
WHY ARE YOU SCARED?
WELL, AS I UNDERSTAND IT--
--YESTERDAY I WAS DEAD.
I WOKE UP TO FIND MYSELF IN THIS METAL BODY.
I LEARNED SOMEONE THAT LOOKS LIKE MY HUSBAND IS A MASS-MURDERING ZEALOT PREPARING TO TAKE OVER THE WORLD.
AND THEN, I WATCHED MY FATHER DIE.

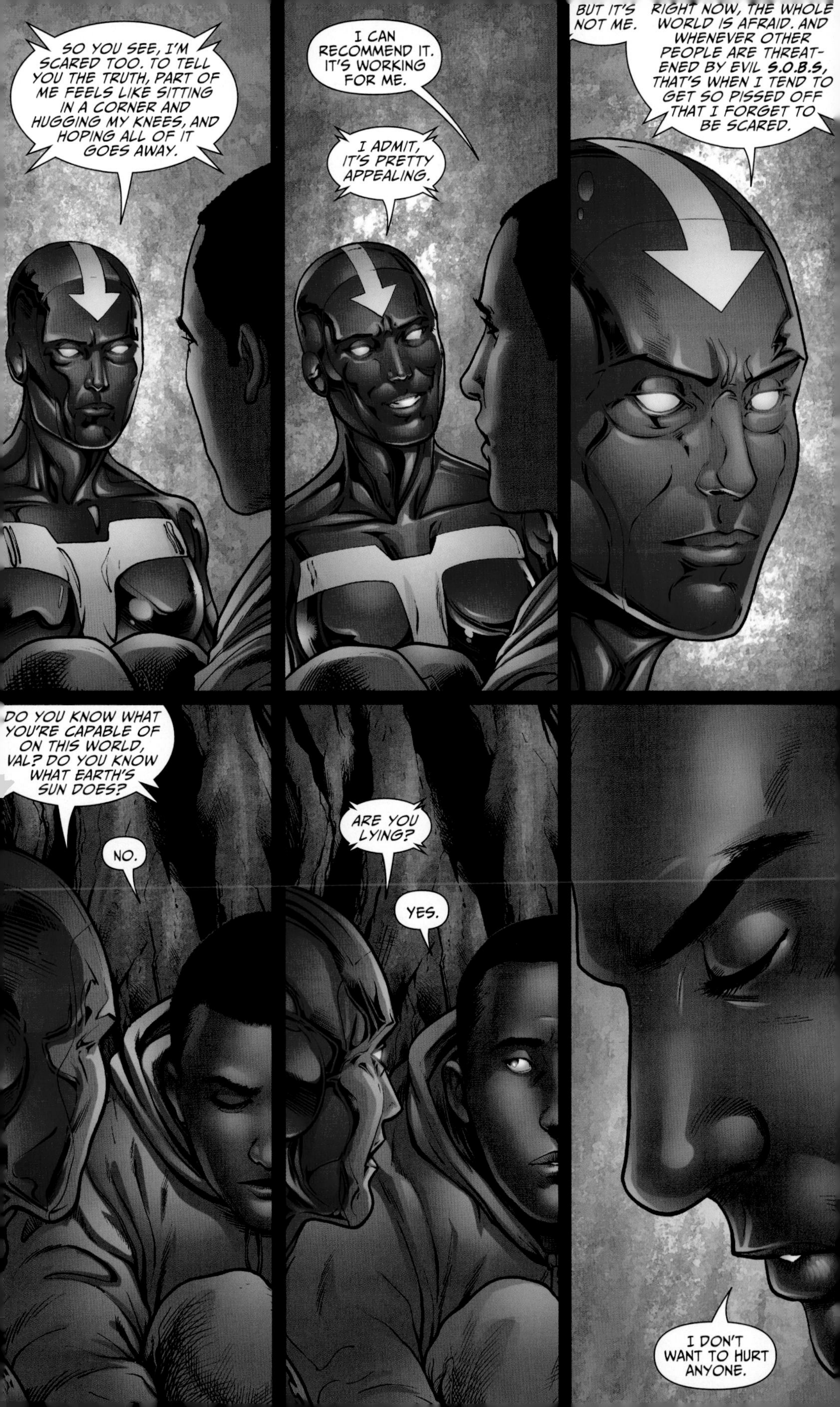

SO YOU SEE, I'M SCARED TOO. TO TELL YOU THE TRUTH, PART OF ME FEELS LIKE SITTING IN A CORNER AND HUGGING MY KNEES, AND HOPING ALL OF IT GOES AWAY.
I ADMIT, IT'S PRETTY APPEALING.
I CAN RECOMMEND IT. IT'S WORKING FOR ME.
BUT IT'S NOT ME.
RIGHT NOW, THE WHOLE WORLD IS AFRAID. AND WHENEVER OTHER PEOPLE ARE THREAT-ENED BY EVIL S.O.B.S, THAT'S WHEN I TEND TO GET SO PISSED OFF THAT I FORGET TO BE SCARED.
DO YOU KNOW WHAT YOU'RE CAPABLE OF ON THIS WORLD, VAL? DO YOU KNOW WHAT EARTH'S SUN DOES?
NO.
ARE YOU LYING?
YES.
I DON'T WANT TO HURT ANYONE.

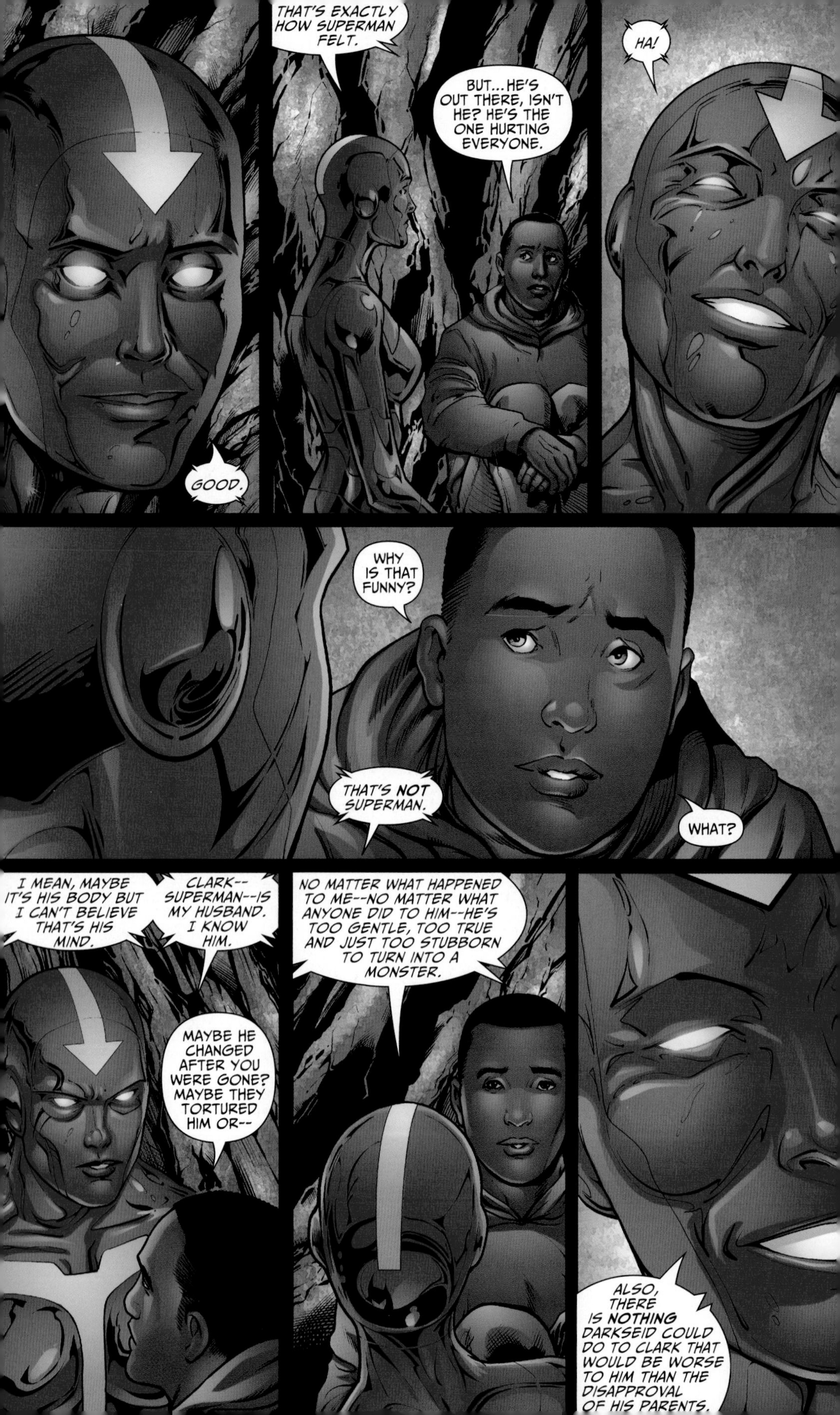
GOOD.
THAT'S EXACTLY HOW SUPERMAN FELT.
BUT... HE'S OUT THERE, ISN'T HE? HE'S THE ONE HURTING EVERYONE.
HA!
WHY IS THAT FUNNY?
THAT'S **NOT** SUPERMAN.
WHAT?
I MEAN, MAYBE IT'S HIS BODY BUT I CAN'T BELIEVE THAT'S HIS MIND.
CLARK-- SUPERMAN--IS MY HUSBAND. I KNOW HIM.
MAYBE HE CHANGED AFTER YOU WERE GONE? MAYBE THEY TORTURED HIM OR--
NO MATTER WHAT HAPPENED TO ME--NO MATTER WHAT ANYONE DID TO HIM--HE'S TOO GENTLE, TOO TRUE AND JUST TOO STUBBORN TO TURN INTO A MONSTER.
ALSO, THERE IS **NOTHING** DARKSEID COULD DO TO CLARK THAT WOULD BE WORSE TO HIM THAN THE DISAPPROVAL OF HIS PARENTS.

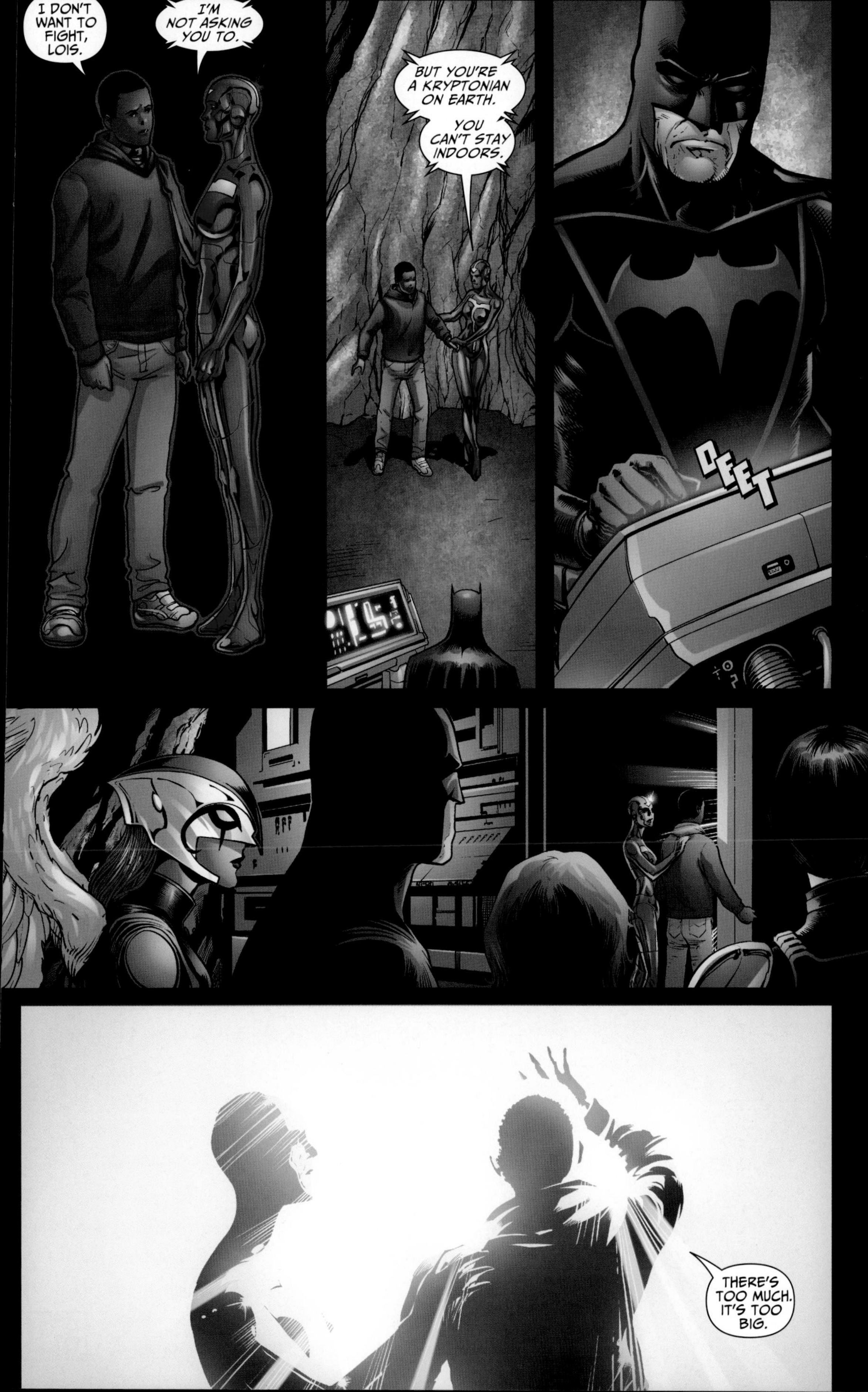
I DON'T WANT TO FIGHT, LOIS.
I'M NOT ASKING YOU TO.
BUT YOU'RE A KRYPTONIAN ON EARTH.
YOU CAN'T STAY INDOORS.
DEET
THERE'S TOO MUCH. IT'S TOO BIG.

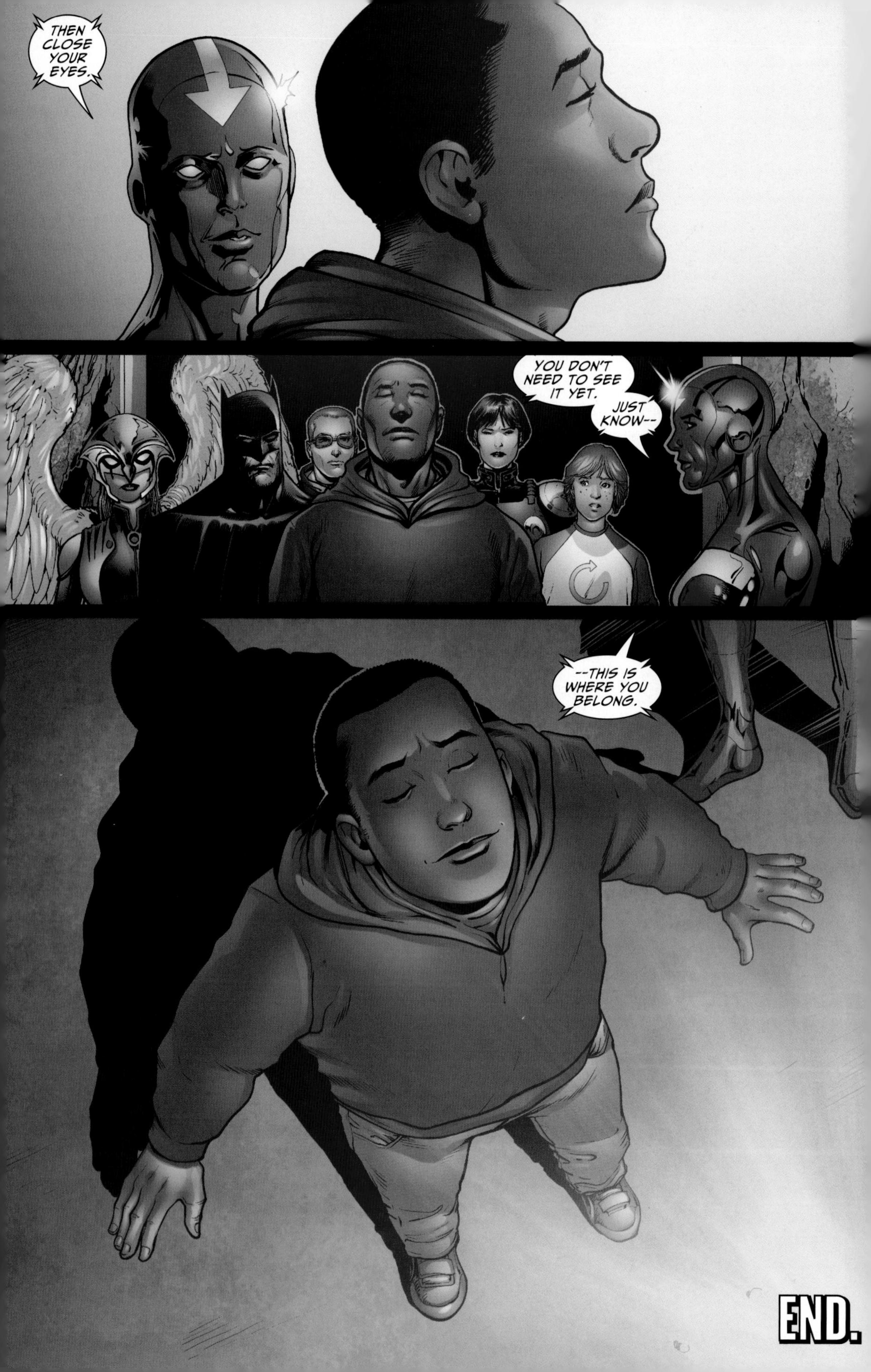
THEN CLOSE YOUR EYES.
YOU DON'T NEED TO SEE IT YET.
JUST KNOW--
--THIS IS WHERE YOU BELONG.
END.

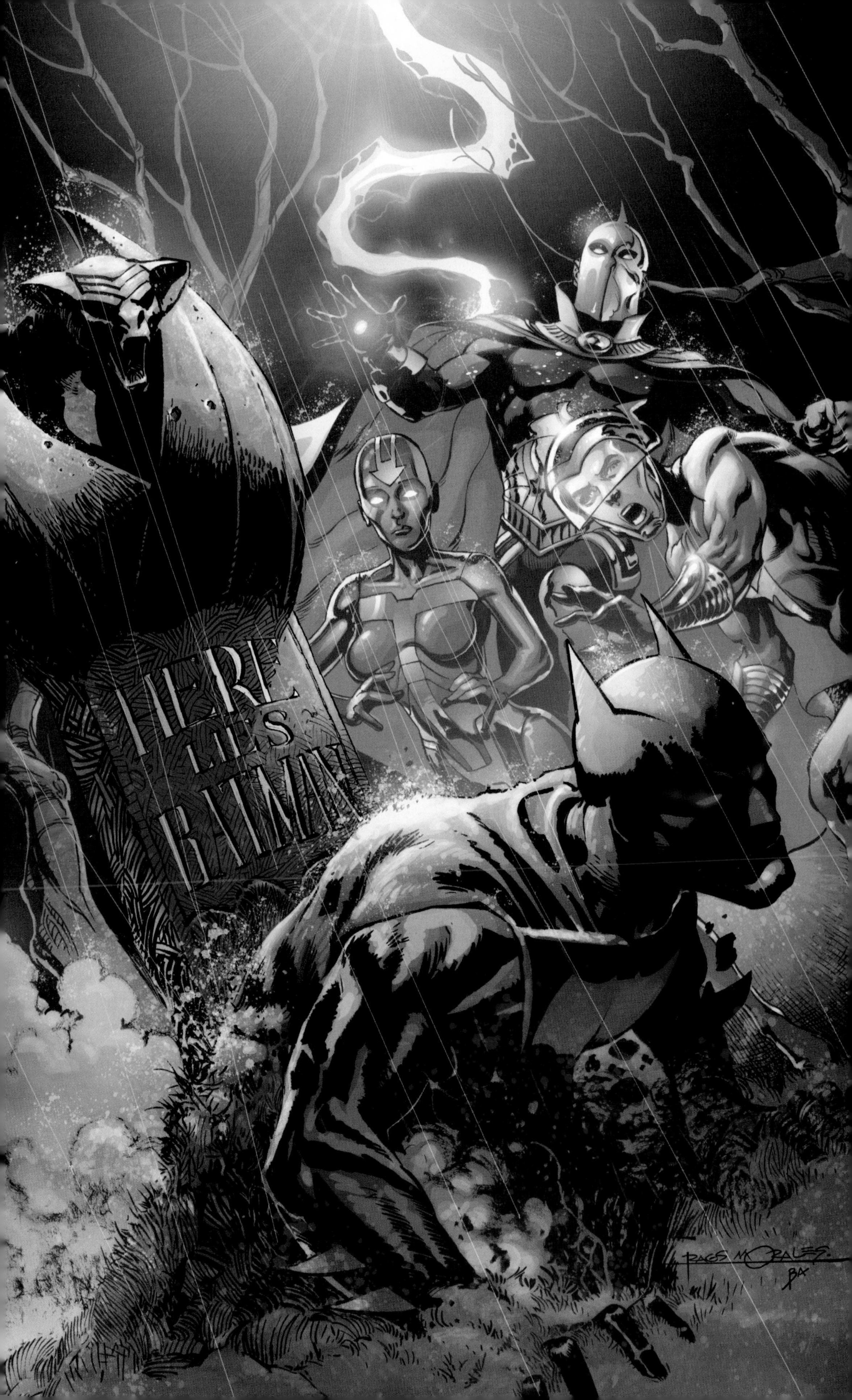
HERE LIES BATMAN

ORIGIN

TOM TAYLOR
writer

ROBSON ROCHA
penciller

SCOTT HANNA
inker

RAGS MORALES & BRAD ANDERSON
cover artists

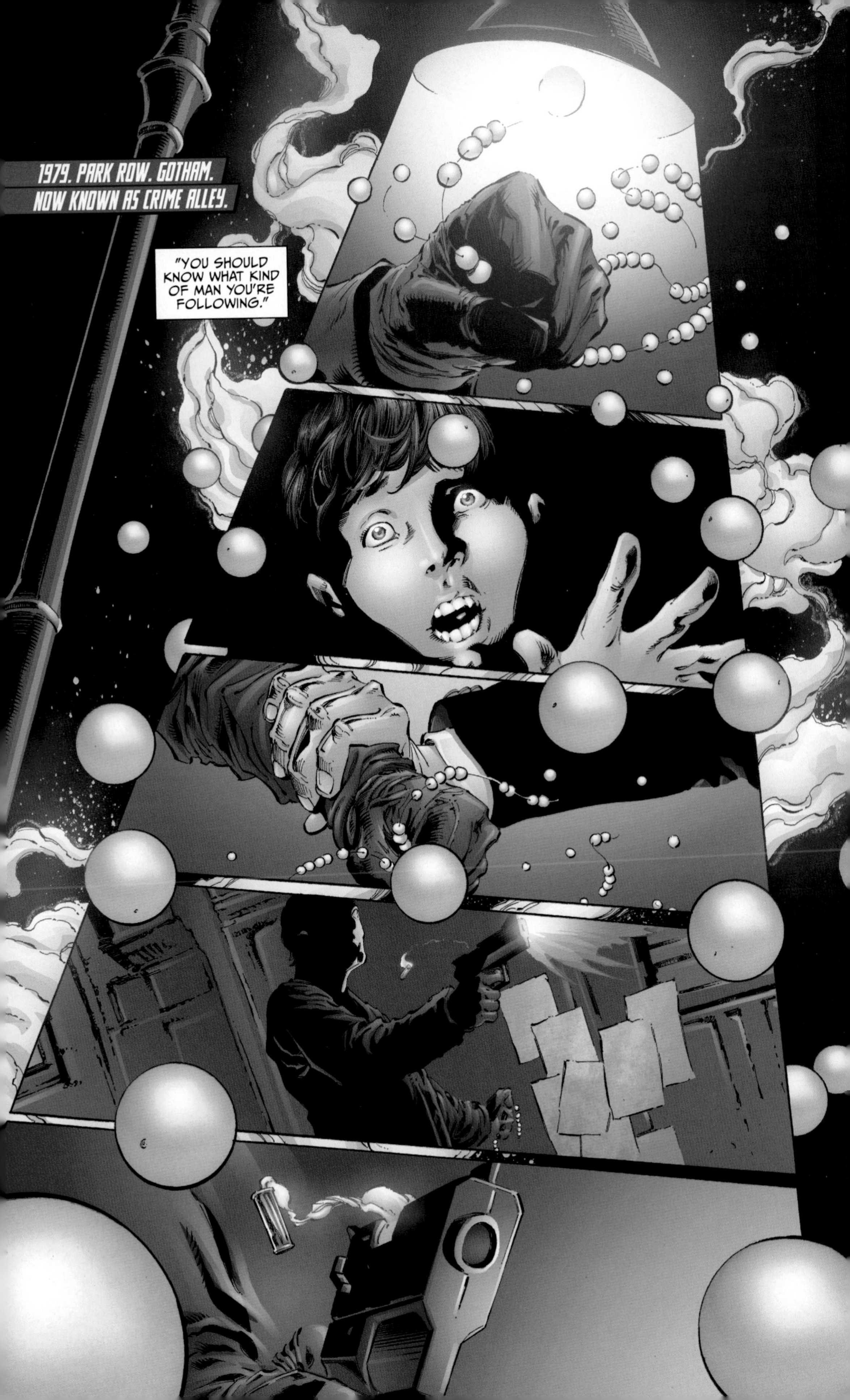
1979. PARK ROW. GOTHAM.
NOW KNOWN AS CRIME ALLEY.
"YOU SHOULD KNOW WHAT KIND OF MAN YOU'RE FOLLOWING."

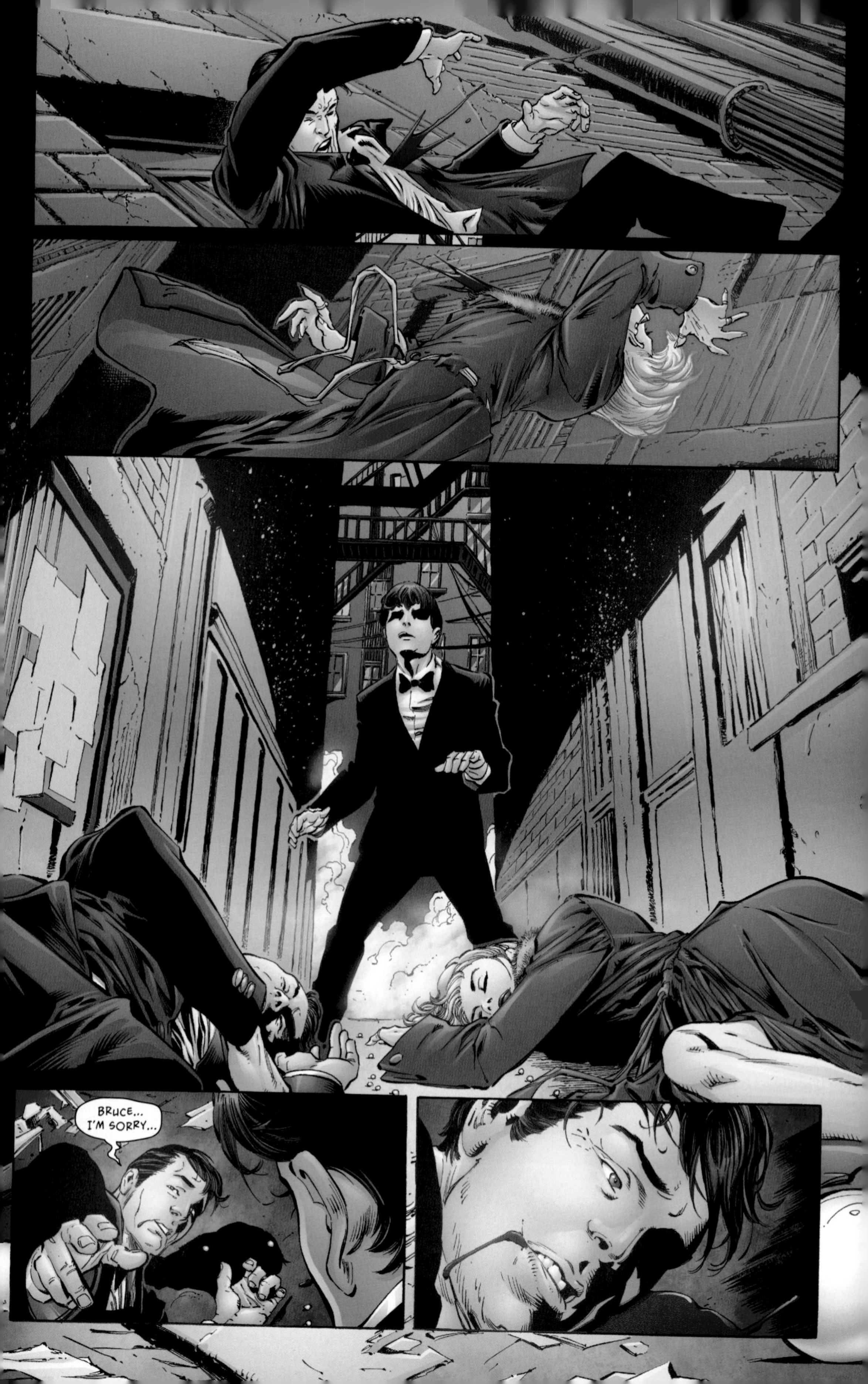
BRUCE... I'M SORRY...

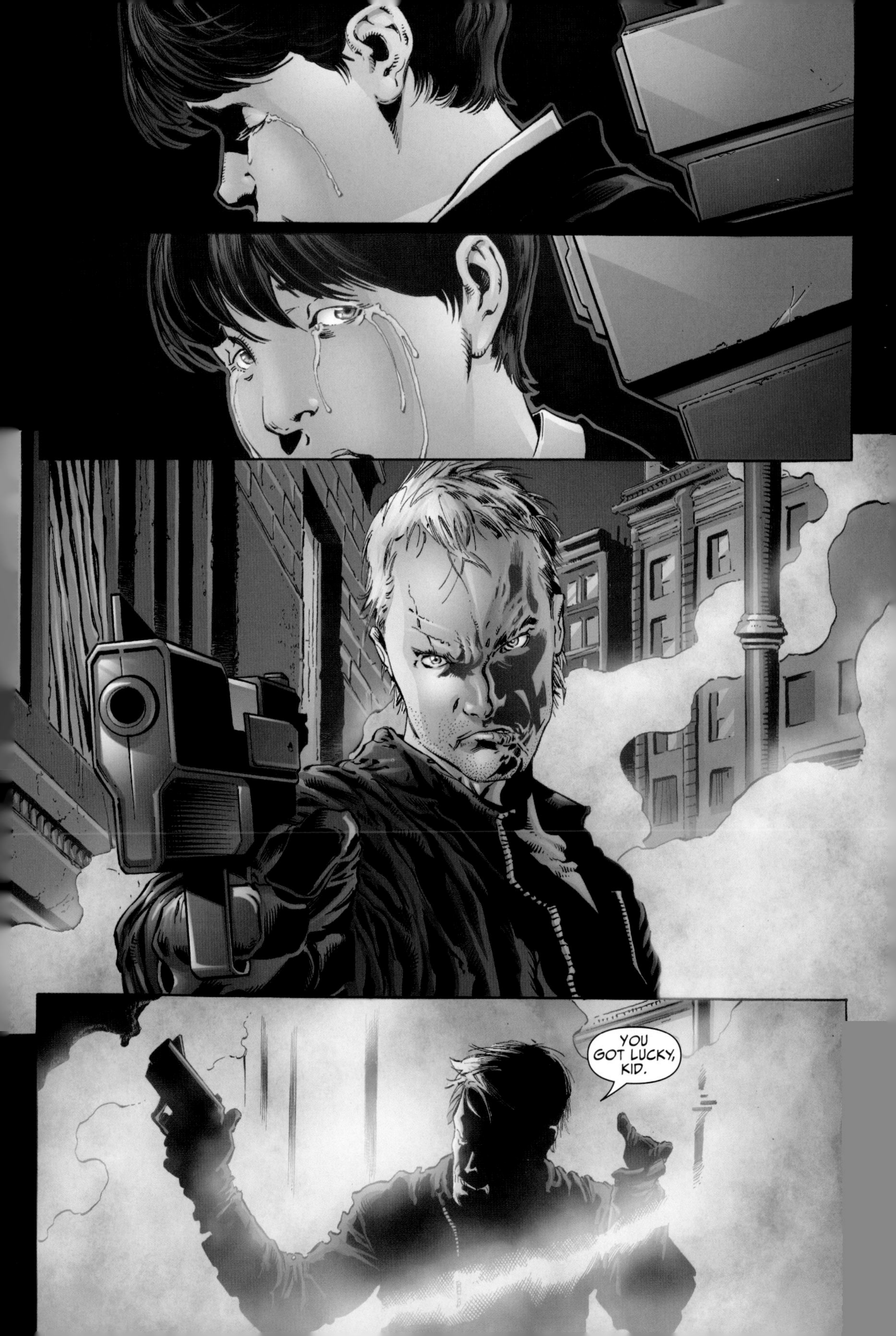
YOU GOT LUCKY, KID.

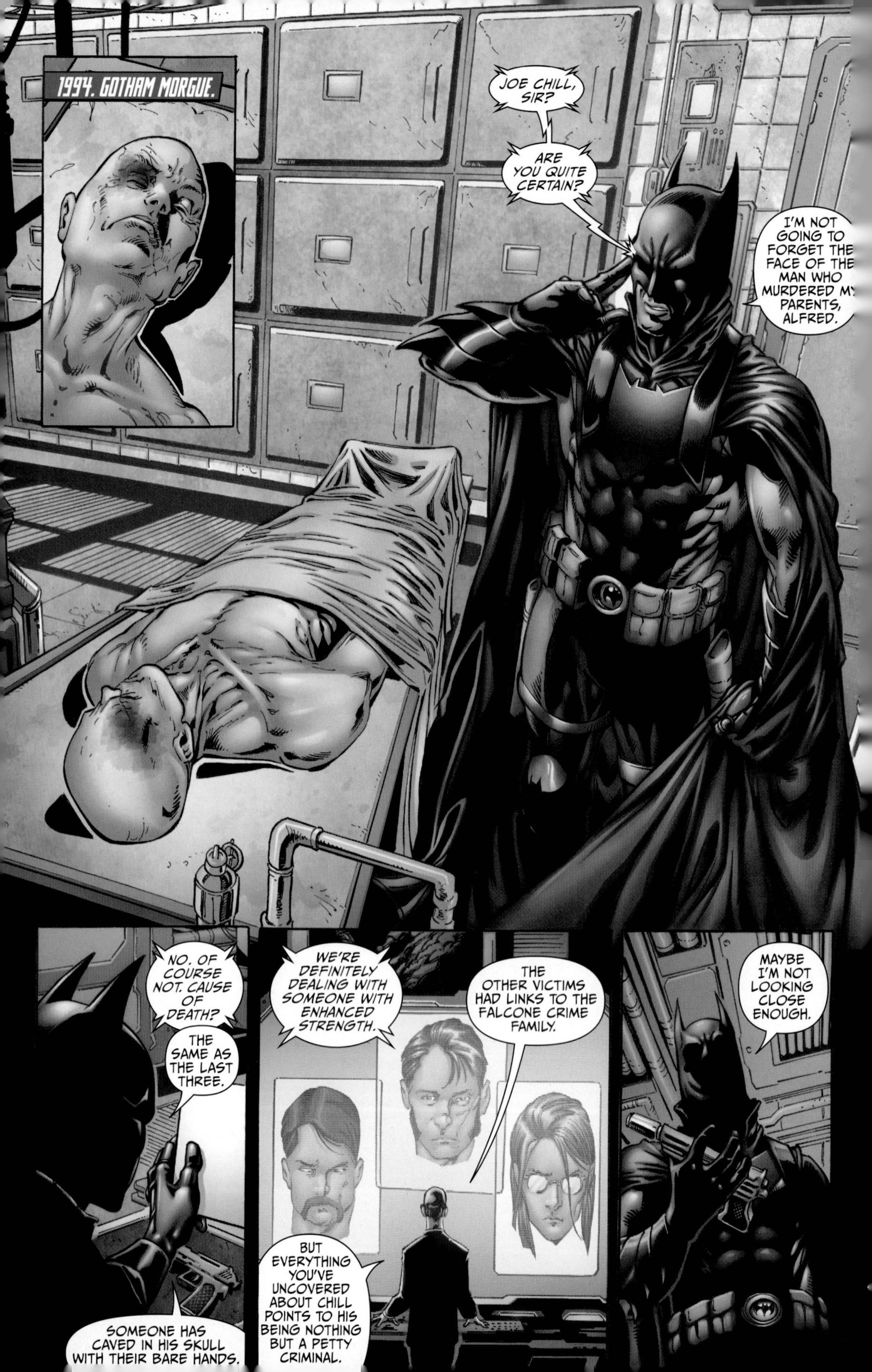
1994. GOTHAM MORGUE.
JOE CHILL, SIR?
ARE YOU QUITE CERTAIN?
I'M NOT GOING TO FORGET THE FACE OF THE MAN WHO MURDERED MY PARENTS, ALFRED.
NO. OF COURSE NOT. CAUSE OF DEATH?
THE SAME AS THE LAST THREE.
SOMEONE HAS CAVED IN HIS SKULL WITH THEIR BARE HANDS.
WE'RE DEFINITELY DEALING WITH SOMEONE WITH ENHANCED STRENGTH.
THE OTHER VICTIMS HAD LINKS TO THE FALCONE CRIME FAMILY.
BUT EVERYTHING YOU'VE UNCOVERED ABOUT CHILL POINTS TO HIS BEING NOTHING BUT A PETTY CRIMINAL.
MAYBE I'M NOT LOOKING CLOSE ENOUGH.

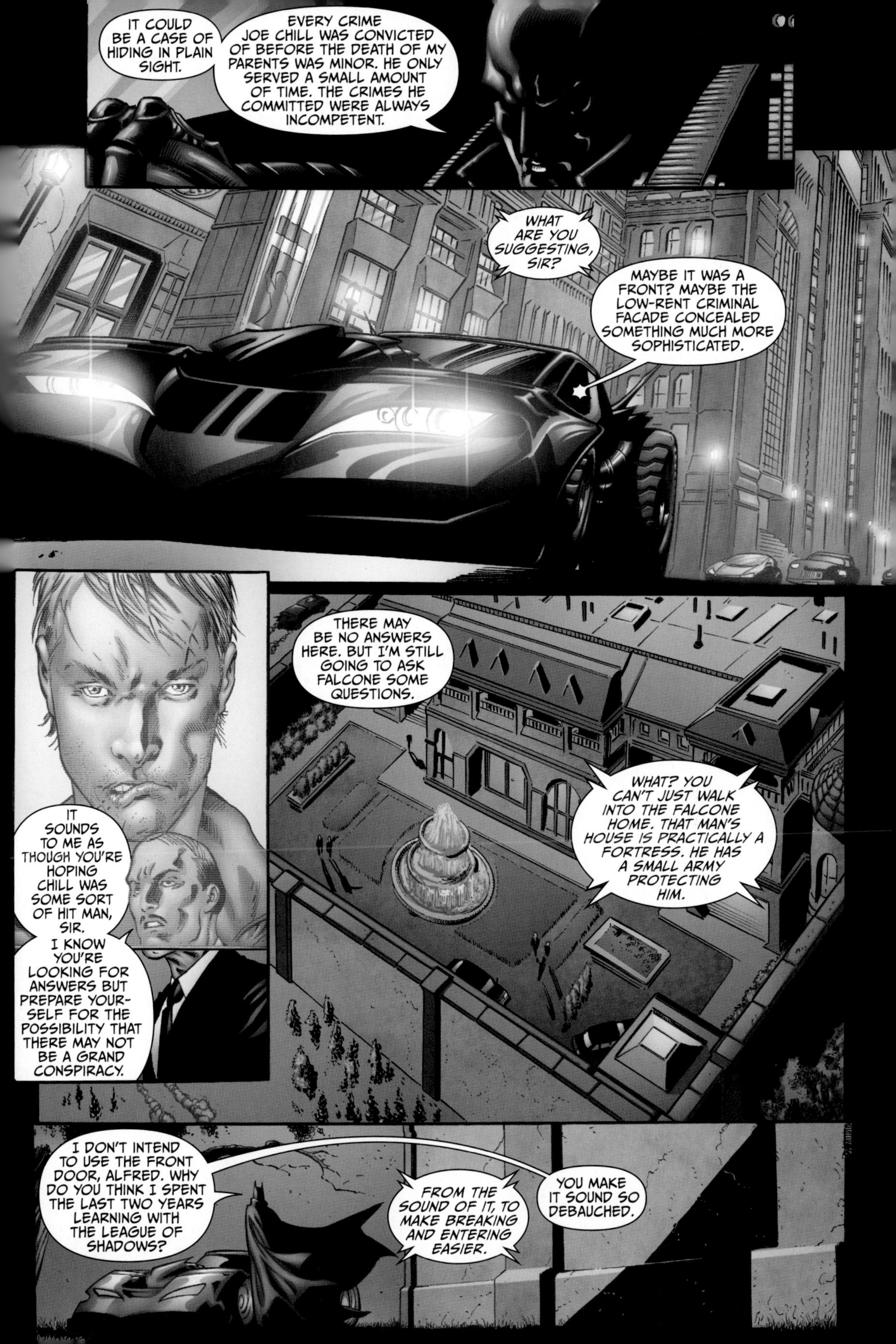
IT COULD BE A CASE OF HIDING IN PLAIN SIGHT.
EVERY CRIME JOE CHILL WAS CONVICTED OF BEFORE THE DEATH OF MY PARENTS WAS MINOR. HE ONLY SERVED A SMALL AMOUNT OF TIME. THE CRIMES HE COMMITTED WERE ALWAYS INCOMPETENT.
WHAT ARE YOU SUGGESTING, SIR?
MAYBE IT WAS A FRONT? MAYBE THE LOW-RENT CRIMINAL FACADE CONCEALED SOMETHING MUCH MORE SOPHISTICATED.
IT SOUNDS TO ME AS THOUGH YOU'RE HOPING CHILL WAS SOME SORT OF HIT MAN, SIR.
I KNOW YOU'RE LOOKING FOR ANSWERS BUT PREPARE YOURSELF FOR THE POSSIBILITY THAT THERE MAY NOT BE A GRAND CONSPIRACY.
THERE MAY BE NO ANSWERS HERE. BUT I'M STILL GOING TO ASK FALCONE SOME QUESTIONS.
WHAT? YOU CAN'T JUST WALK INTO THE FALCONE HOME. THAT MAN'S HOUSE IS PRACTICALLY A FORTRESS. HE HAS A SMALL ARMY PROTECTING HIM.
I DON'T INTEND TO USE THE FRONT DOOR, ALFRED. WHY DO YOU THINK I SPENT THE LAST TWO YEARS LEARNING WITH THE LEAGUE OF SHADOWS?
FROM THE SOUND OF IT, TO MAKE BREAKING AND ENTERING EASIER.
YOU MAKE IT SOUND SO DEBAUCHED.

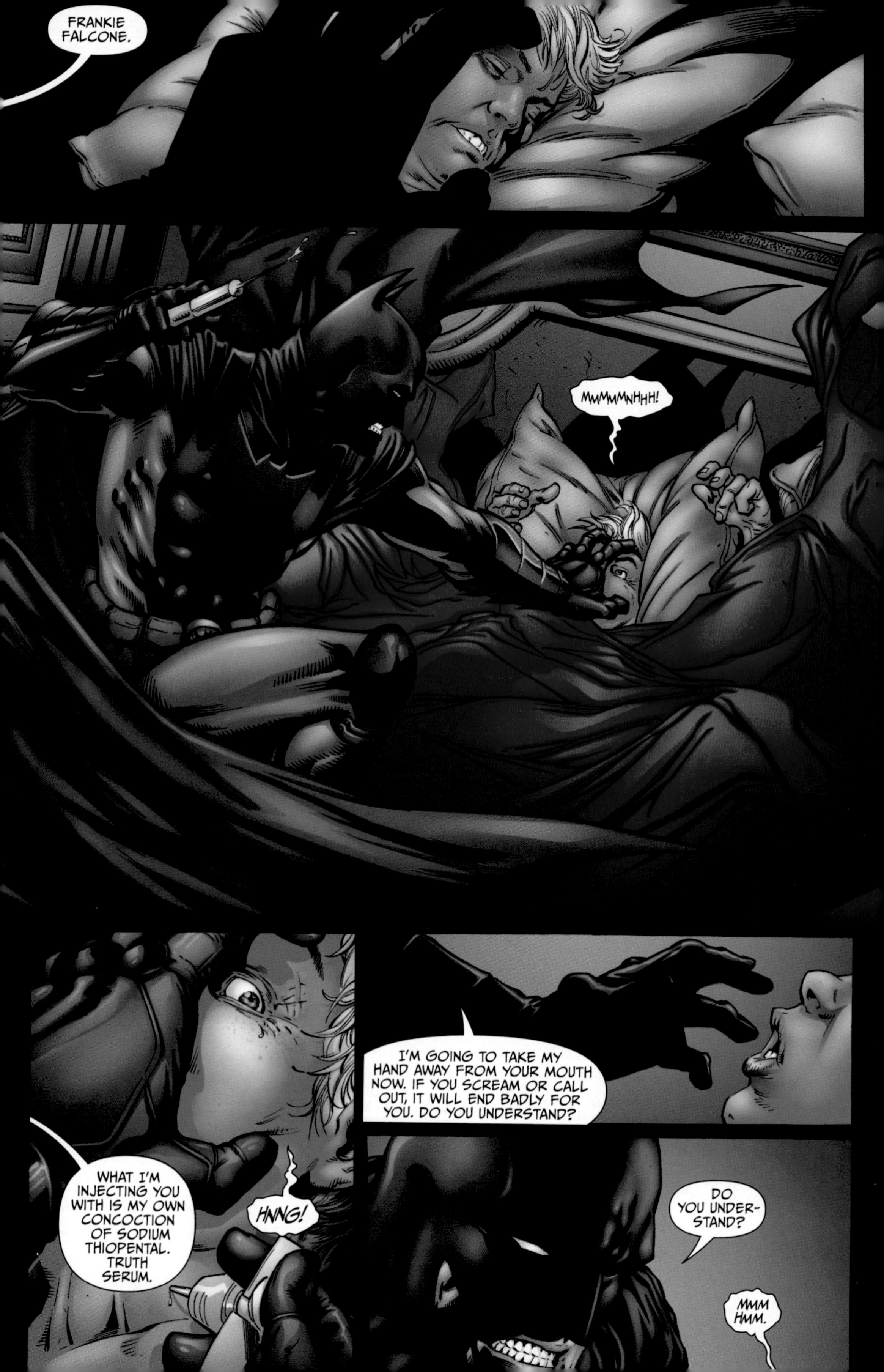
FRANKIE FALCONE.
MMMMMNHHH!
WHAT I'M INJECTING YOU WITH IS MY OWN CONCOCTION OF SODIUM THIOPENTAL. TRUTH SERUM.
HNNG!
I'M GOING TO TAKE MY HAND AWAY FROM YOUR MOUTH NOW. IF YOU SCREAM OR CALL OUT, IT WILL END BADLY FOR YOU. DO YOU UNDERSTAND?
DO YOU UNDER-STAND?
MMM HMM.

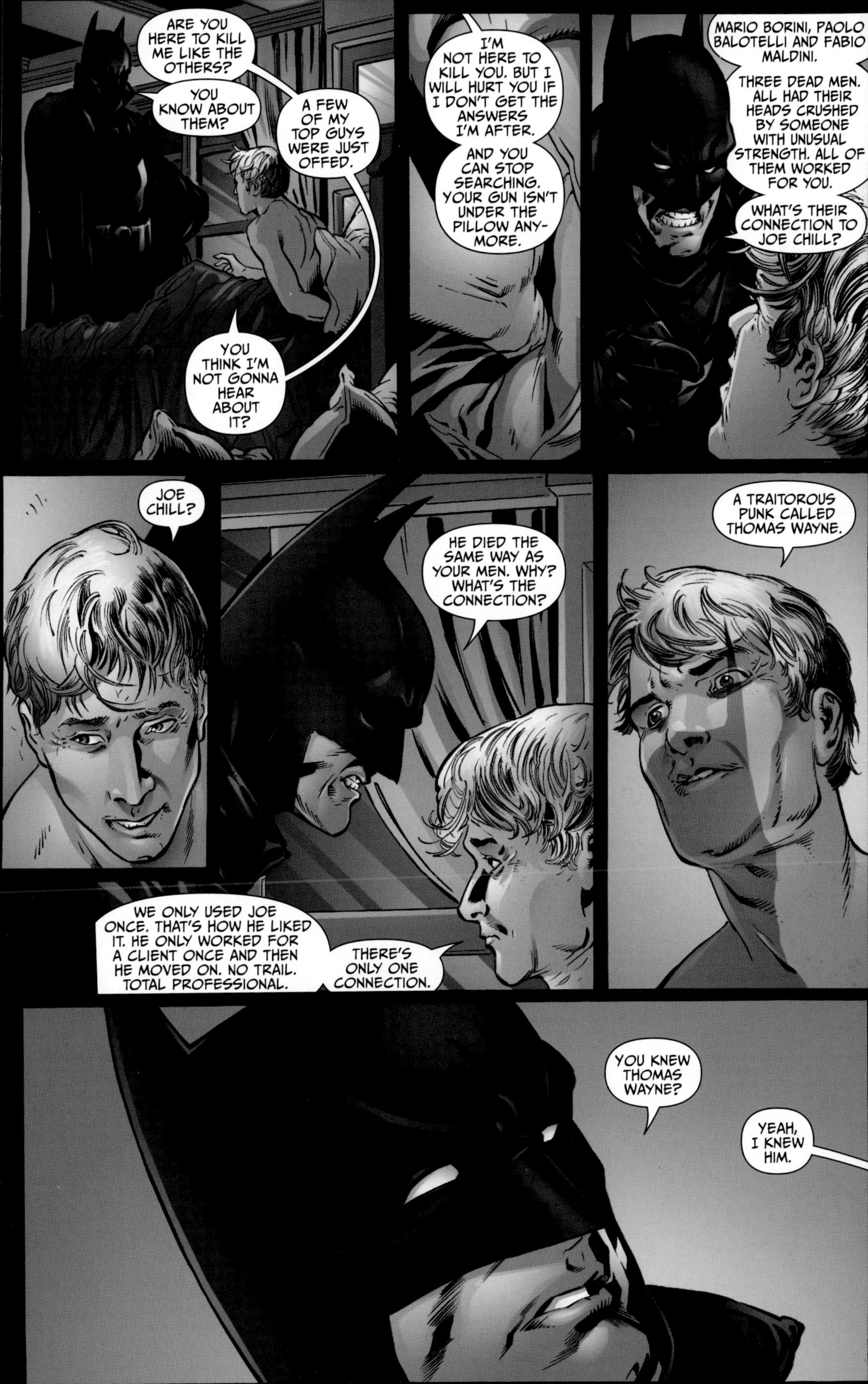
ARE YOU HERE TO KILL ME LIKE THE OTHERS?
YOU KNOW ABOUT THEM?
A FEW OF MY TOP GUYS WERE JUST OFFED.
YOU THINK I'M NOT GONNA HEAR ABOUT IT?
I'M NOT HERE TO KILL YOU. BUT I WILL HURT YOU IF I DON'T GET THE ANSWERS I'M AFTER.
AND YOU CAN STOP SEARCHING. YOUR GUN ISN'T UNDER THE PILLOW ANY-MORE.
MARIO BORINI, PAOLO BALOTELLI AND FABIO MALDINI.
THREE DEAD MEN. ALL HAD THEIR HEADS CRUSHED BY SOMEONE WITH UNUSUAL STRENGTH. ALL OF THEM WORKED FOR YOU.
WHAT'S THEIR CONNECTION TO JOE CHILL?
JOE CHILL?
HE DIED THE SAME WAY AS YOUR MEN. WHY? WHAT'S THE CONNECTION?
WE ONLY USED JOE ONCE. THAT'S HOW HE LIKED IT. HE ONLY WORKED FOR A CLIENT ONCE AND THEN HE MOVED ON. NO TRAIL. TOTAL PROFESSIONAL.
THERE'S ONLY ONE CONNECTION.
A TRAITOROUS PUNK CALLED THOMAS WAYNE.
YOU KNEW THOMAS WAYNE?
YEAH, I KNEW HIM.

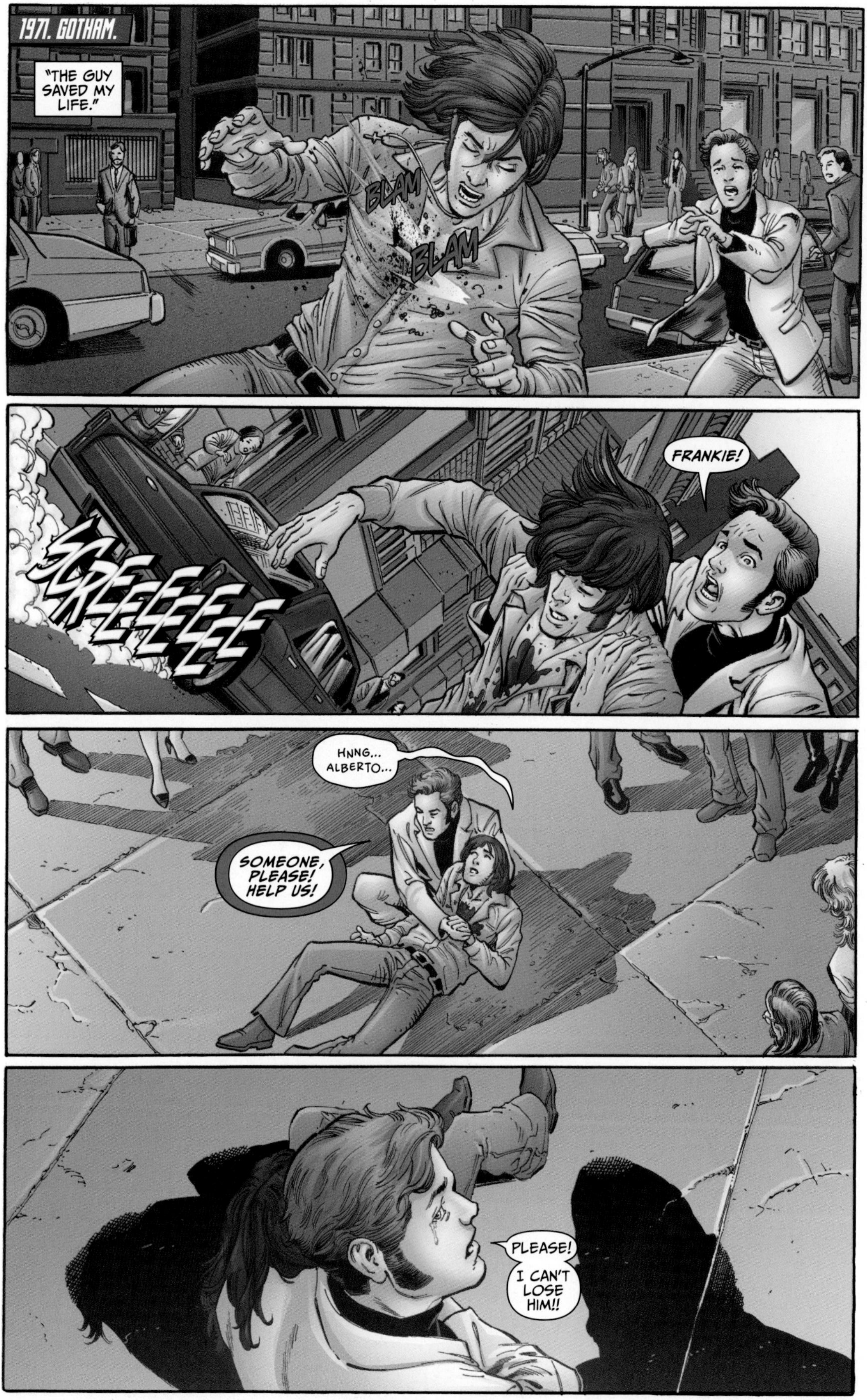
1971. GOTHAM.
"THE GUY SAVED MY LIFE."
BLAM
BLAM
FRANKIE!
SCREEEEEEE
HNNG... ALBERTO...
SOMEONE, PLEASE! HELP US!
PLEASE!
I CAN'T LOSE HIM!!

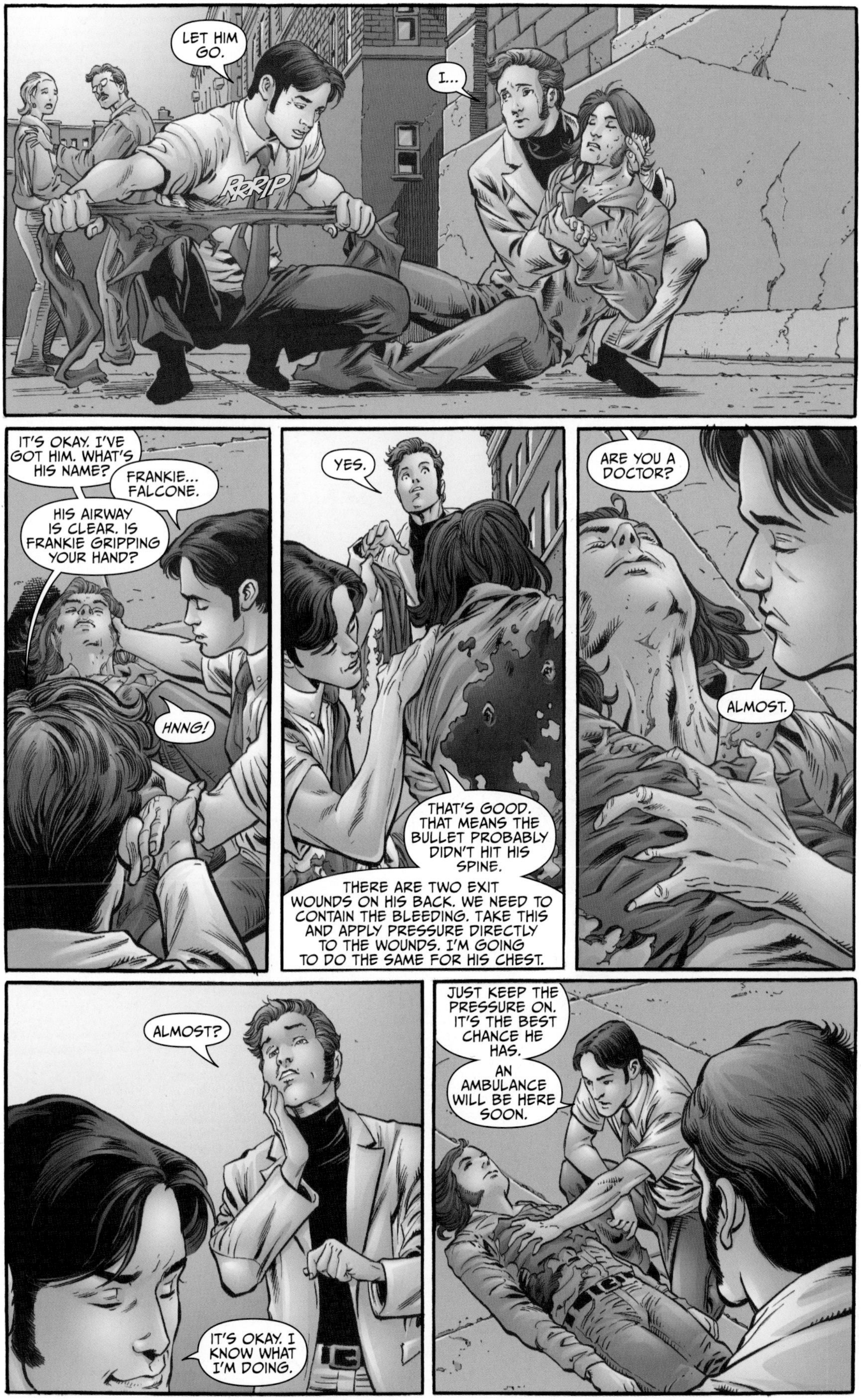
LET HIM GO.
RRRIP
I...
IT'S OKAY. I'VE GOT HIM. WHAT'S HIS NAME?
FRANKIE... FALCONE.
HIS AIRWAY IS CLEAR. IS FRANKIE GRIPPING YOUR HAND?
HNNG!
YES.
THAT'S GOOD. THAT MEANS THE BULLET PROBABLY DIDN'T HIT HIS SPINE.
THERE ARE TWO EXIT WOUNDS ON HIS BACK. WE NEED TO CONTAIN THE BLEEDING. TAKE THIS AND APPLY PRESSURE DIRECTLY TO THE WOUNDS. I'M GOING TO DO THE SAME FOR HIS CHEST.
ARE YOU A DOCTOR?
ALMOST.
ALMOST?
IT'S OKAY. I KNOW WHAT I'M DOING.
JUST KEEP THE PRESSURE ON. IT'S THE BEST CHANCE HE HAS.
AN AMBULANCE WILL BE HERE SOON.

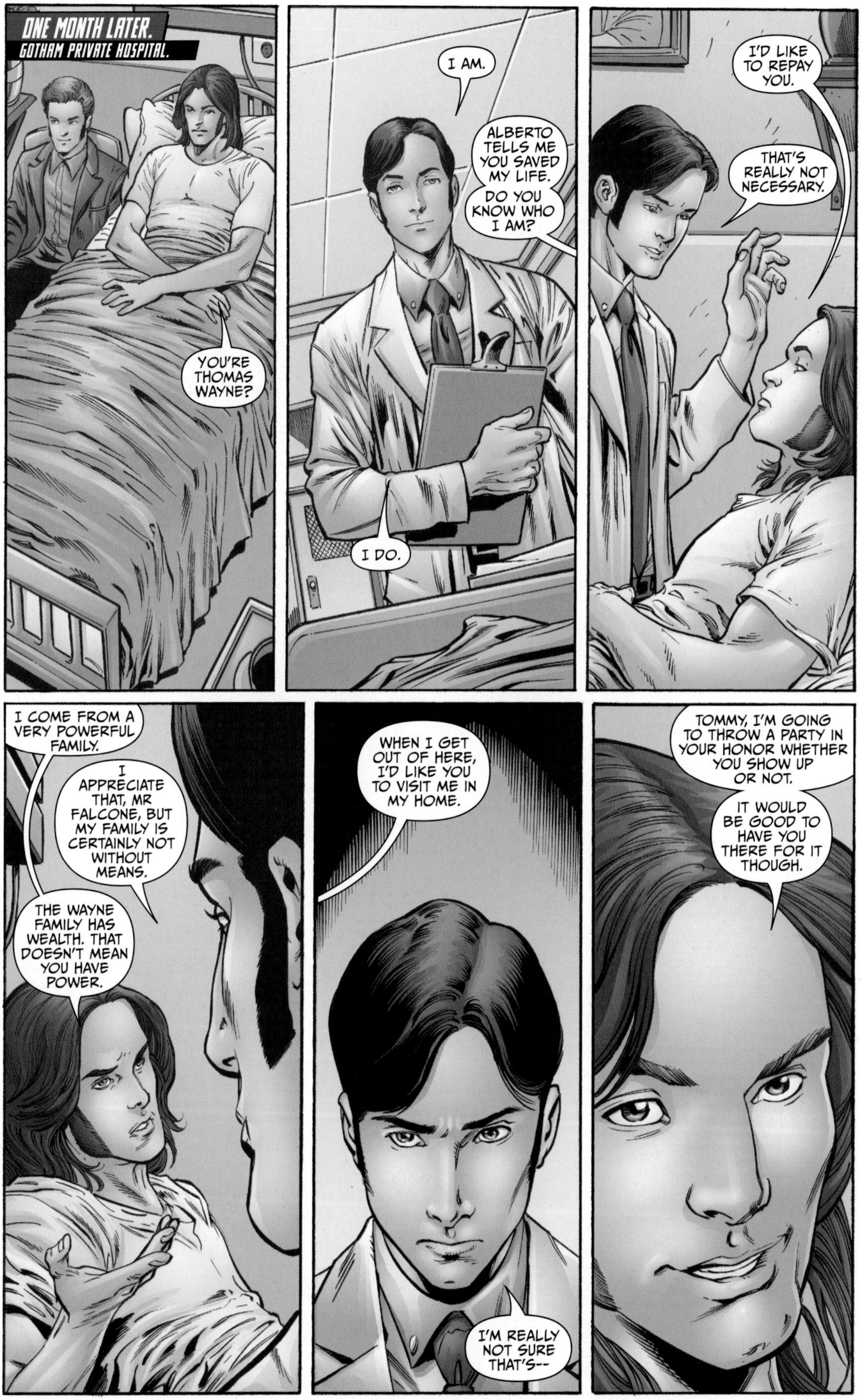
ONE MONTH LATER.
GOTHAM PRIVATE HOSPITAL.
YOU'RE THOMAS WAYNE?
I AM.
ALBERTO TELLS ME YOU SAVED MY LIFE.
DO YOU KNOW WHO I AM?
I DO.
I'D LIKE TO REPAY YOU.
THAT'S REALLY NOT NECESSARY.
I COME FROM A VERY POWERFUL FAMILY.
I APPRECIATE THAT, MR FALCONE, BUT MY FAMILY IS CERTAINLY NOT WITHOUT MEANS.
THE WAYNE FAMILY HAS WEALTH. THAT DOESN'T MEAN YOU HAVE POWER.
WHEN I GET OUT OF HERE, I'D LIKE YOU TO VISIT ME IN MY HOME.
I'M REALLY NOT SURE THAT'S--
TOMMY, I'M GOING TO THROW A PARTY IN YOUR HONOR WHETHER YOU SHOW UP OR NOT.
IT WOULD BE GOOD TO HAVE YOU THERE FOR IT THOUGH.

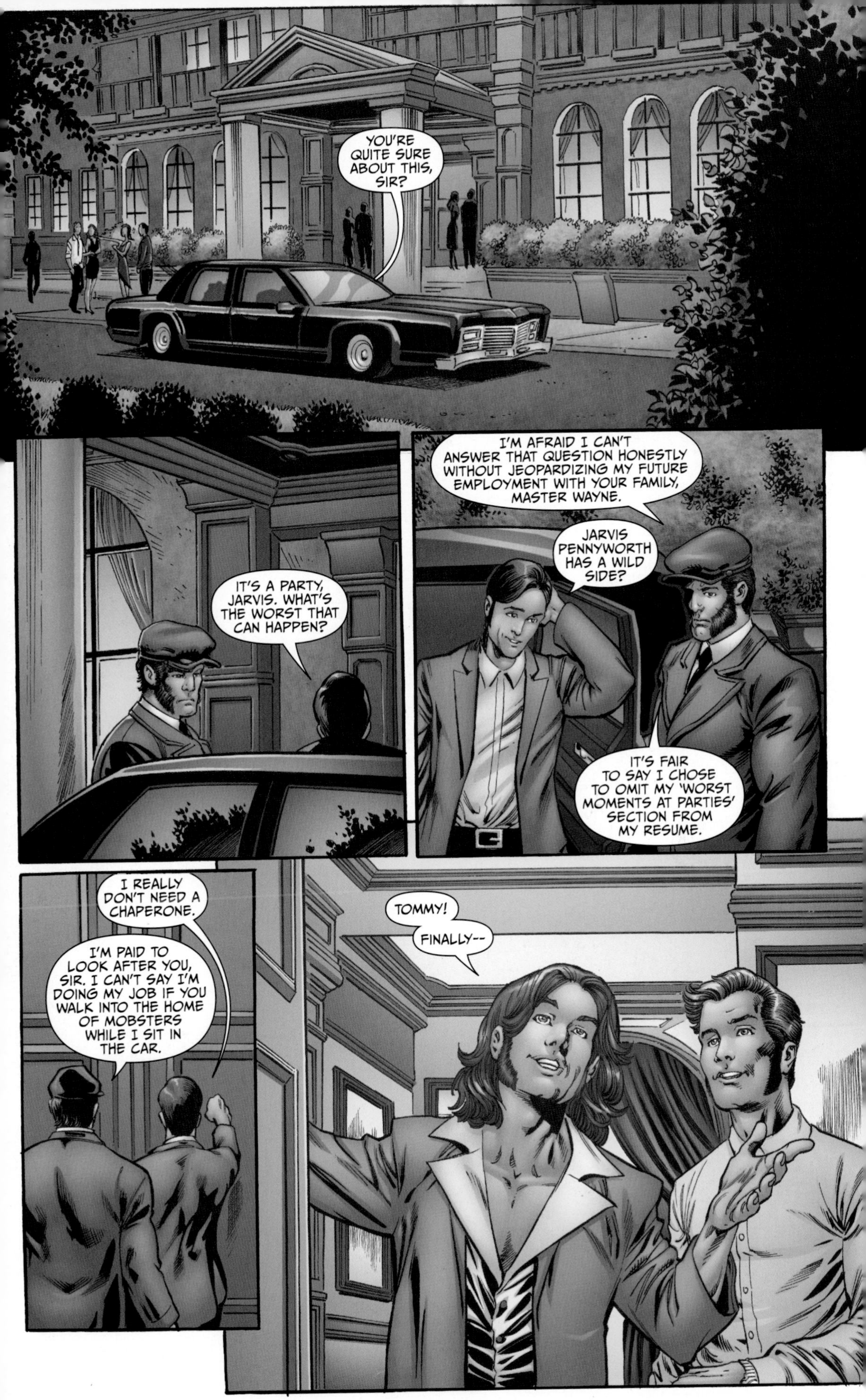
YOU'RE QUITE SURE ABOUT THIS, SIR?
IT'S A PARTY, JARVIS. WHAT'S THE WORST THAT CAN HAPPEN?
I'M AFRAID I CAN'T ANSWER THAT QUESTION HONESTLY WITHOUT JEOPARDIZING MY FUTURE EMPLOYMENT WITH YOUR FAMILY, MASTER WAYNE.
JARVIS PENNYWORTH HAS A WILD SIDE?
IT'S FAIR TO SAY I CHOSE TO OMIT MY 'WORST MOMENTS AT PARTIES' SECTION FROM MY RESUME.
I REALLY DON'T NEED A CHAPERONE.
I'M PAID TO LOOK AFTER YOU, SIR. I CAN'T SAY I'M DOING MY JOB IF YOU WALK INTO THE HOME OF MOBSTERS WHILE I SIT IN THE CAR.
TOMMY!
FINALLY--

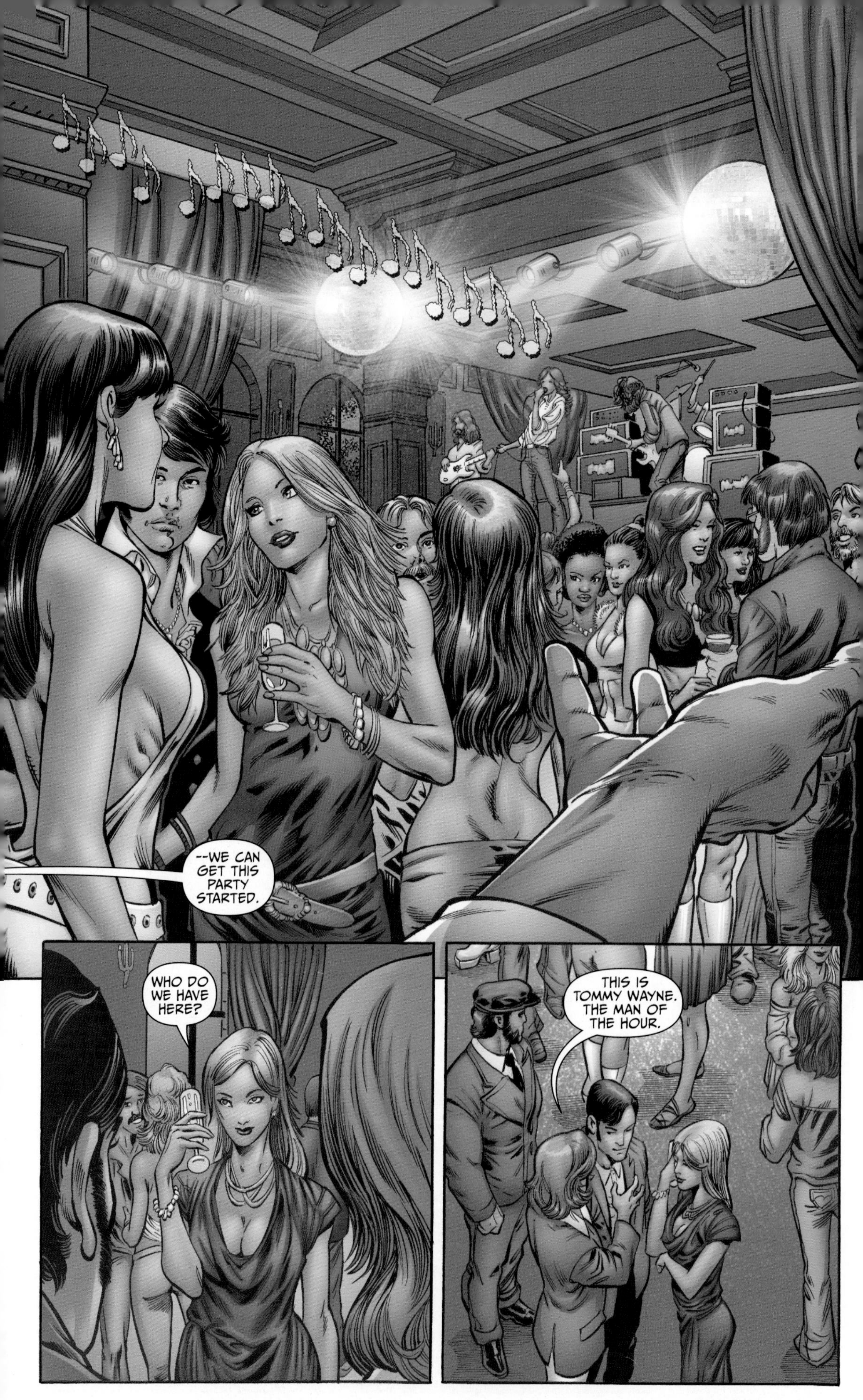
--WE CAN GET THIS PARTY STARTED.
WHO DO WE HAVE HERE?
THIS IS TOMMY WAYNE. THE MAN OF THE HOUR.

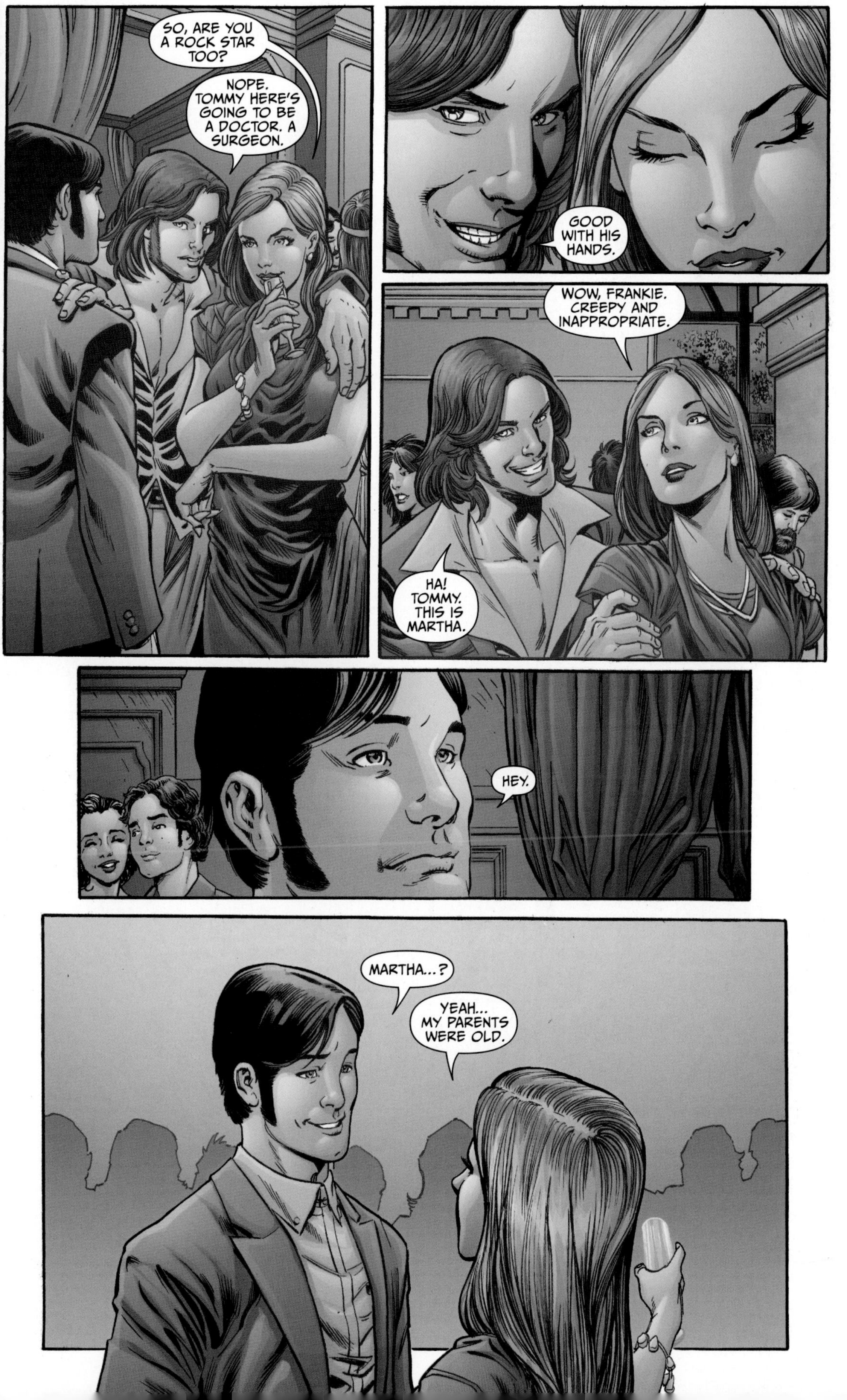
SO, ARE YOU A ROCK STAR TOO?
NOPE. TOMMY HERE'S GOING TO BE A DOCTOR. A SURGEON.
GOOD WITH HIS HANDS.
WOW, FRANKIE. CREEPY AND INAPPROPRIATE.
HA! TOMMY. THIS IS MARTHA.
HEY.
MARTHA...?
YEAH... MY PARENTS WERE OLD.

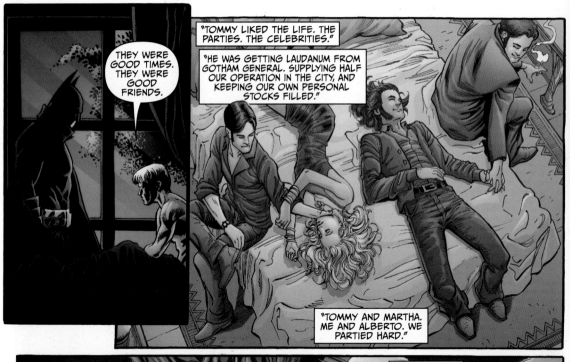

THEY WERE GOOD TIMES. THEY WERE GOOD FRIENDS.

"TOMMY LIKED THE LIFE. THE PARTIES. THE CELEBRITIES."

"HE WAS GETTING LAUDANUM FROM GOTHAM GENERAL. SUPPLYING HALF OUR OPERATION IN THE CITY, AND KEEPING OUR OWN PERSONAL STOCKS FILLED."

"TOMMY AND MARTHA. ME AND ALBERTO. WE PARTIED HARD."

"PARTIED TOO HARD FOR ALBERTO."

I STILL MISS THAT BOY. HE WAS WAY OUT OF MY LEAGUE.

IF YOU WERE ALL SUCH GOOD FRIENDS, WHAT HAPPENED?

WHAT HAPPENED?

1973.

CONGRATULATIONS
- FRANKIE

"THEY HAD A KID."

IT NEEDS TO STOP, THOMAS! YOU HAVE A SON NOW. WHAT SORT OF EXAMPLE ARE YOU SETTING?

"AND TOMMY TRIED TO LEAVE ME."

I'M SORRY, FRANKIE. I NEED TO STRAIGHTEN OUT.

WE HAVE AN ARRANGEMENT. I DON'T WANT TO BUT I WILL RUIN YOU BEFORE I'LL LET YOU WALK AWAY. THIS IS BUSINESS.

"WE GOT INTO IT."

CRCK

WHATEVER YOU HAVE OVER ME, YOU KNOW I HAVE MORE ON YOU.

I KNOW THINGS, FRANKIE. AND I WILL TALK IF YOU TRY TO HURT ME. I'M PREPARED TO BE PUNISHED FOR MY SINS. ARE YOU?

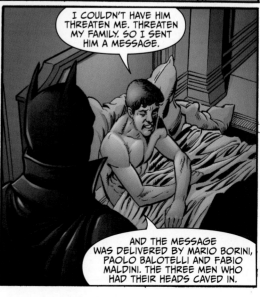

I COULDN'T HAVE HIM THREATEN ME. THREATEN MY FAMILY. SO I SENT HIM A MESSAGE.

AND THE MESSAGE WAS DELIVERED BY MARIO BORINI, PAOLO BALOTELLI AND FABIO MALDINI. THE THREE MEN WHO HAD THEIR HEADS CAVED IN.

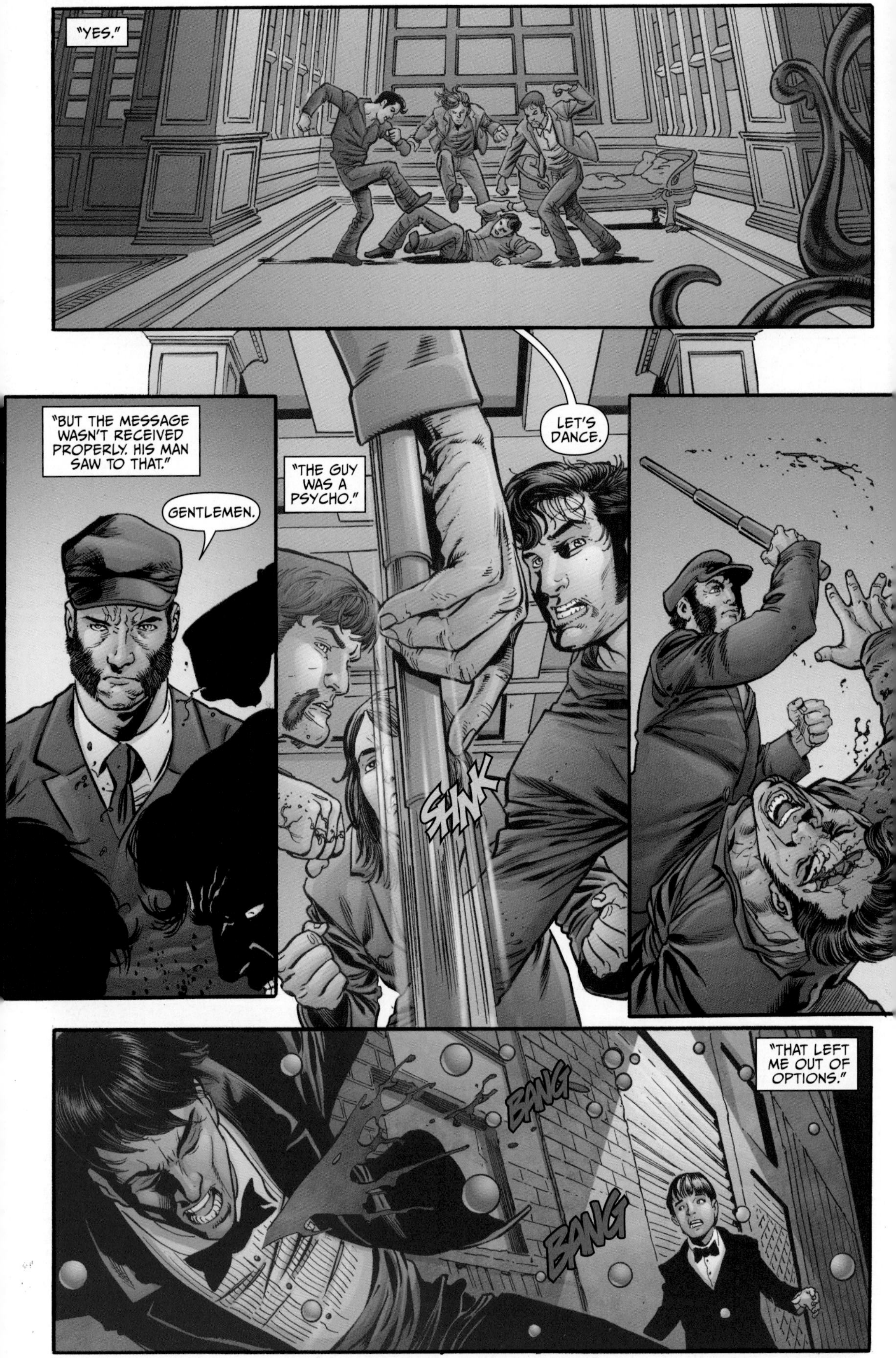
"YES."
"BUT THE MESSAGE WASN'T RECEIVED PROPERLY. HIS MAN SAW TO THAT."
GENTLEMEN.
"THE GUY WAS A PSYCHO."
LET'S DANCE.
SHNK
"THAT LEFT ME OUT OF OPTIONS."
BANG
BANG

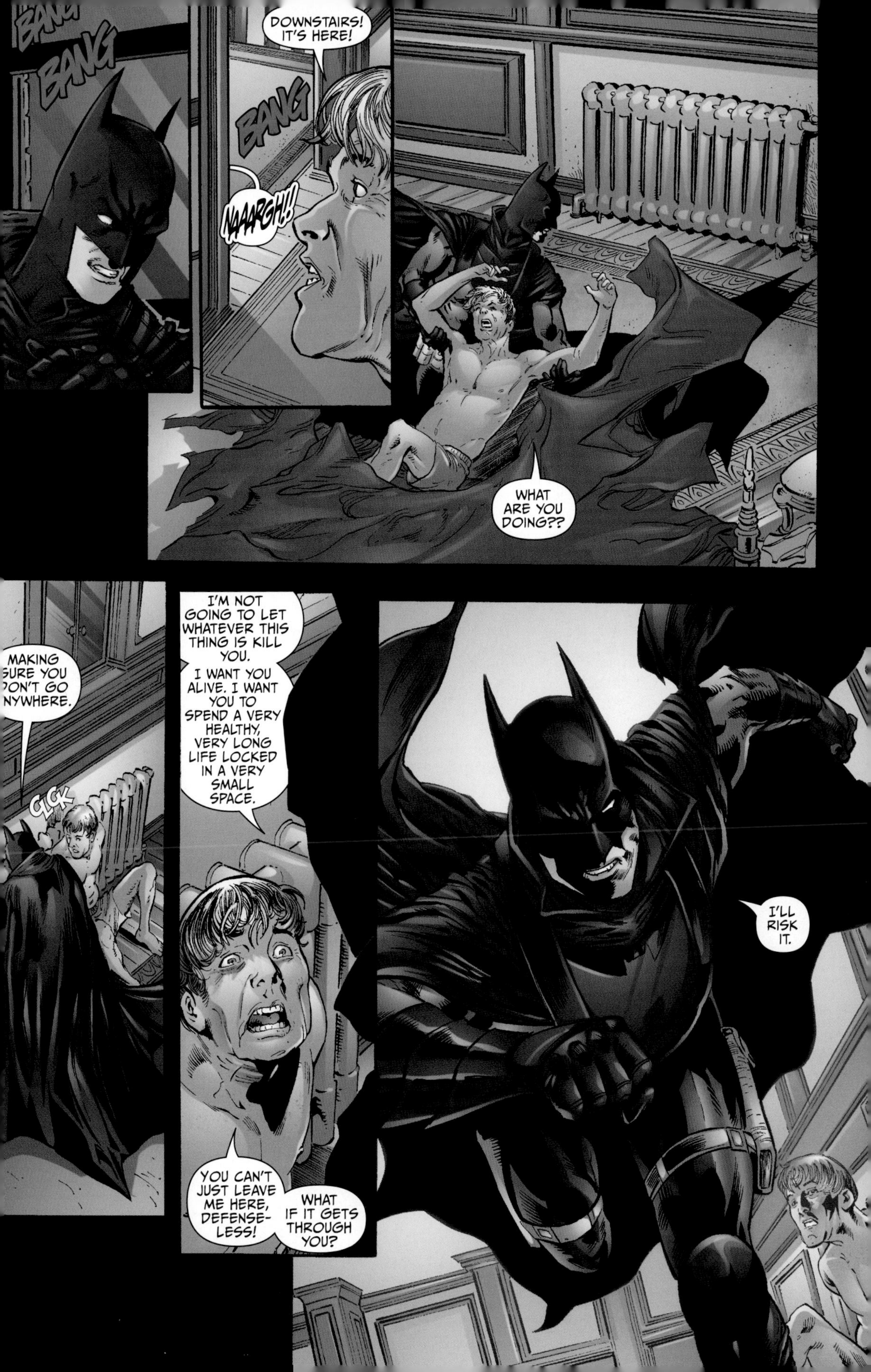
BANG
BANG
DOWNSTAIRS! IT'S HERE!
BANG
NAAARGH!!
WHAT ARE YOU DOING??
MAKING SURE YOU DON'T GO ANYWHERE.
CLCK
I'M NOT GOING TO LET WHATEVER THIS THING IS KILL YOU.
I WANT YOU ALIVE. I WANT YOU TO SPEND A VERY HEALTHY, VERY LONG LIFE LOCKED IN A VERY SMALL SPACE.
YOU CAN'T JUST LEAVE ME HERE, DEFENSELESS!
WHAT IF IT GETS THROUGH YOU?
I'LL RISK IT.

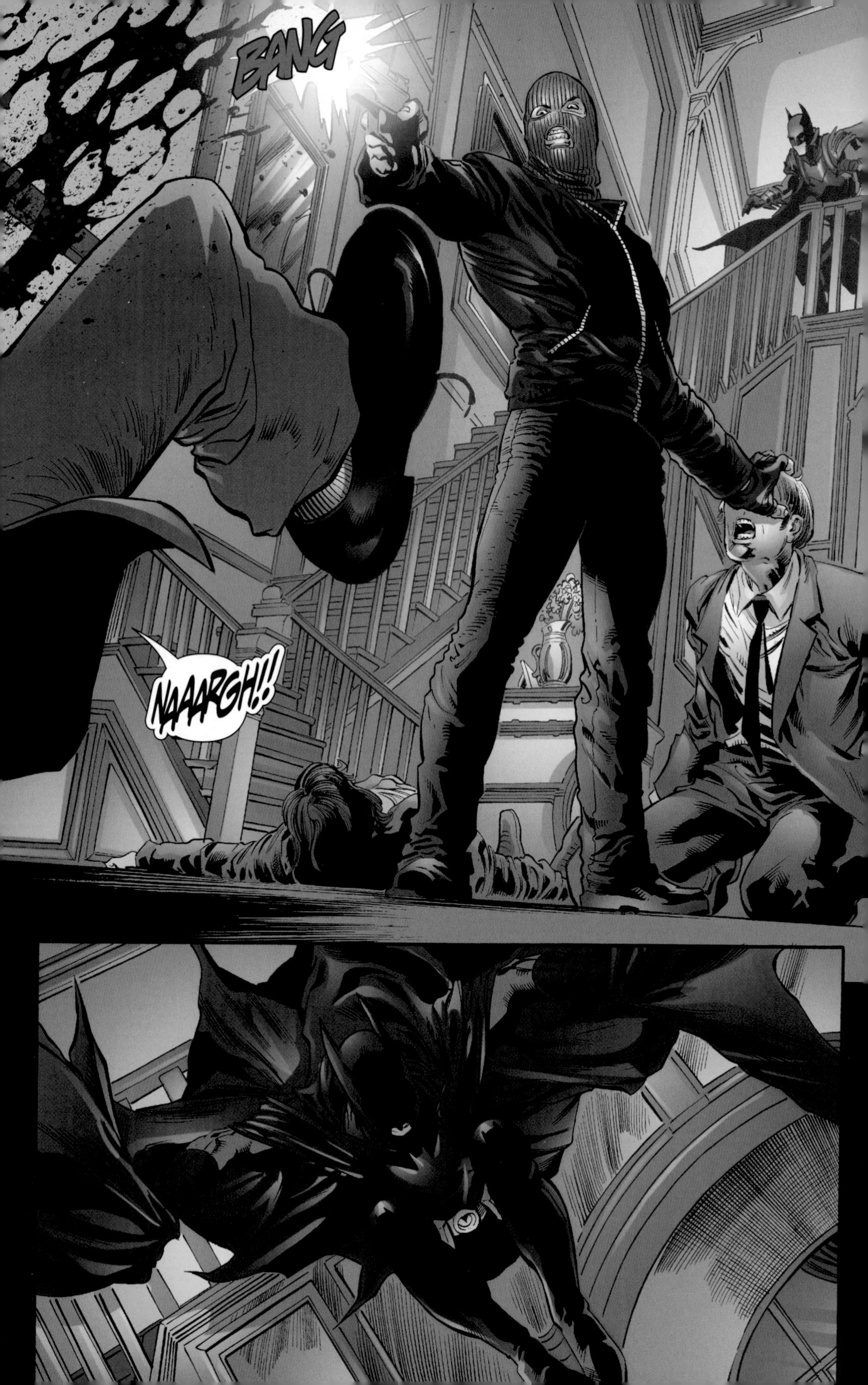
BANG
NAAARGH!!

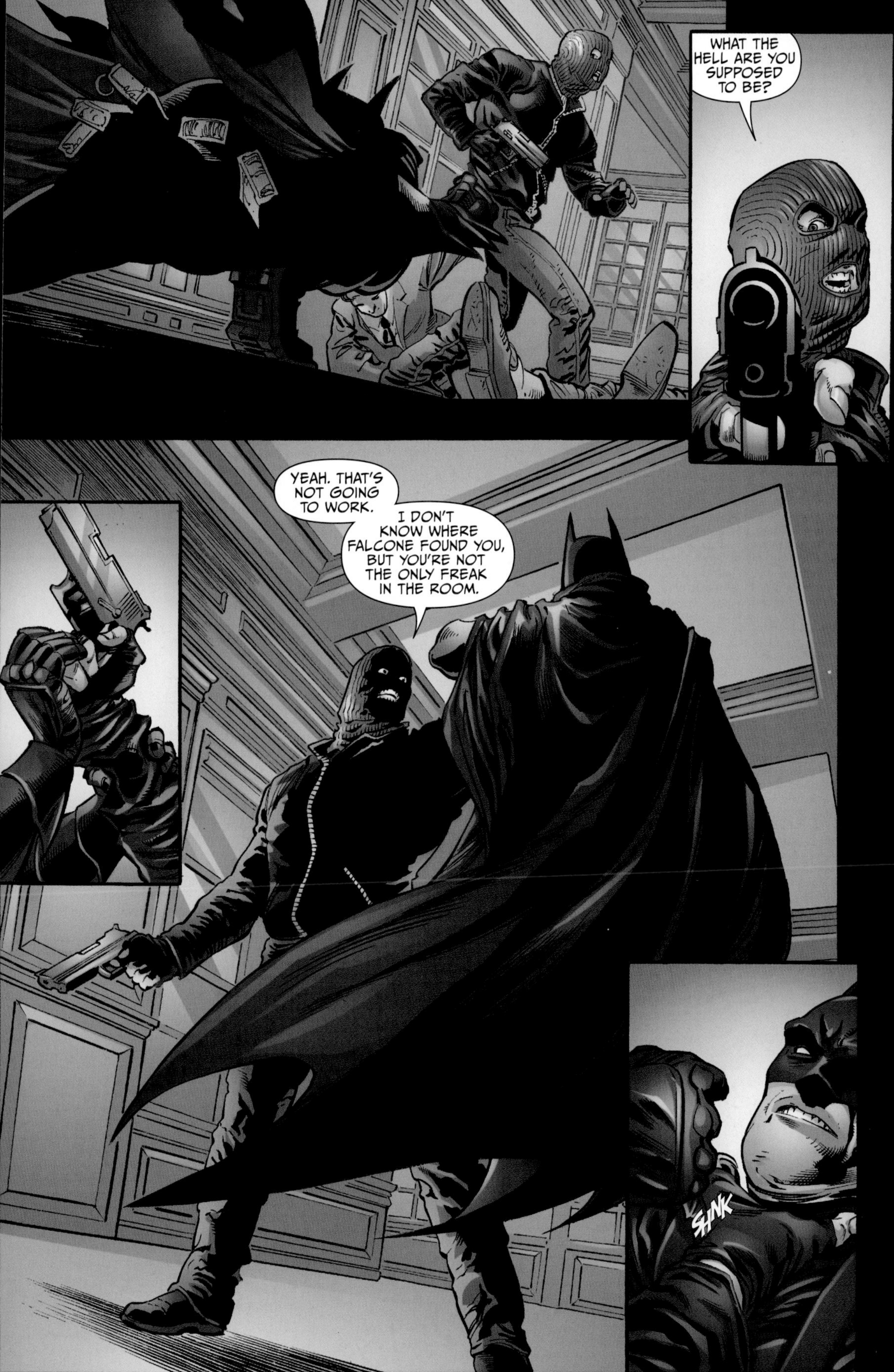
WHAT THE HELL ARE YOU SUPPOSED TO BE?
YEAH. THAT'S NOT GOING TO WORK.
I DON'T KNOW WHERE FALCONE FOUND YOU, BUT YOU'RE NOT THE ONLY FREAK IN THE ROOM.
SHNK

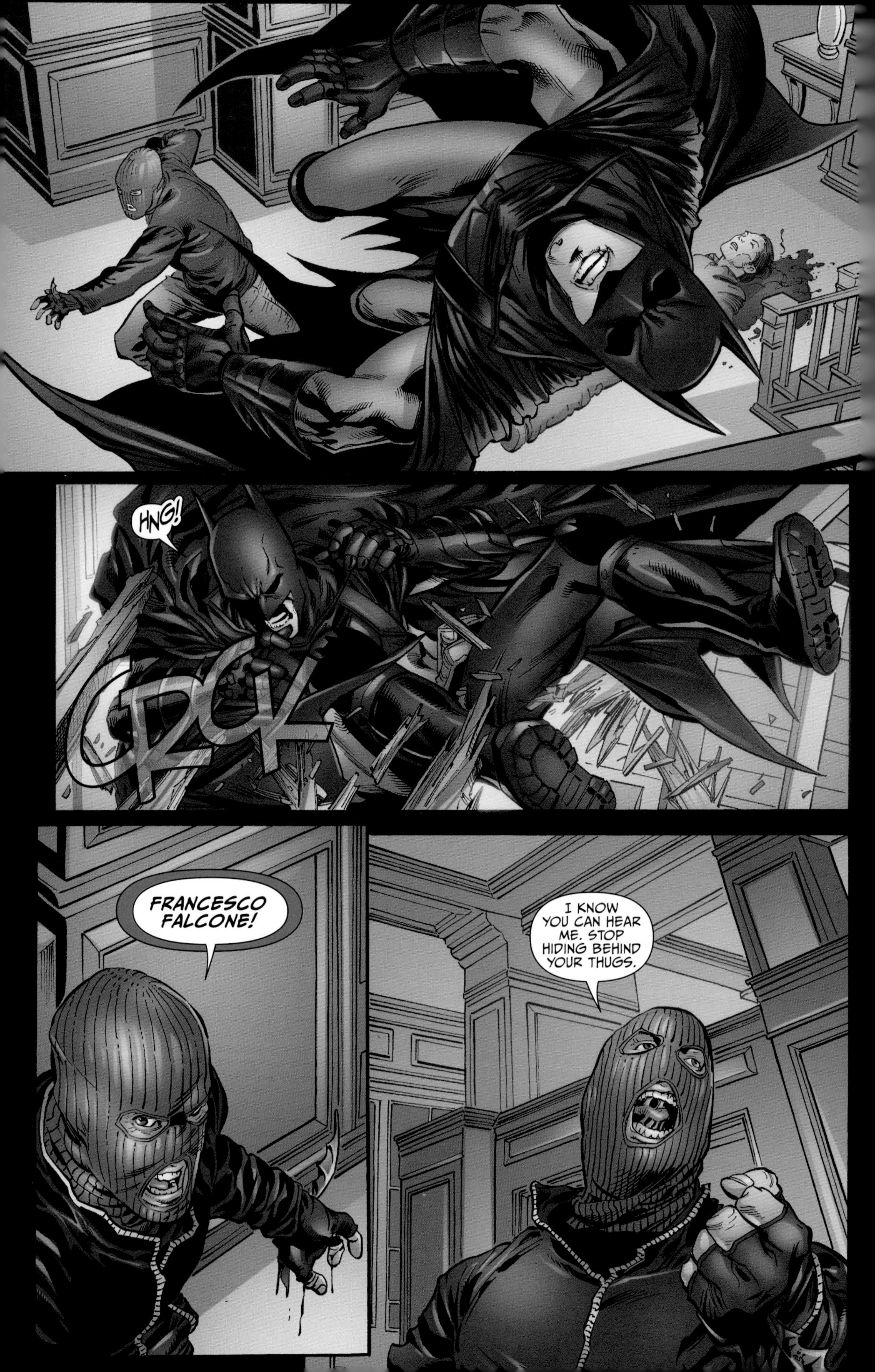
HNG!
CRCK
FRANCESCO FALCONE!
I KNOW YOU CAN HEAR ME. STOP HIDING BEHIND YOUR THUGS.

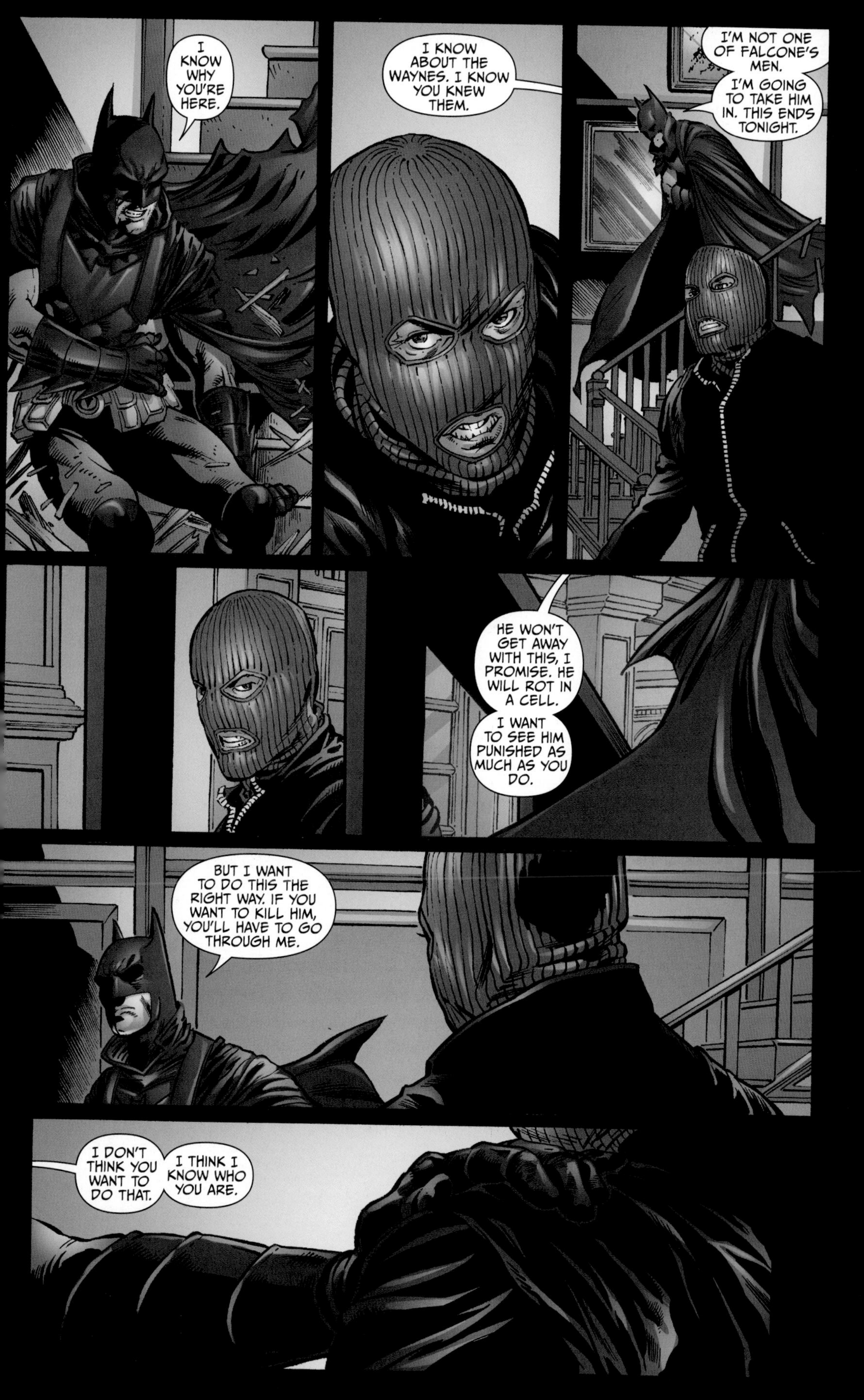
I KNOW WHY YOU'RE HERE.
I KNOW ABOUT THE WAYNES. I KNOW YOU KNEW THEM.
I'M NOT ONE OF FALCONE'S MEN.
I'M GOING TO TAKE HIM IN. THIS ENDS TONIGHT.
HE WON'T GET AWAY WITH THIS, I PROMISE. HE WILL ROT IN A CELL.
I WANT TO SEE HIM PUNISHED AS MUCH AS YOU DO.
BUT I WANT TO DO THIS THE RIGHT WAY. IF YOU WANT TO KILL HIM, YOU'LL HAVE TO GO THROUGH ME.
I DON'T THINK YOU WANT TO DO THAT.
I THINK I KNOW WHO YOU ARE.

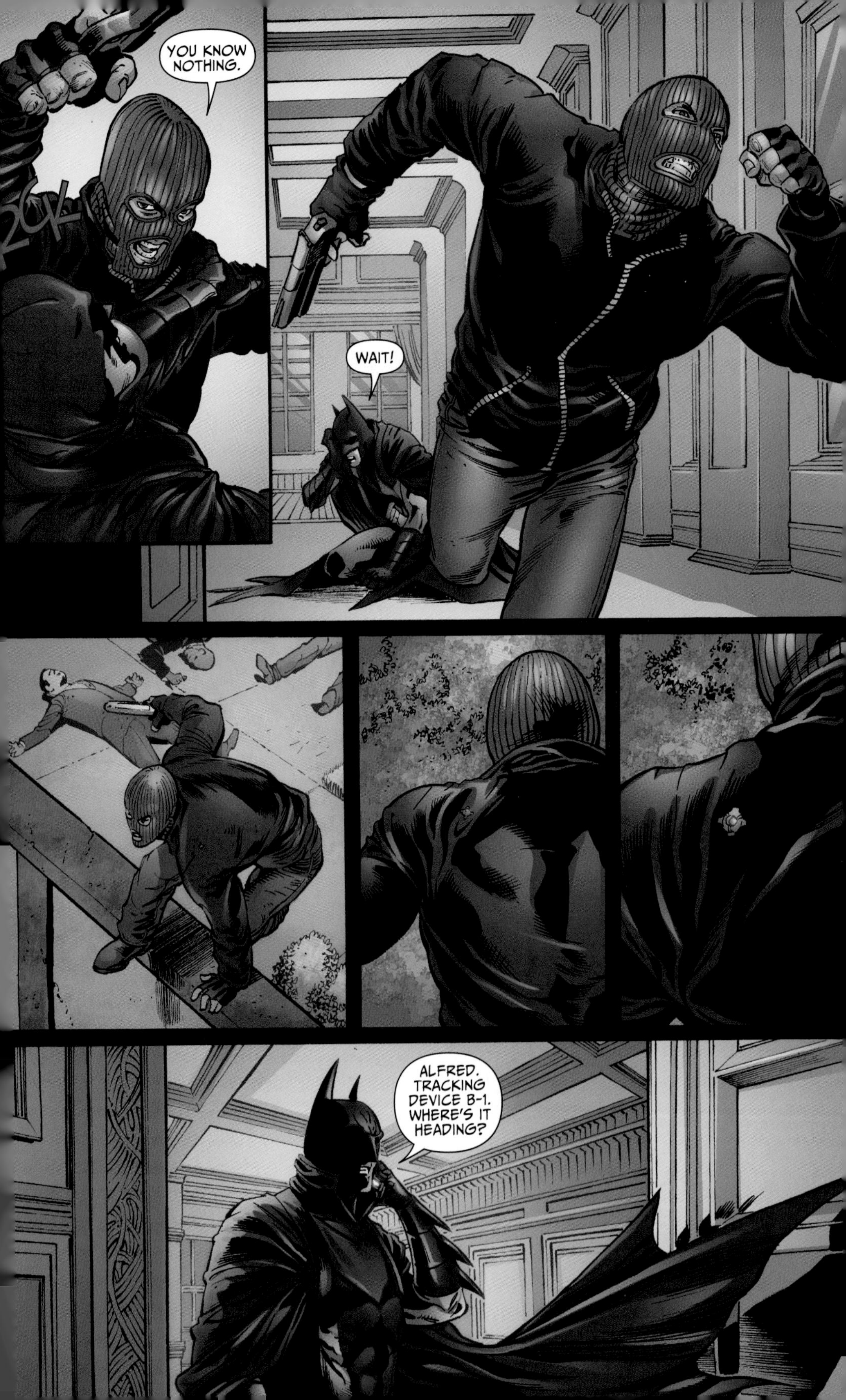
YOU KNOW NOTHING.
WAIT!
ALFRED. TRACKING DEVICE B-1. WHERE'S IT HEADING?

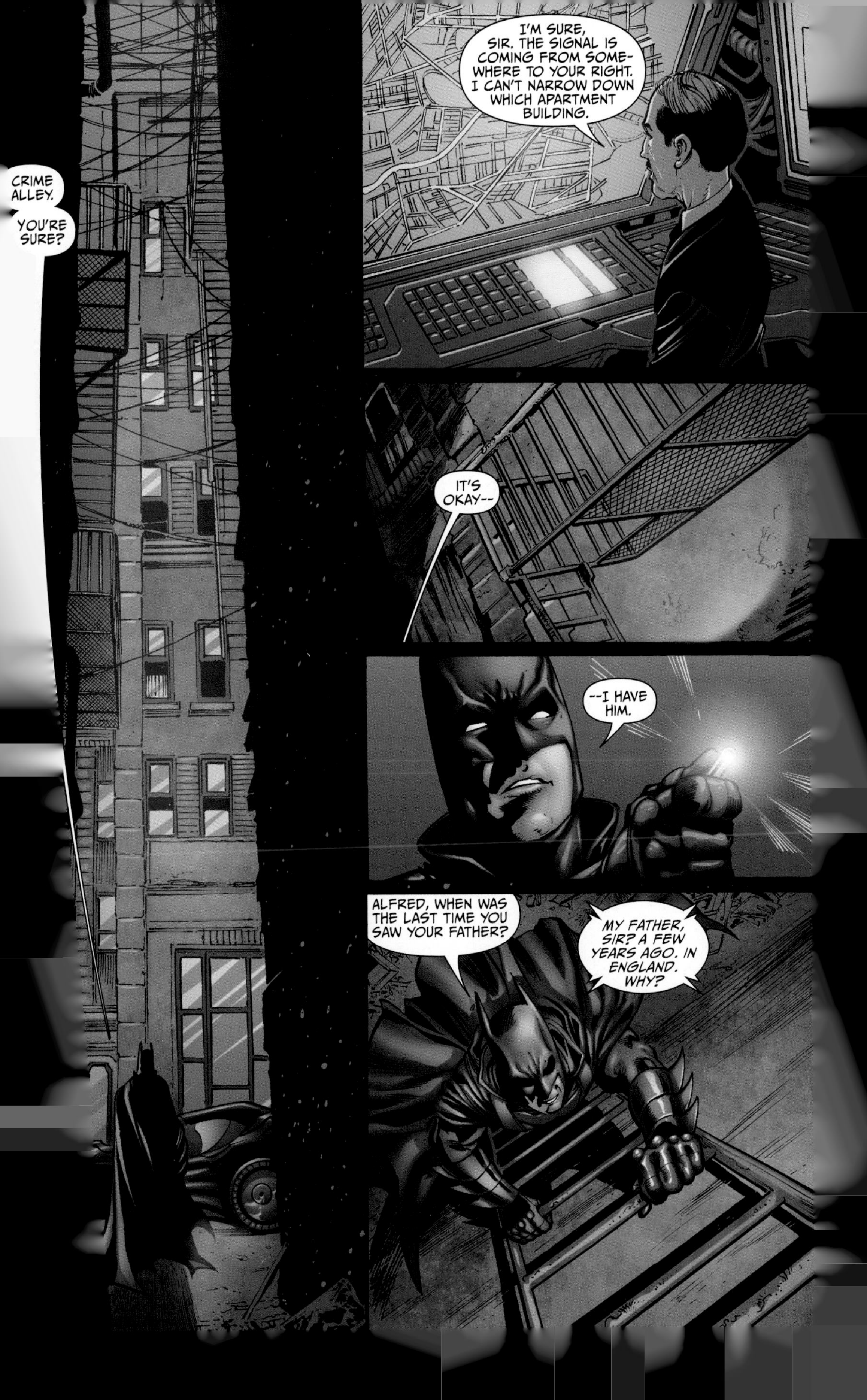
CRIME ALLEY.
YOU'RE SURE?
I'M SURE, SIR. THE SIGNAL IS COMING FROM SOME-WHERE TO YOUR RIGHT. I CAN'T NARROW DOWN WHICH APARTMENT BUILDING.
IT'S OKAY--
--I HAVE HIM.
ALFRED, WHEN WAS THE LAST TIME YOU SAW YOUR FATHER?
MY FATHER, SIR? A FEW YEARS AGO. IN ENGLAND. WHY?

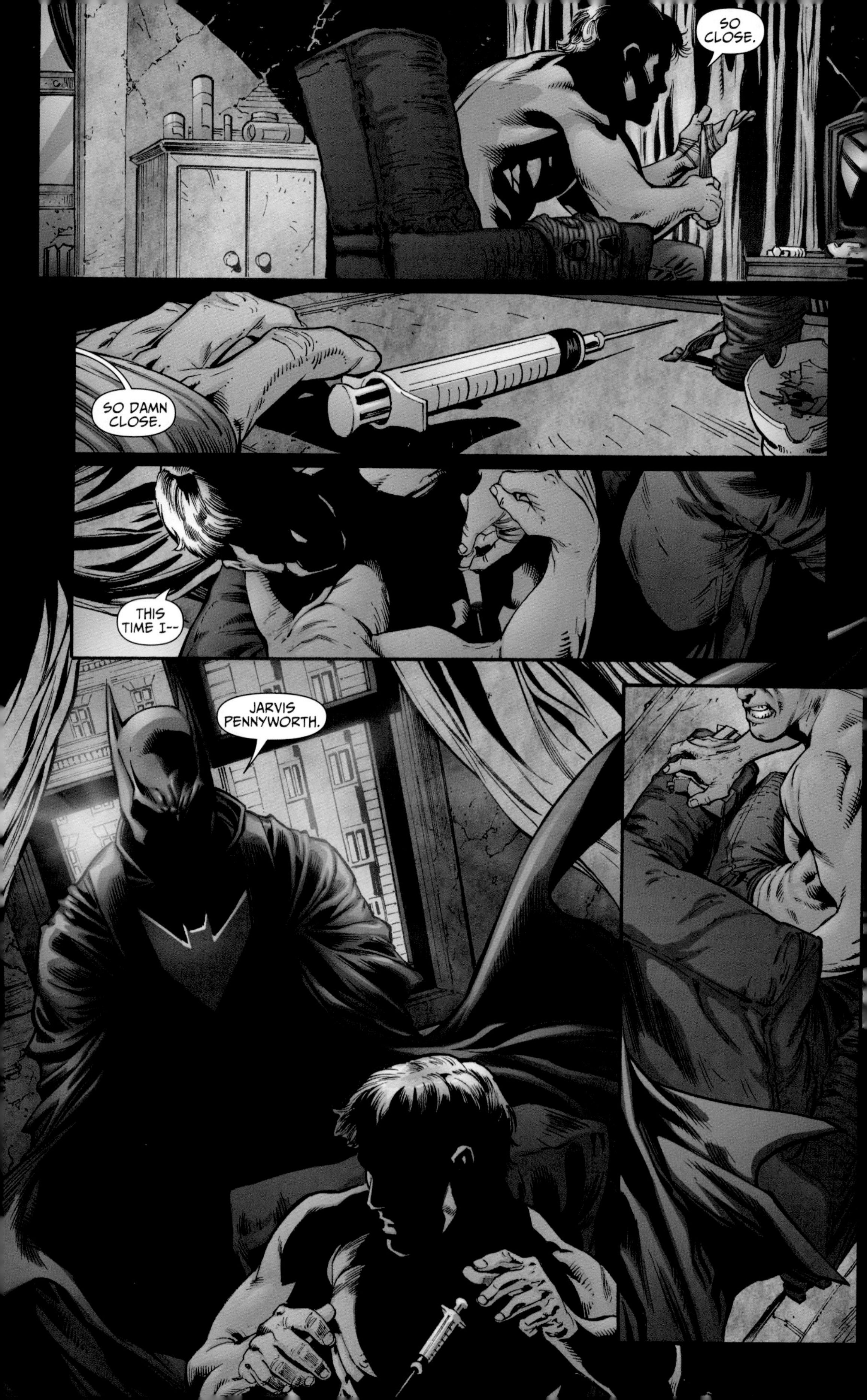
SO CLOSE.
SO DAMN CLOSE.
THIS TIME I--
JARVIS PENNYWORTH.

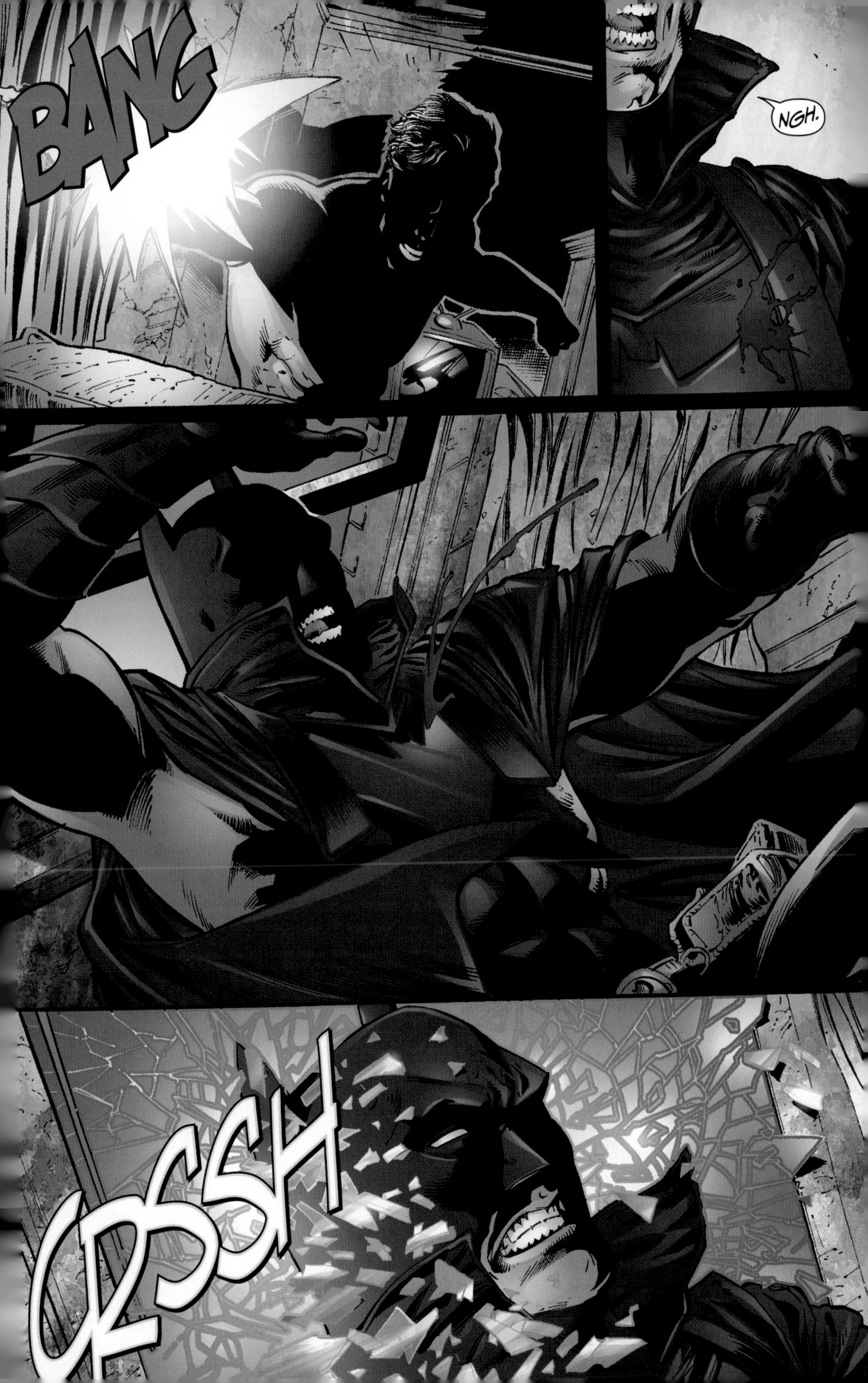
BANG
NGH.
CRSSH

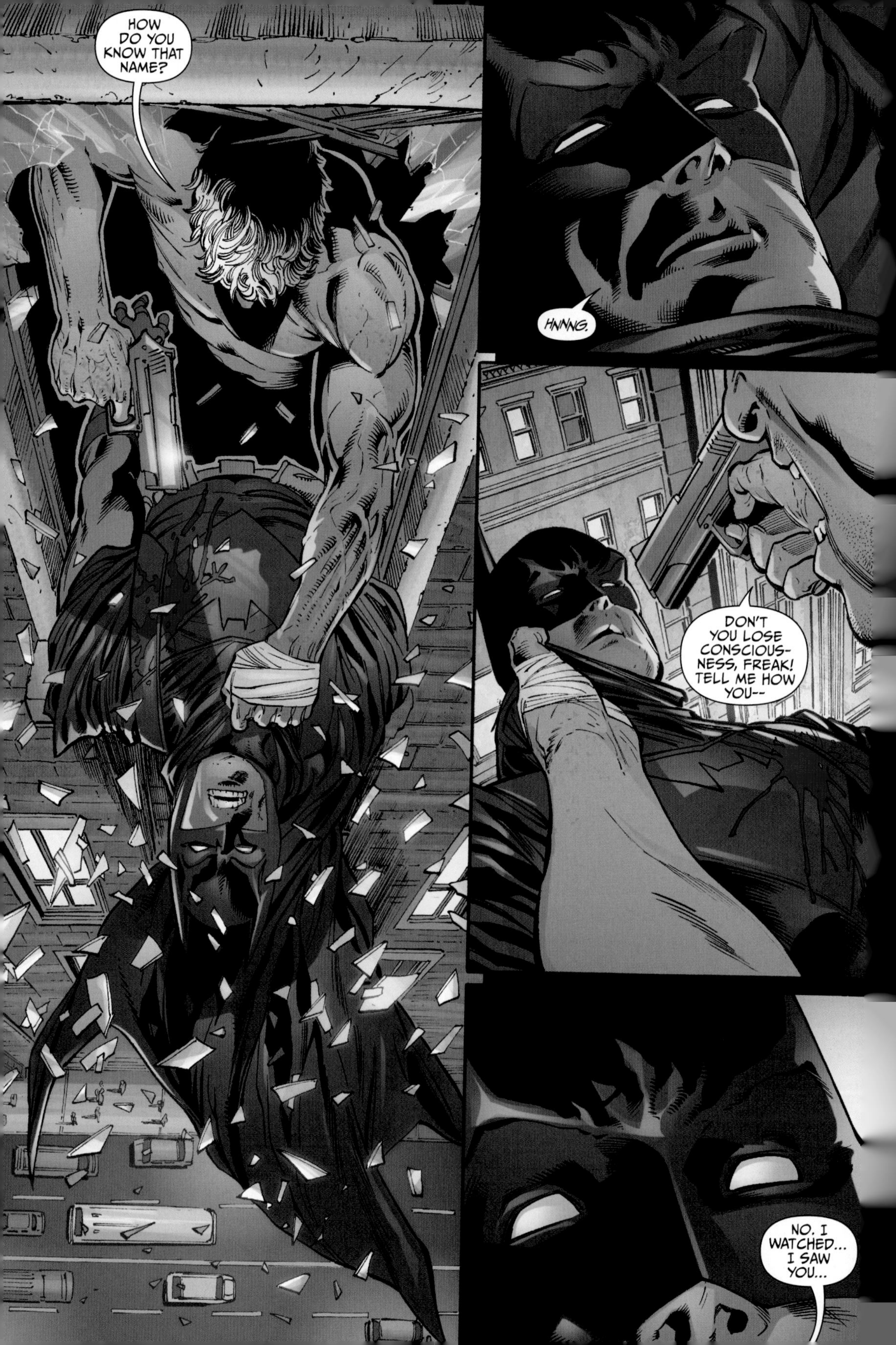
HOW DO YOU KNOW THAT NAME?
HNNNG.
DON'T YOU LOSE CONSCIOUS-NESS, FREAK! TELL ME HOW YOU--
NO. I WATCHED... I SAW YOU...

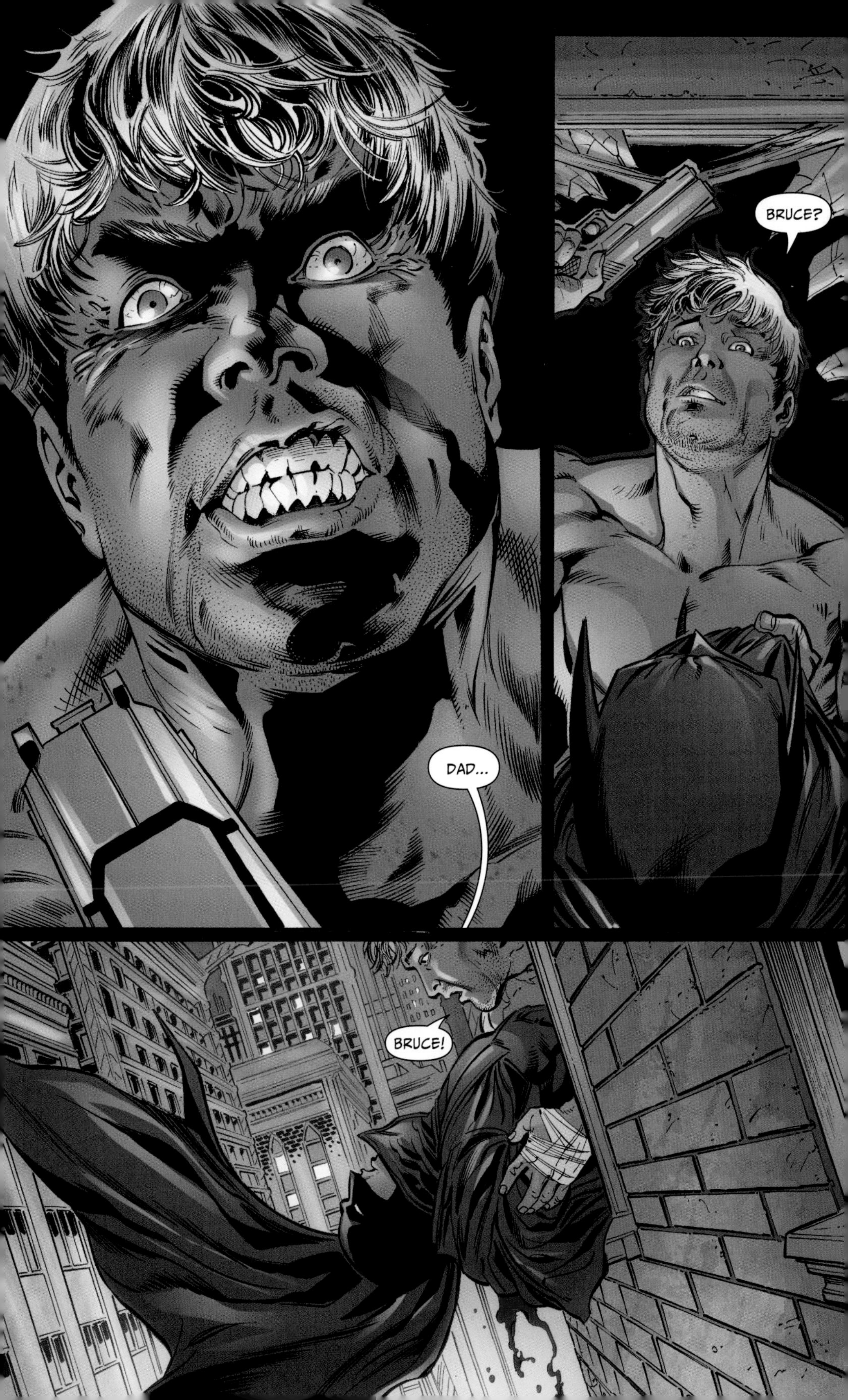
BRUCE?
DAD...
BRUCE!

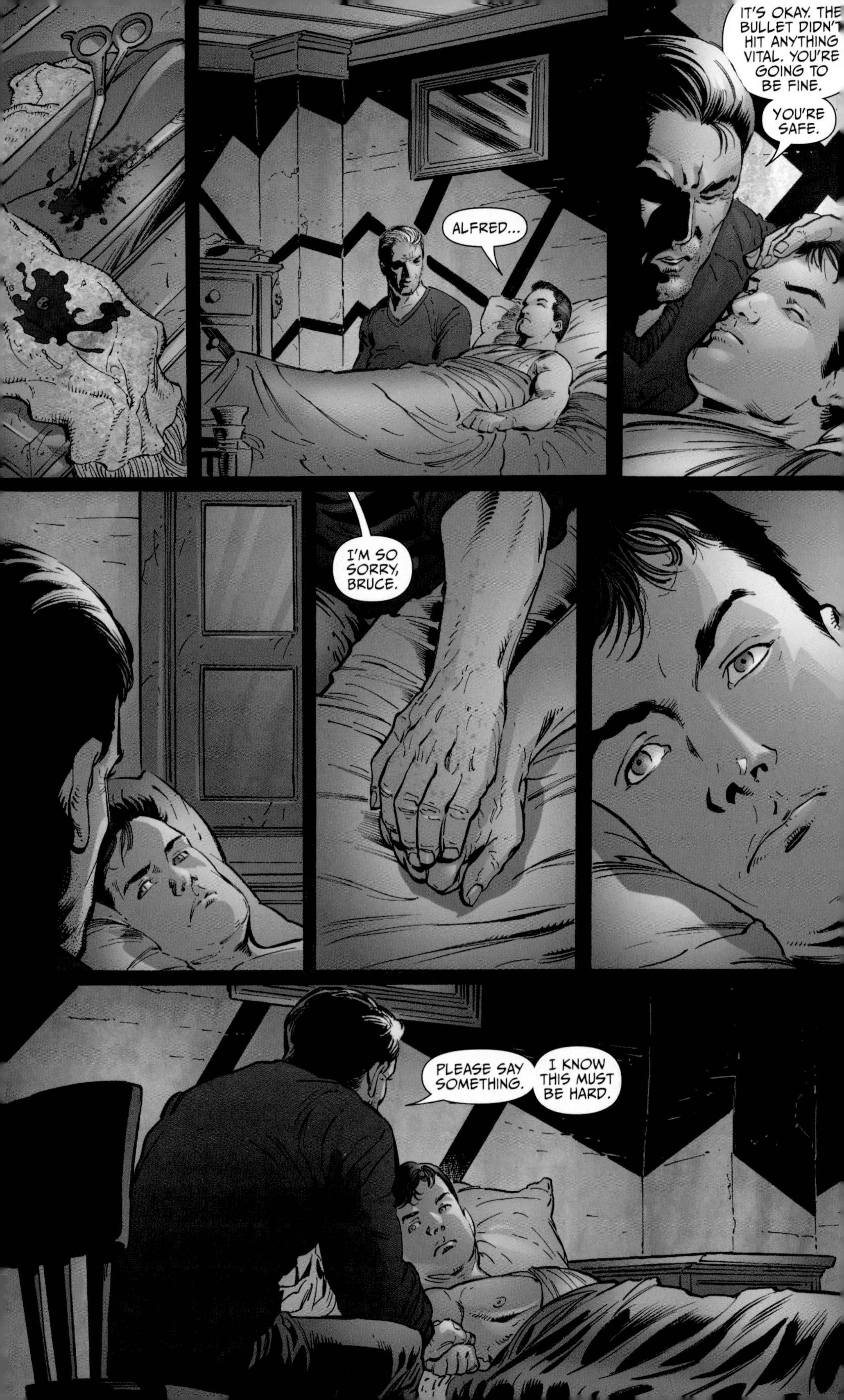
ALFRED...
IT'S OKAY. THE BULLET DIDN'T HIT ANYTHING VITAL. YOU'RE GOING TO BE FINE.
YOU'RE SAFE.
I'M SO SORRY, BRUCE.
PLEASE SAY SOMETHING.
I KNOW THIS MUST BE HARD.

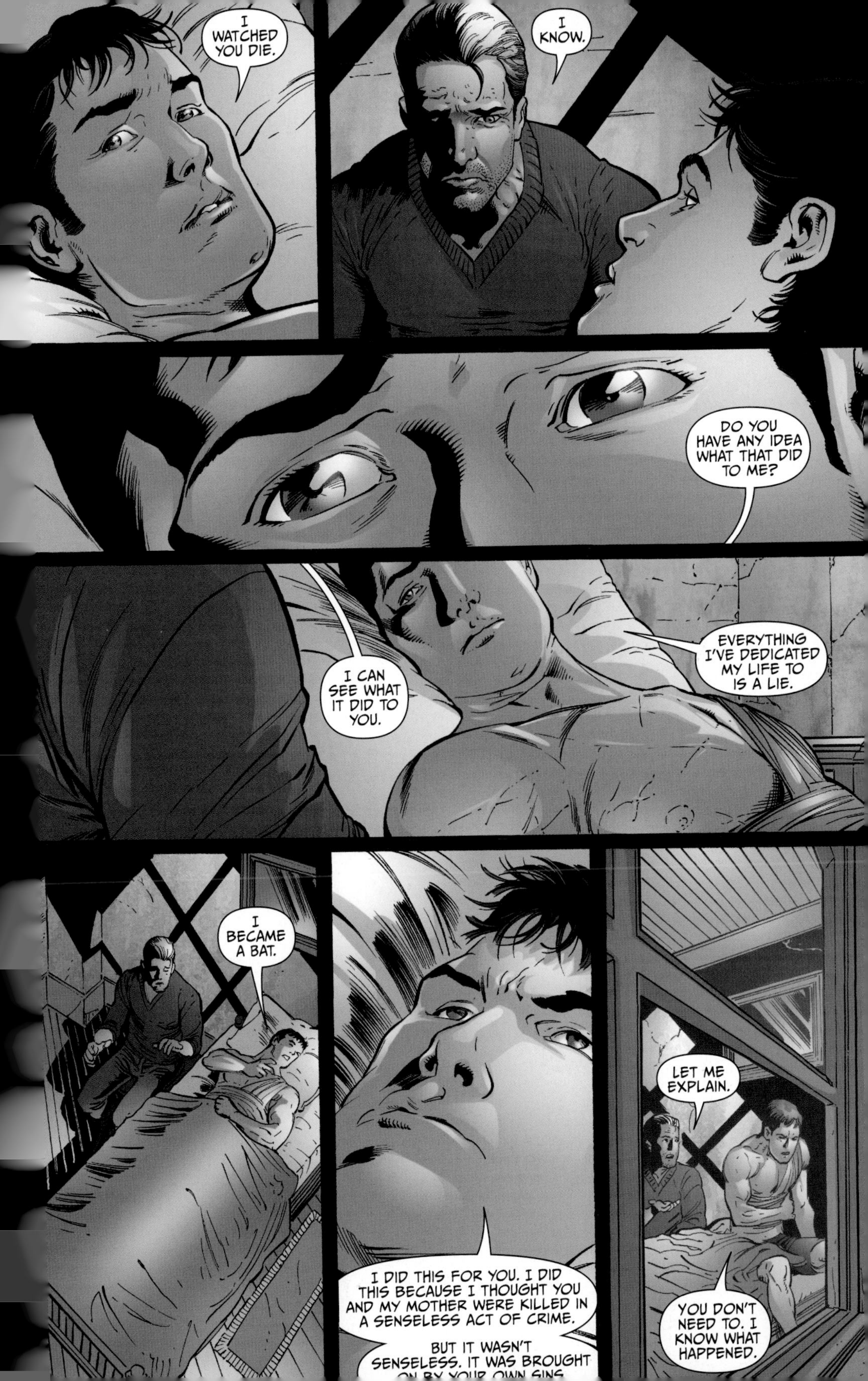
I WATCHED YOU DIE.
I KNOW.
DO YOU HAVE ANY IDEA WHAT THAT DID TO ME?
I CAN SEE WHAT IT DID TO YOU.
EVERYTHING I'VE DEDICATED MY LIFE TO IS A LIE.
I BECAME A BAT.
I DID THIS FOR YOU. I DID THIS BECAUSE I THOUGHT YOU AND MY MOTHER WERE KILLED IN A SENSELESS ACT OF CRIME.
BUT IT WASN'T SENSELESS. IT WAS BROUGHT
LET ME EXPLAIN.
YOU DON'T NEED TO. I KNOW WHAT HAPPENED.

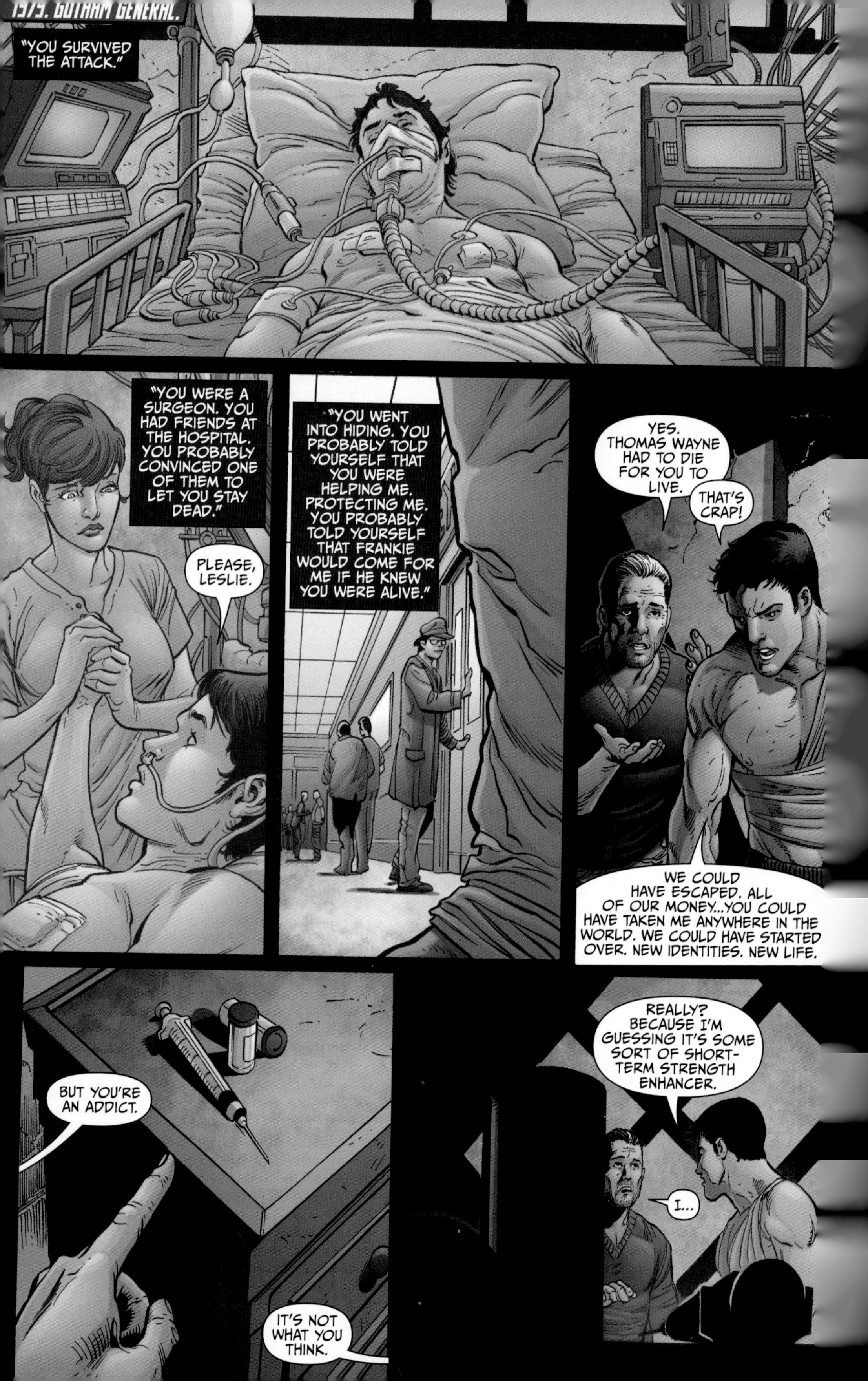
GOTHAM GENERAL.
"YOU SURVIVED THE ATTACK."
"YOU WERE A SURGEON. YOU HAD FRIENDS AT THE HOSPITAL. YOU PROBABLY CONVINCED ONE OF THEM TO LET YOU STAY DEAD."
PLEASE, LESLIE.
"YOU WENT INTO HIDING. YOU PROBABLY TOLD YOURSELF THAT YOU WERE HELPING ME. PROTECTING ME. YOU PROBABLY TOLD YOURSELF THAT FRANKIE WOULD COME FOR ME IF HE KNEW YOU WERE ALIVE."
YES. THOMAS WAYNE HAD TO DIE FOR YOU TO LIVE.
THAT'S CRAP!
WE COULD HAVE ESCAPED. ALL OF OUR MONEY...YOU COULD HAVE TAKEN ME ANYWHERE IN THE WORLD. WE COULD HAVE STARTED OVER. NEW IDENTITIES. NEW LIFE.
BUT YOU'RE AN ADDICT.
IT'S NOT WHAT YOU THINK.
REALLY? BECAUSE I'M GUESSING IT'S SOME SORT OF SHORT-TERM STRENGTH ENHANCER.
I...

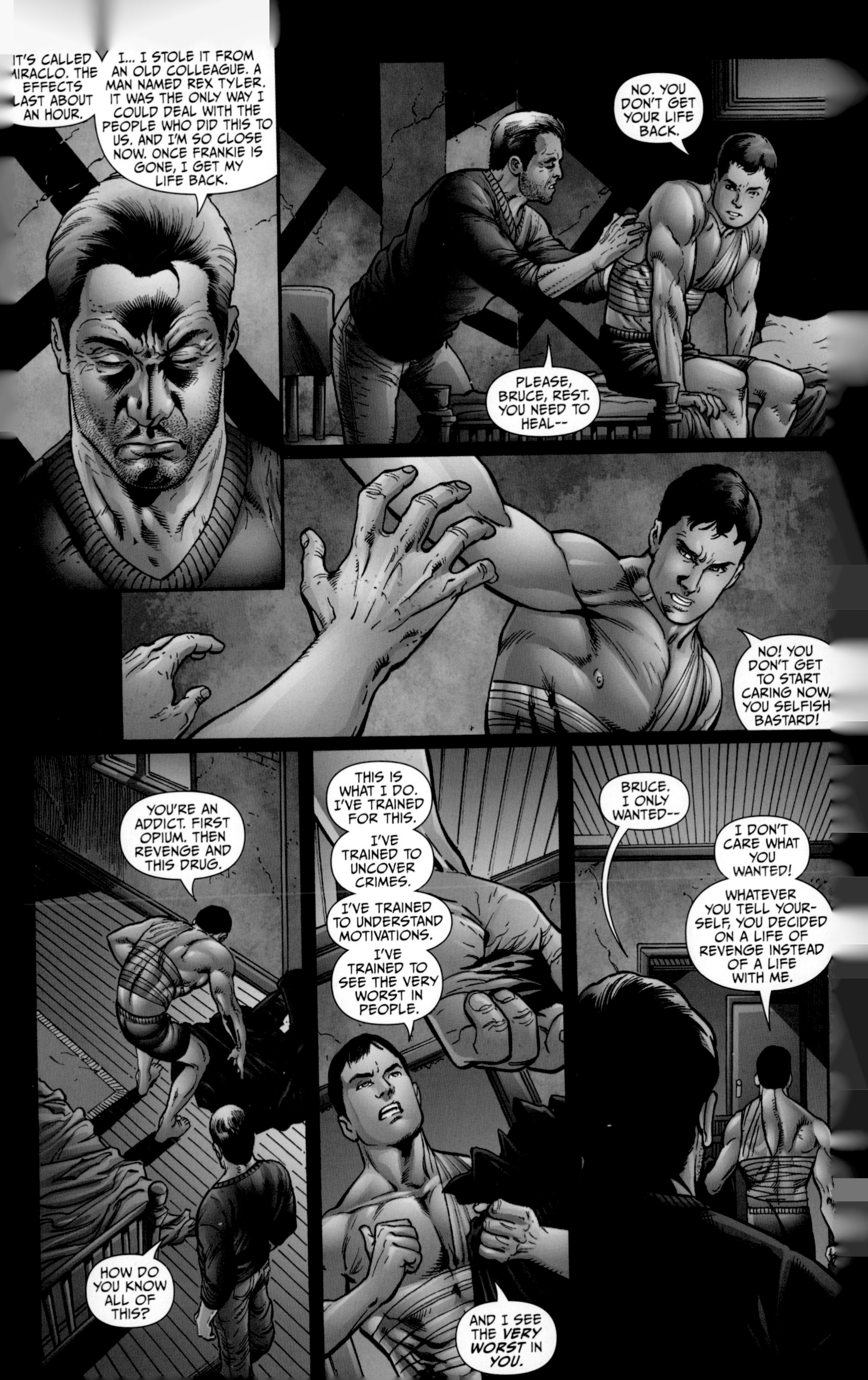
IT'S CALLED MIRACLO. THE EFFECTS LAST ABOUT AN HOUR.
I... I STOLE IT FROM AN OLD COLLEAGUE. A MAN NAMED REX TYLER. IT WAS THE ONLY WAY I COULD DEAL WITH THE PEOPLE WHO DID THIS TO US. AND I'M SO CLOSE NOW. ONCE FRANKIE IS GONE, I GET MY LIFE BACK.
NO. YOU DON'T GET YOUR LIFE BACK.
PLEASE, BRUCE, REST. YOU NEED TO HEAL--
NO! YOU DON'T GET TO START CARING NOW, YOU SELFISH BASTARD!
YOU'RE AN ADDICT. FIRST OPIUM. THEN REVENGE AND THIS DRUG.
HOW DO YOU KNOW ALL OF THIS?
THIS IS WHAT I DO. I'VE TRAINED FOR THIS.
I'VE TRAINED TO UNCOVER CRIMES.
I'VE TRAINED TO UNDERSTAND MOTIVATIONS.
I'VE TRAINED TO SEE THE VERY WORST IN PEOPLE.
AND I SEE THE VERY WORST IN YOU.
BRUCE. I ONLY WANTED--
I DON'T CARE WHAT YOU WANTED!
WHATEVER YOU TELL YOURSELF, YOU DECIDED ON A LIFE OF REVENGE INSTEAD OF A LIFE WITH ME.

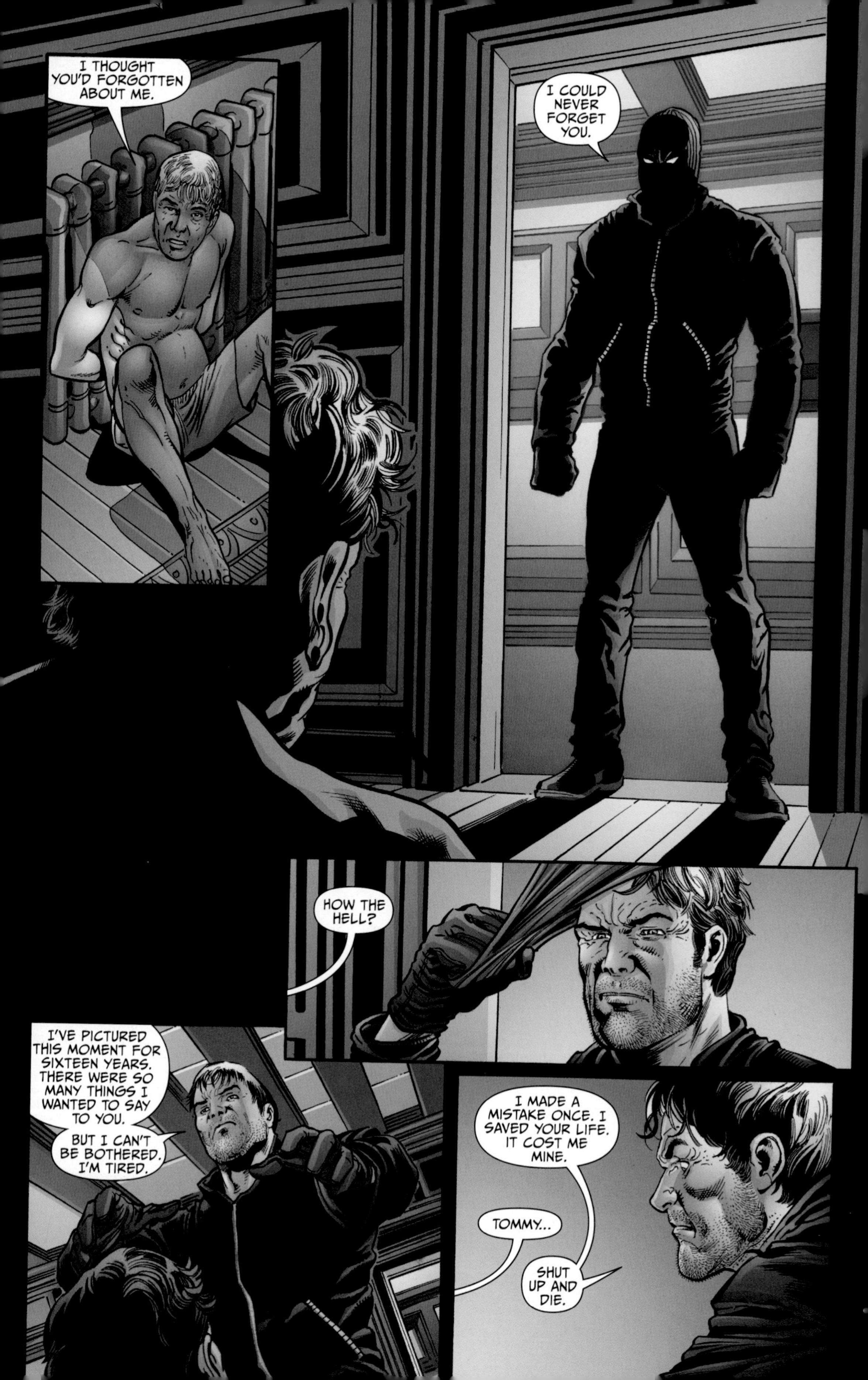
I THOUGHT YOU'D FORGOTTEN ABOUT ME.
I COULD NEVER FORGET YOU.
HOW THE HELL?
I'VE PICTURED THIS MOMENT FOR SIXTEEN YEARS. THERE WERE SO MANY THINGS I WANTED TO SAY TO YOU.
BUT I CAN'T BE BOTHERED. I'M TIRED.
I MADE A MISTAKE ONCE. I SAVED YOUR LIFE. IT COST ME MINE.
TOMMY...
SHUT UP AND DIE.

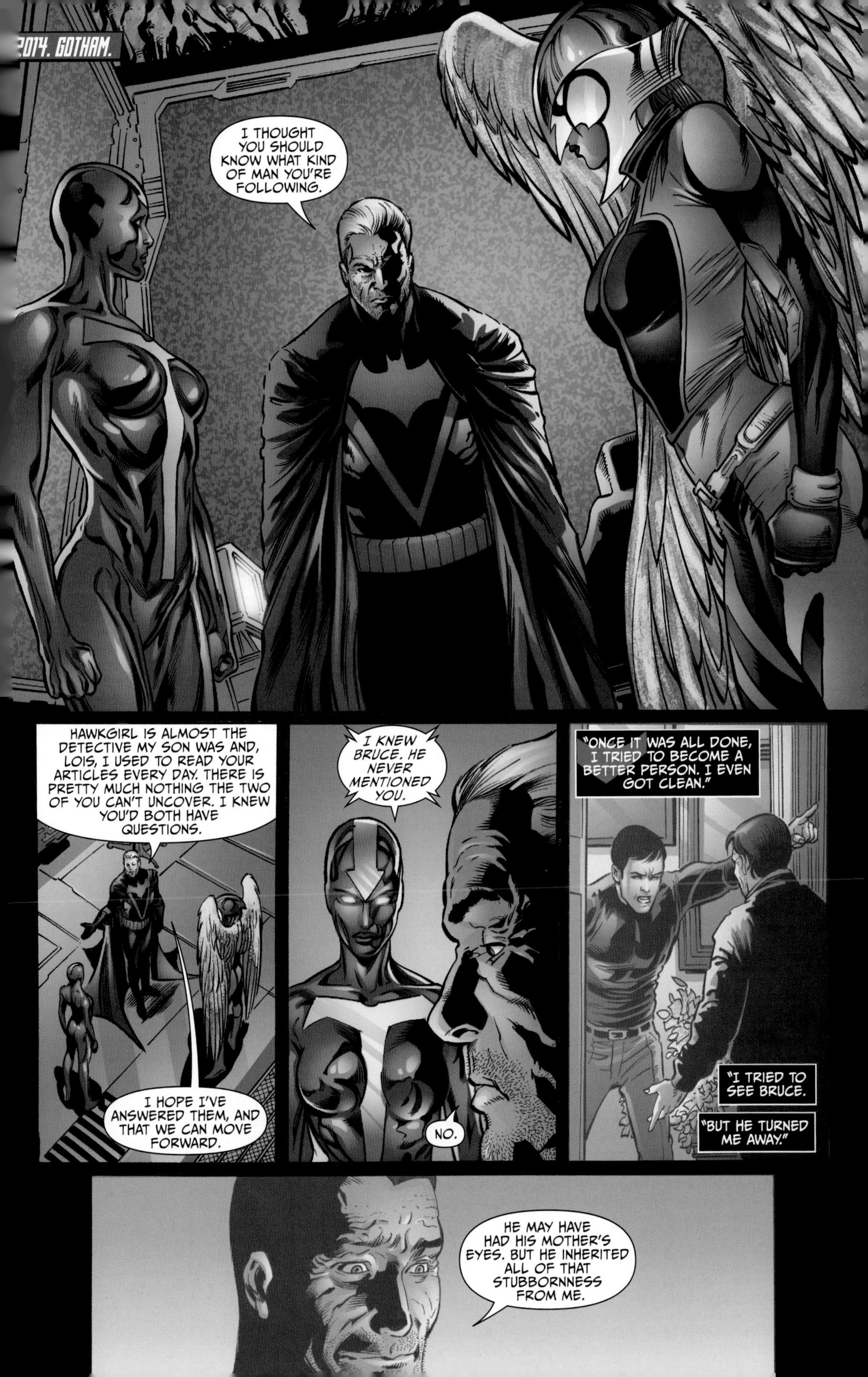
2014. GOTHAM.
I THOUGHT YOU SHOULD KNOW WHAT KIND OF MAN YOU'RE FOLLOWING.
HAWKGIRL IS ALMOST THE DETECTIVE MY SON WAS AND, LOIS, I USED TO READ YOUR ARTICLES EVERY DAY. THERE IS PRETTY MUCH NOTHING THE TWO OF YOU CAN'T UNCOVER. I KNEW YOU'D BOTH HAVE QUESTIONS.
I HOPE I'VE ANSWERED THEM, AND THAT WE CAN MOVE FORWARD.
I KNEW BRUCE. HE NEVER MENTIONED YOU.
NO.
"ONCE IT WAS ALL DONE, I TRIED TO BECOME A BETTER PERSON. I EVEN GOT CLEAN."
"I TRIED TO SEE BRUCE.
"BUT HE TURNED ME AWAY."
HE MAY HAVE HAD HIS MOTHER'S EYES. BUT HE INHERITED ALL OF THAT STUBBORNNESS FROM ME.

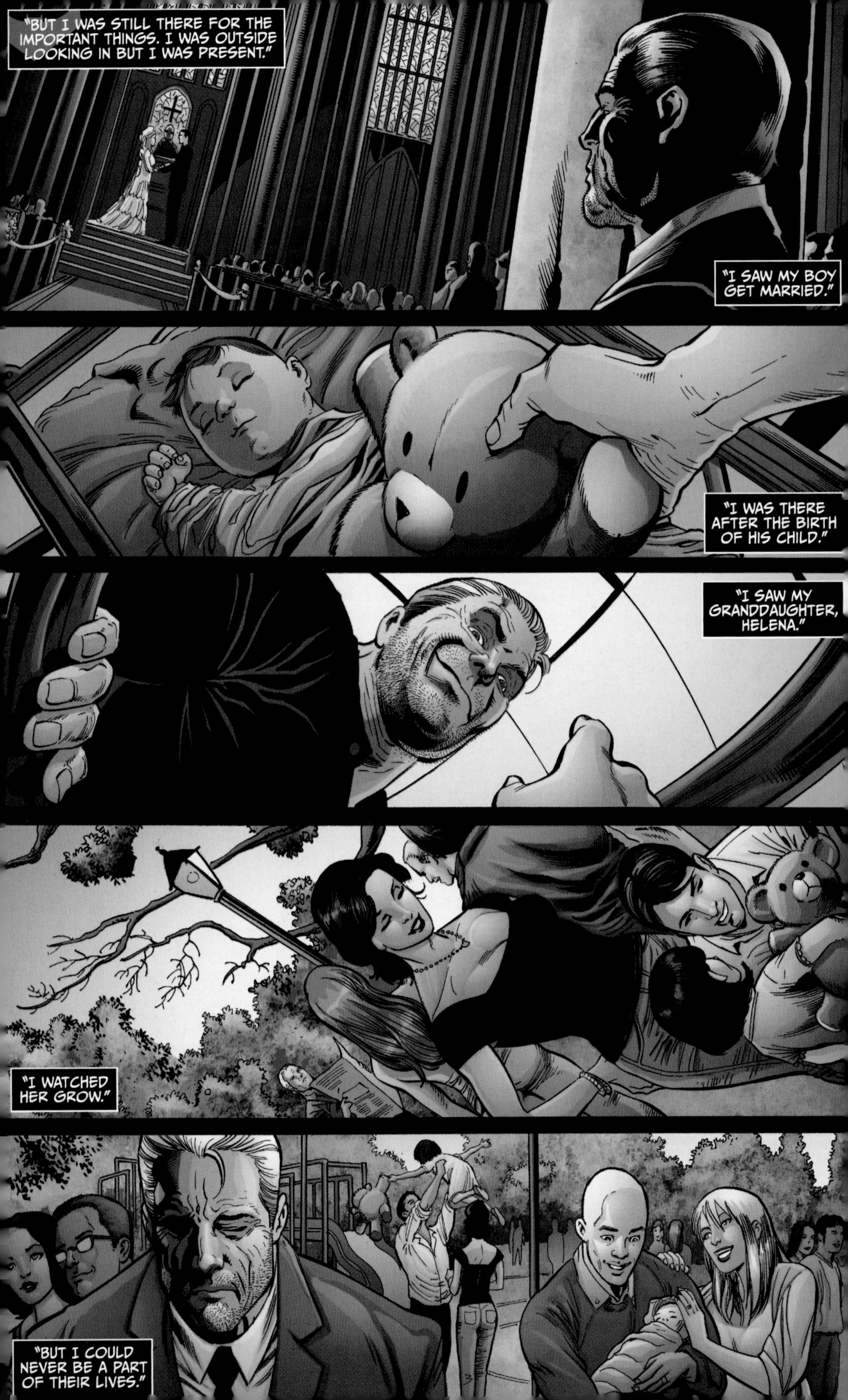
"BUT I WAS STILL THERE FOR THE IMPORTANT THINGS. I WAS OUTSIDE LOOKING IN BUT I WAS PRESENT."
"I SAW MY BOY GET MARRIED."
"I WAS THERE AFTER THE BIRTH OF HIS CHILD."
"I SAW MY GRANDDAUGHTER, HELENA."
"I WATCHED HER GROW."
"BUT I COULD NEVER BE A PART OF THEIR LIVES."

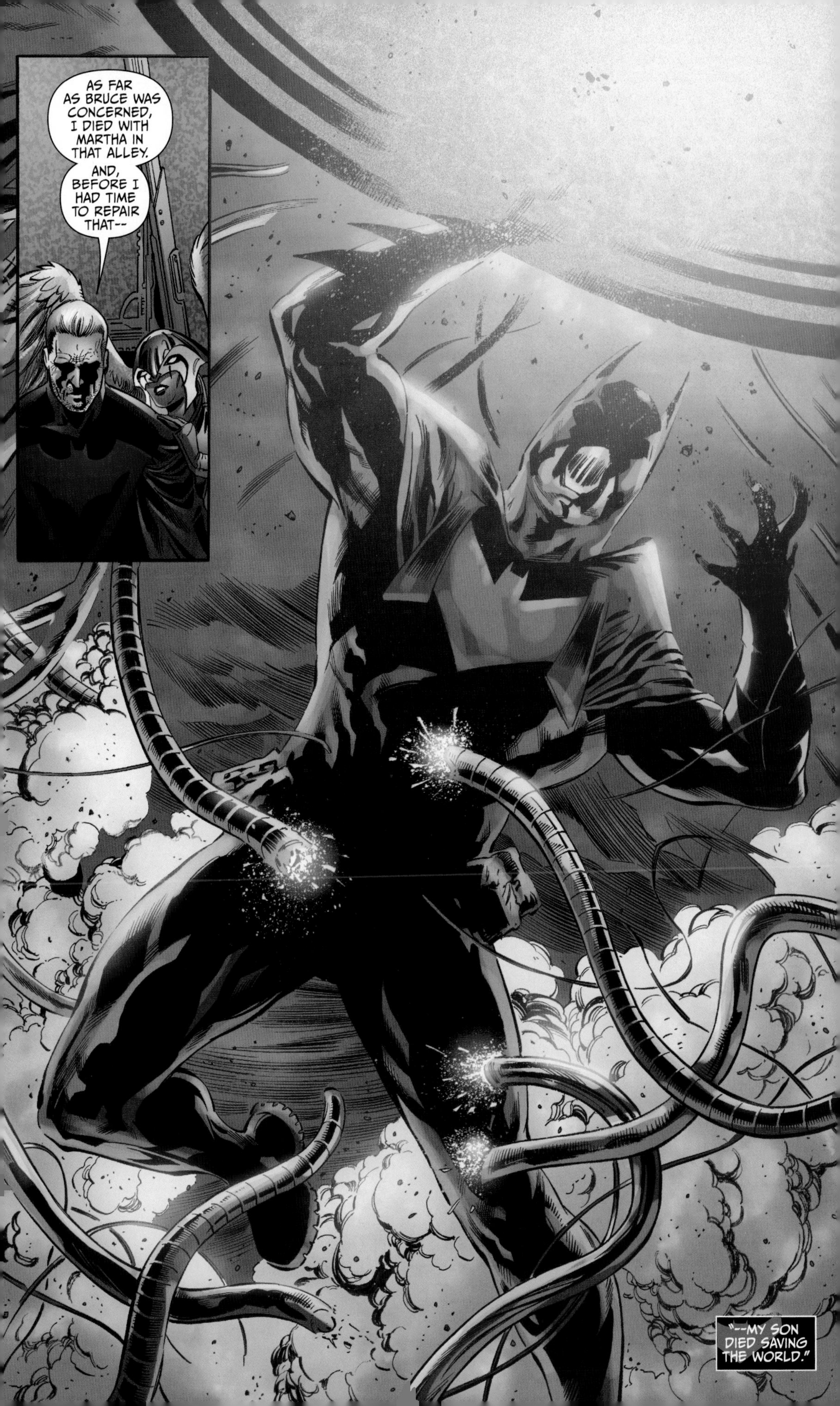
AS FAR AS BRUCE WAS CONCERNED, I DIED WITH MARTHA IN THAT ALLEY.
AND, BEFORE I HAD TIME TO REPAIR THAT--
"--MY SON DIED SAVING THE WORLD."

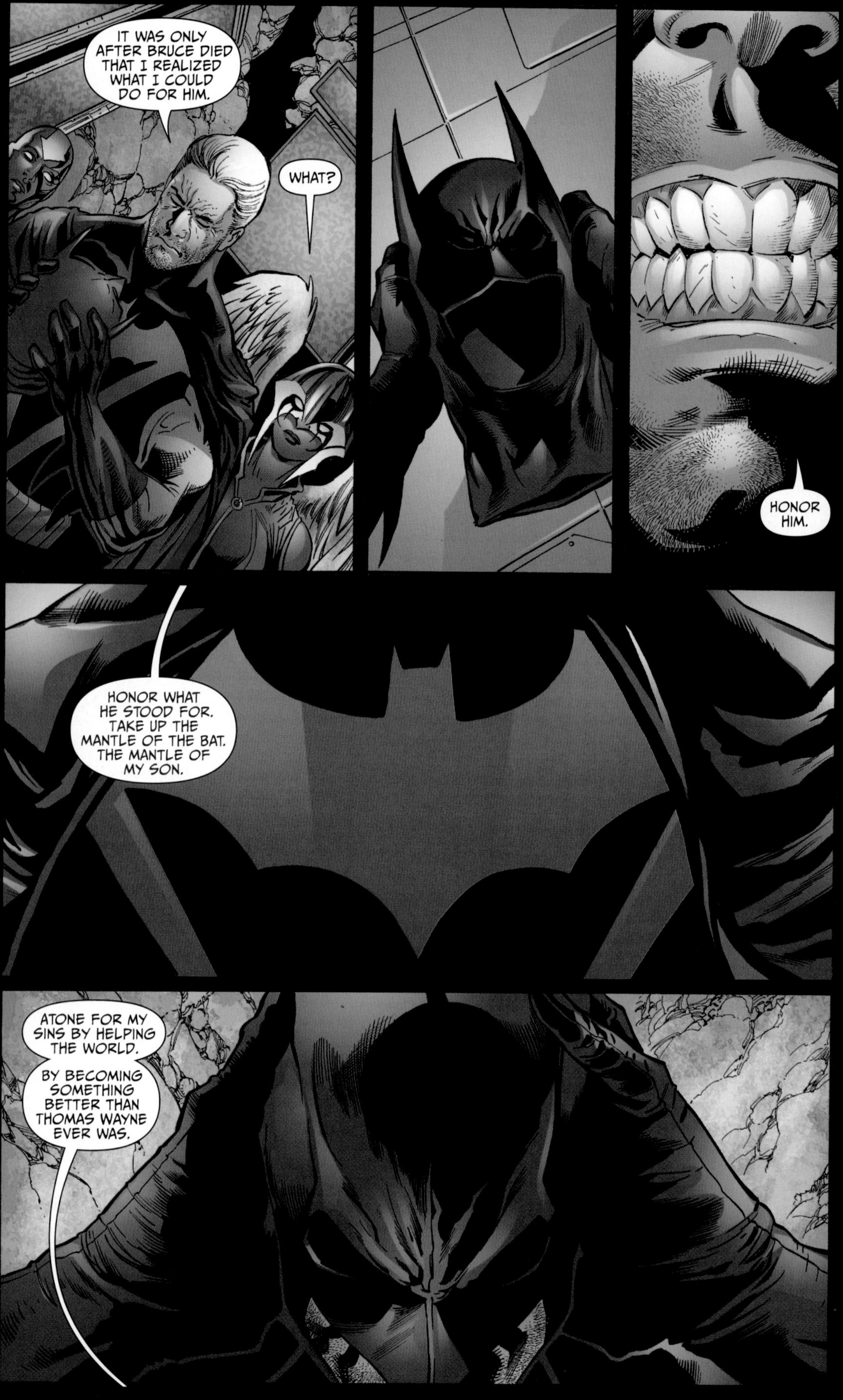
IT WAS ONLY AFTER BRUCE DIED THAT I REALIZED WHAT I COULD DO FOR HIM.
WHAT?
HONOR HIM.
HONOR WHAT HE STOOD FOR. TAKE UP THE MANTLE OF THE BAT. THE MANTLE OF MY SON.
ATONE FOR MY SINS BY HELPING THE WORLD.
BY BECOMING SOMETHING BETTER THAN THOMAS WAYNE EVER WAS.

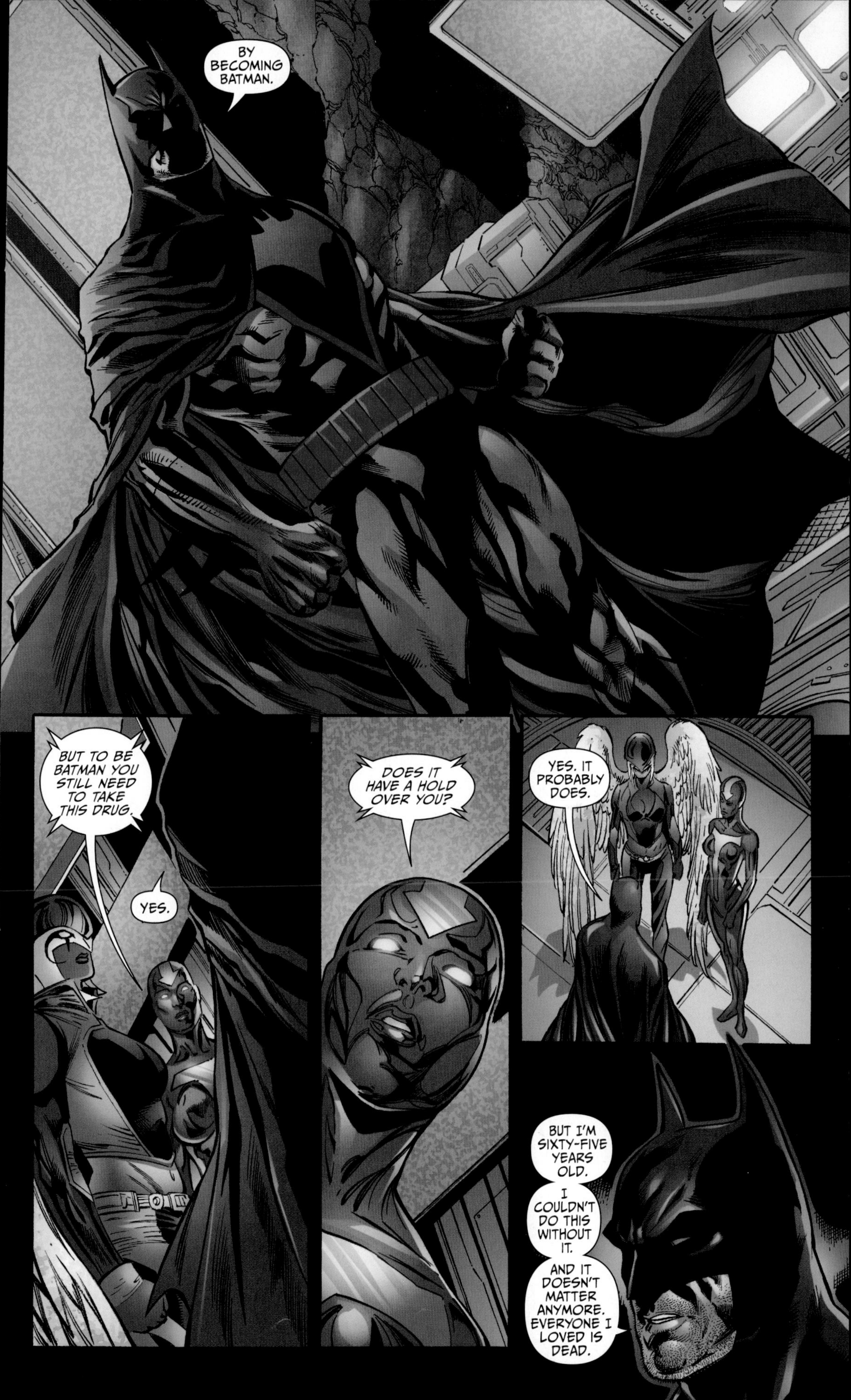
BY BECOMING BATMAN.
BUT TO BE BATMAN YOU STILL NEED TO TAKE THIS DRUG.
YES.
DOES IT HAVE A HOLD OVER YOU?
YES. IT PROBABLY DOES.
BUT I'M SIXTY-FIVE YEARS OLD.
I COULDN'T DO THIS WITHOUT IT.
AND IT DOESN'T MATTER ANYMORE. EVERYONE I LOVED IS DEAD.

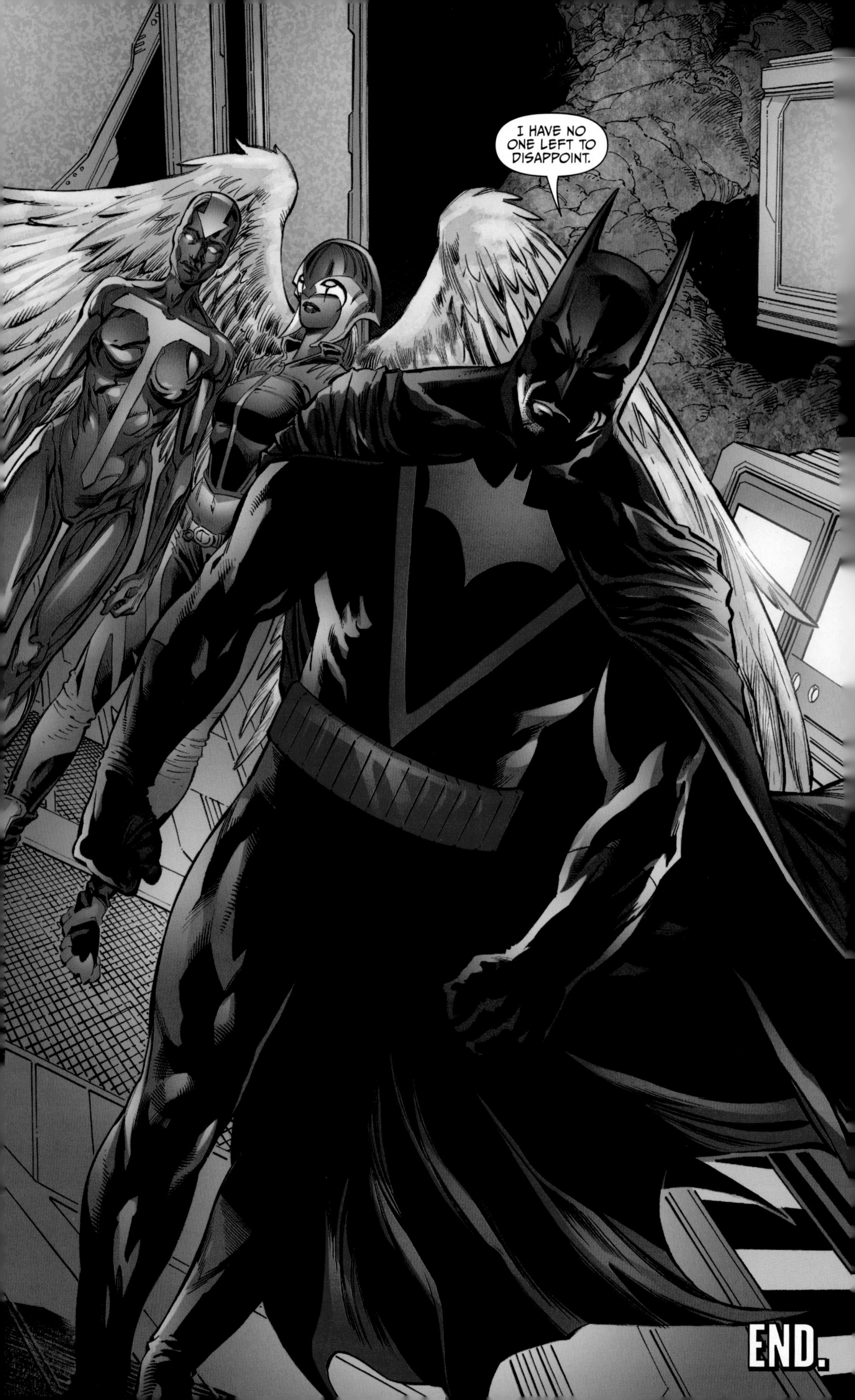
I HAVE NO ONE LEFT TO DISAPPOINT.
END.

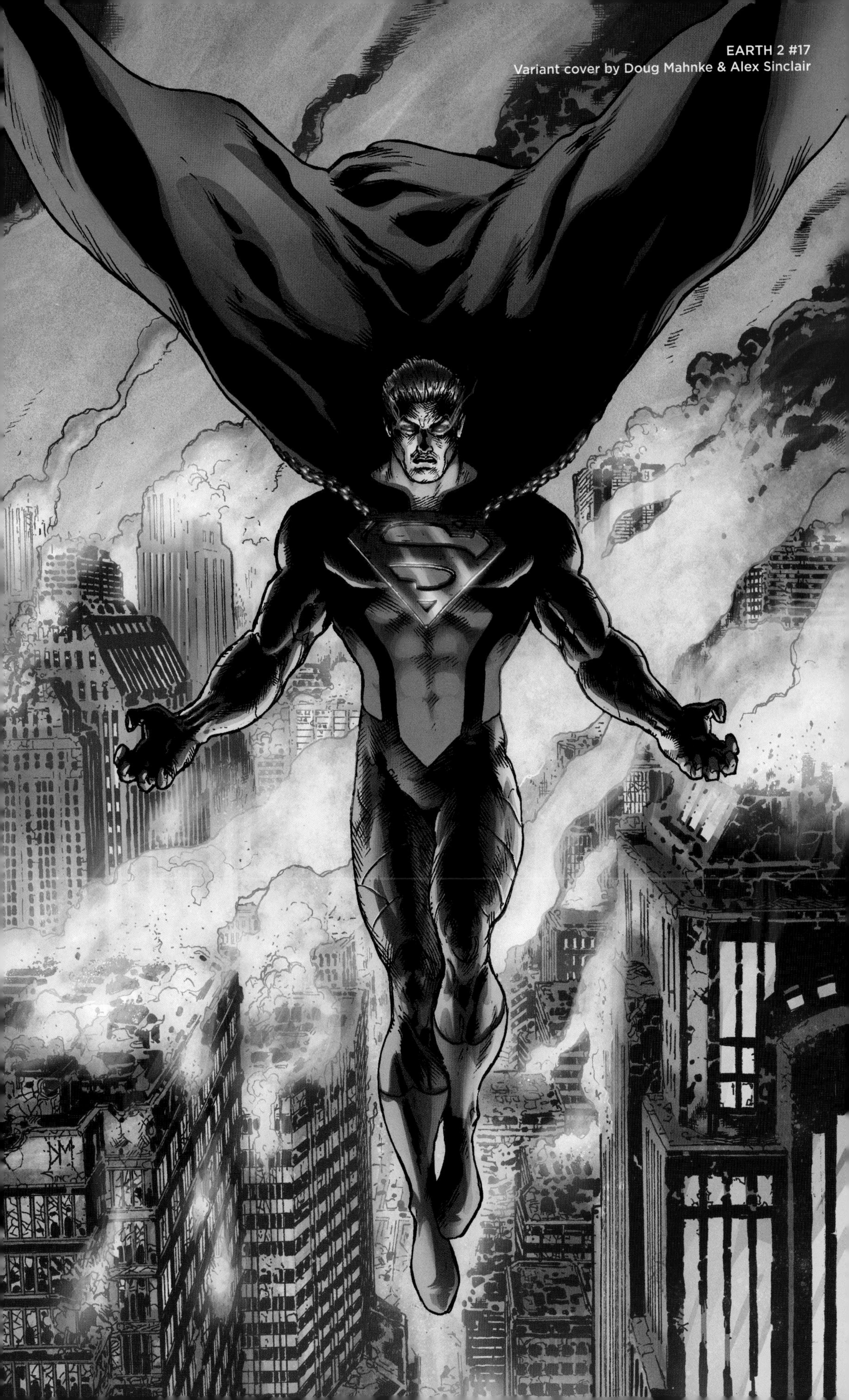

EARTH 2 #17
Variant cover by Doug Mahnke & Alex Sinclair

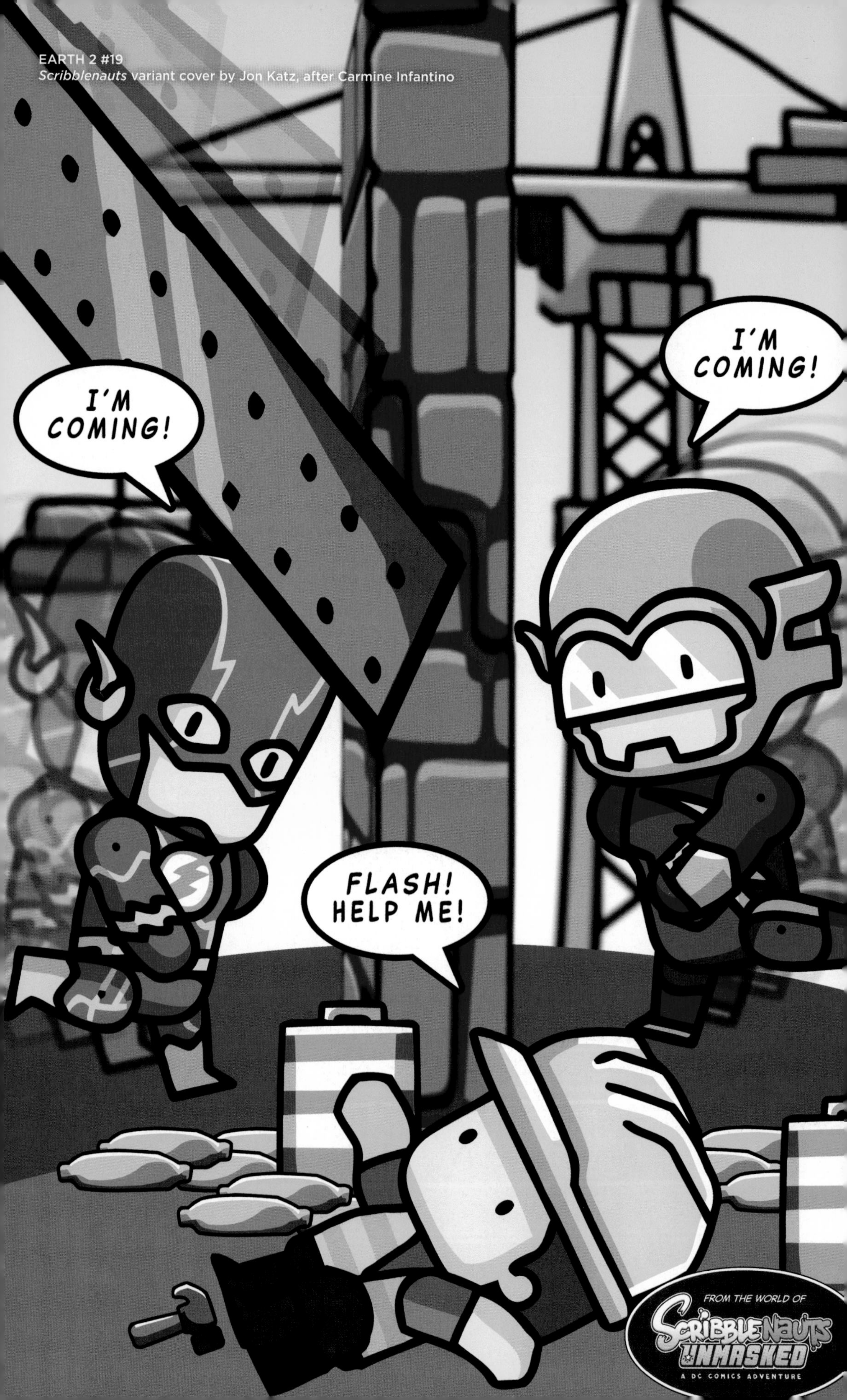
I'M COMING!
I'M COMING!
FLASH! HELP ME!
FROM THE WORLD OF
SCRIBBLENAUTS UNMASKED
A DC COMICS ADVENTURE

EARTH 2 #19
Scribblenauts variant cover by Jon Katz, after Carmine Infantino

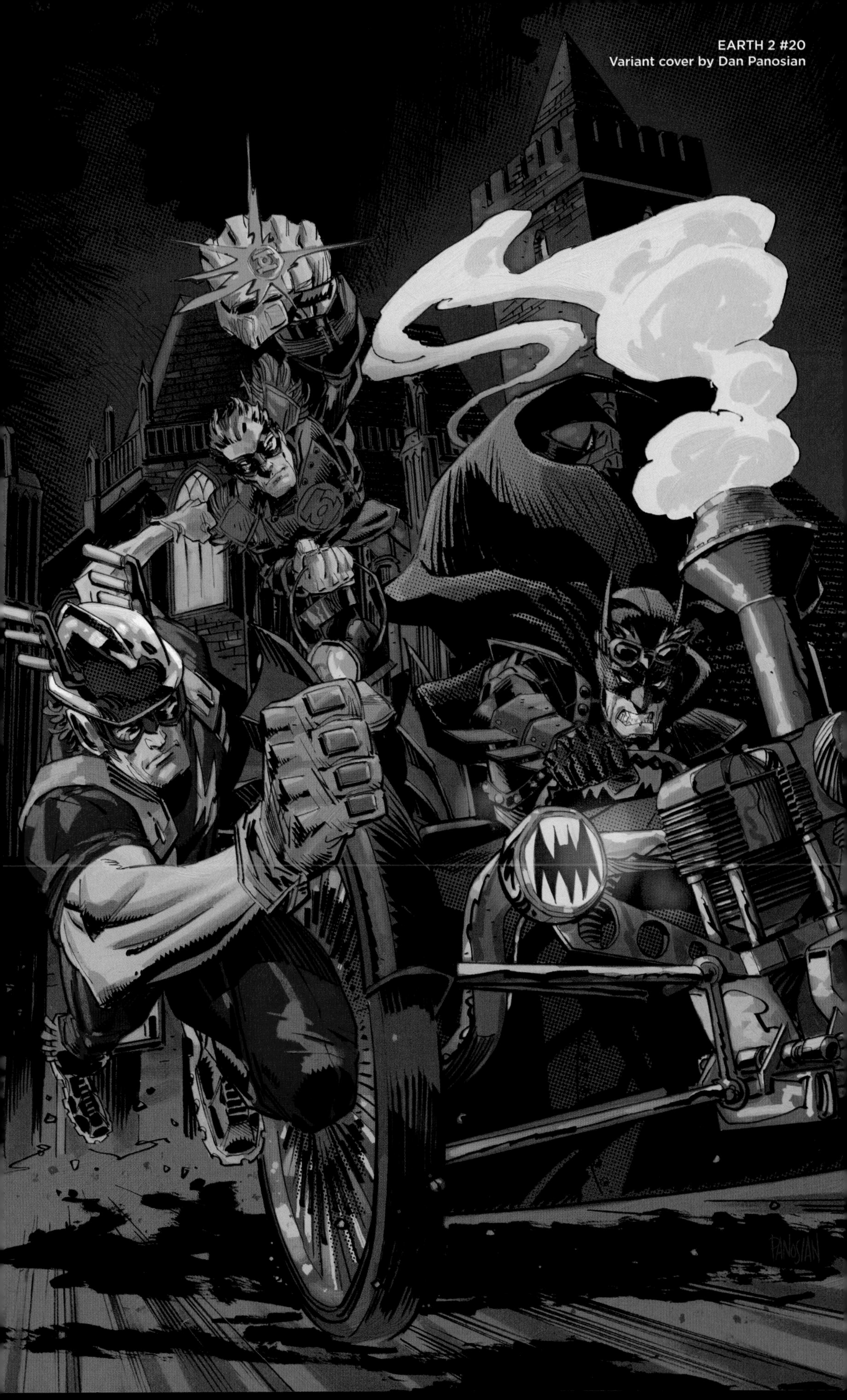
PANOSIAN

EARTH 2 #20
Variant cover by Dan Panosian

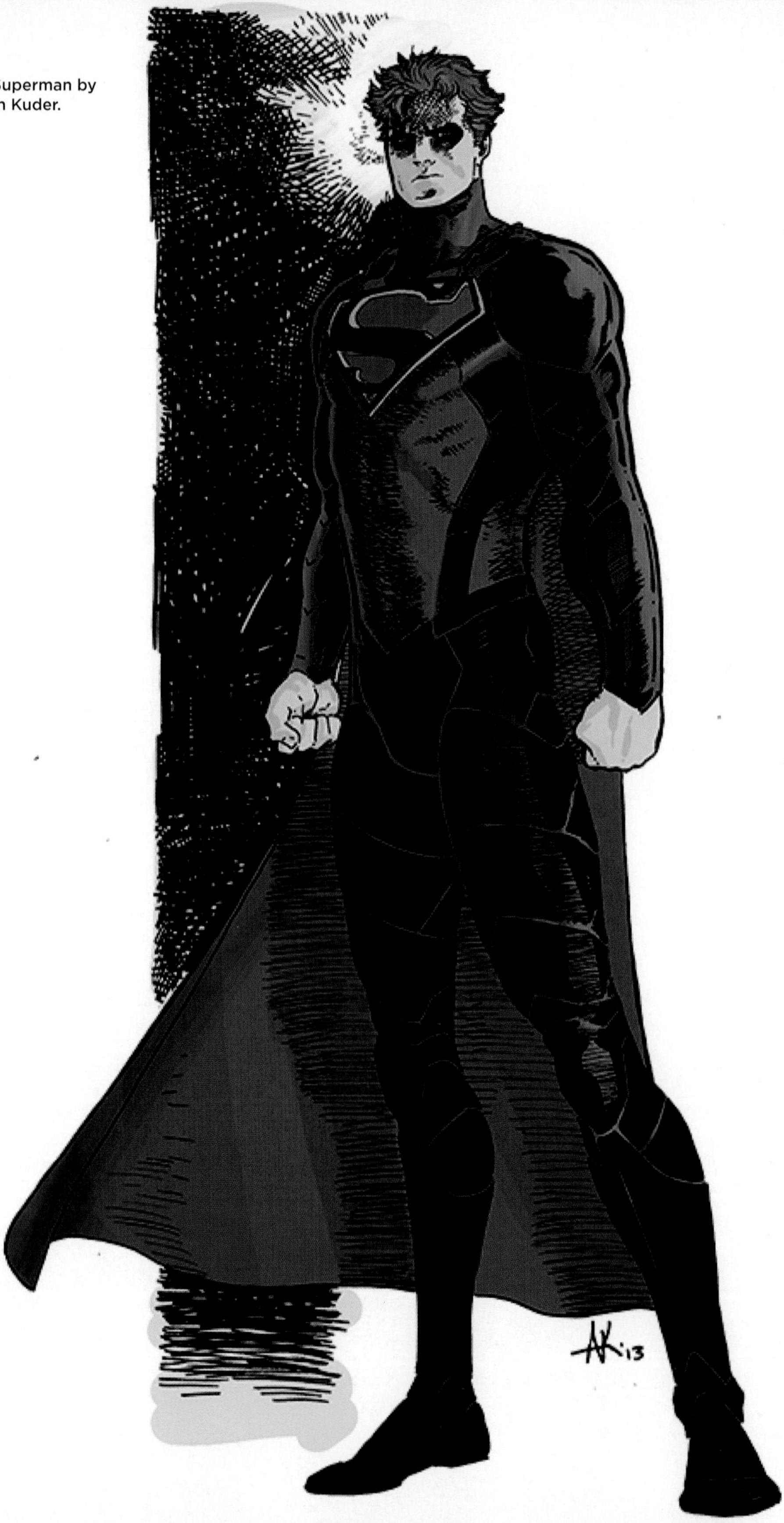
AK '13

Evil Superman by Aaron Kuder.

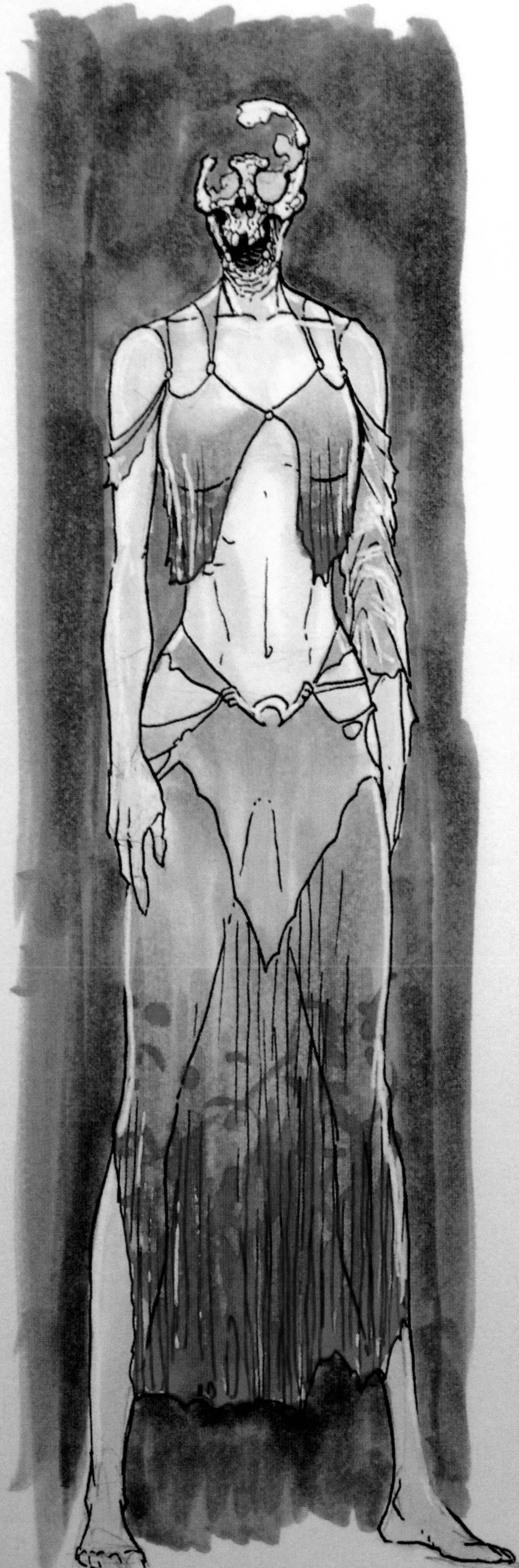

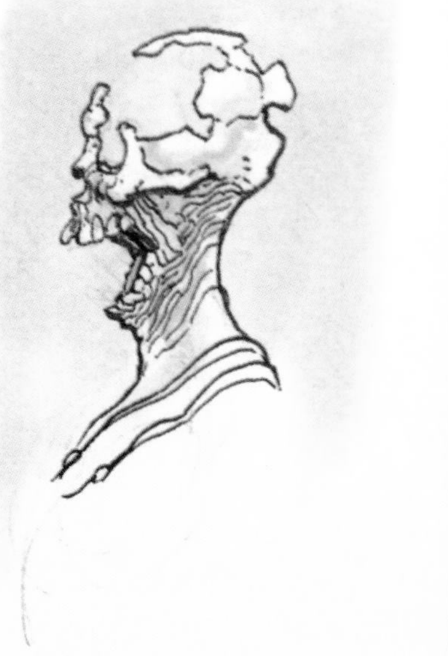

Beguiler and Bedlam
designs by Aaron Kuder.

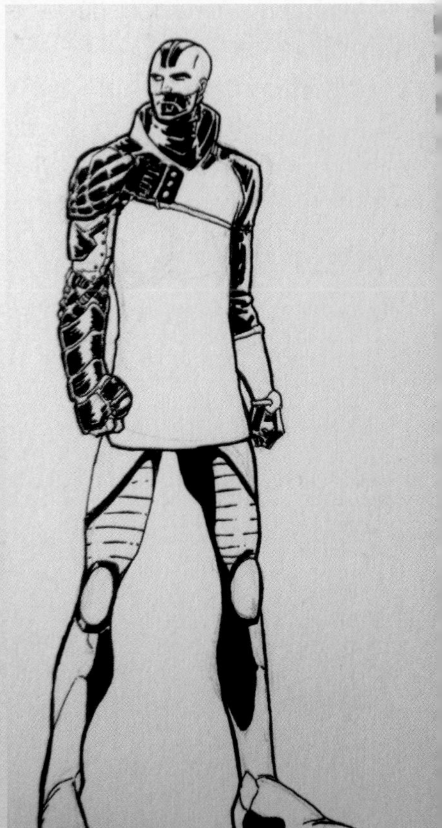

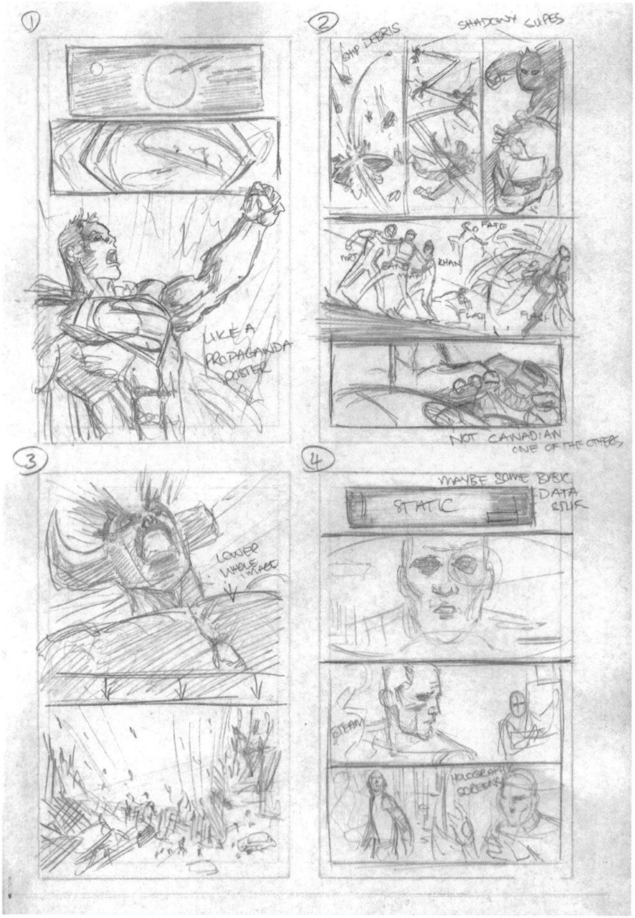
SHIP DEBRIS
LIKE A
PROPAGANDA
POSTER
NOT CANADIAN
ONE OF THE OTHERS
MAYBE SOME BASIC
DATA
STUFF
STATIC
LOWER
WHOLE
IMAGE

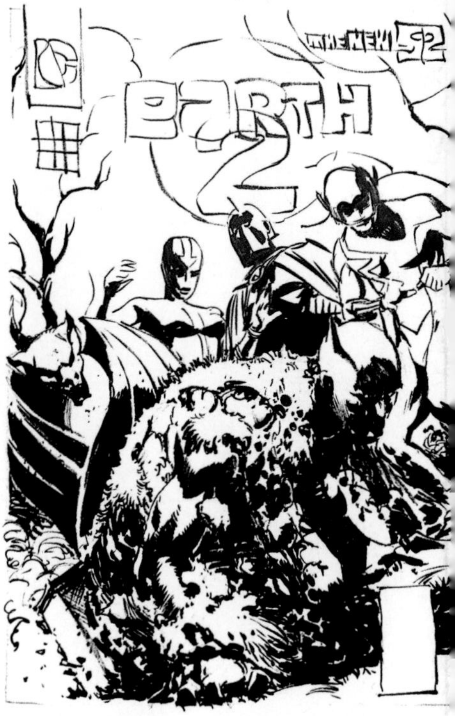
THE NEW 52
EARTH
2

EARTH 2 ANNUAL #2
Cover sketch by Rags Morales.

Thumbnail layouts for EARTH 2 #17 pages 1-4 (top) and 5-6 (bottom) by Nicola Scott.

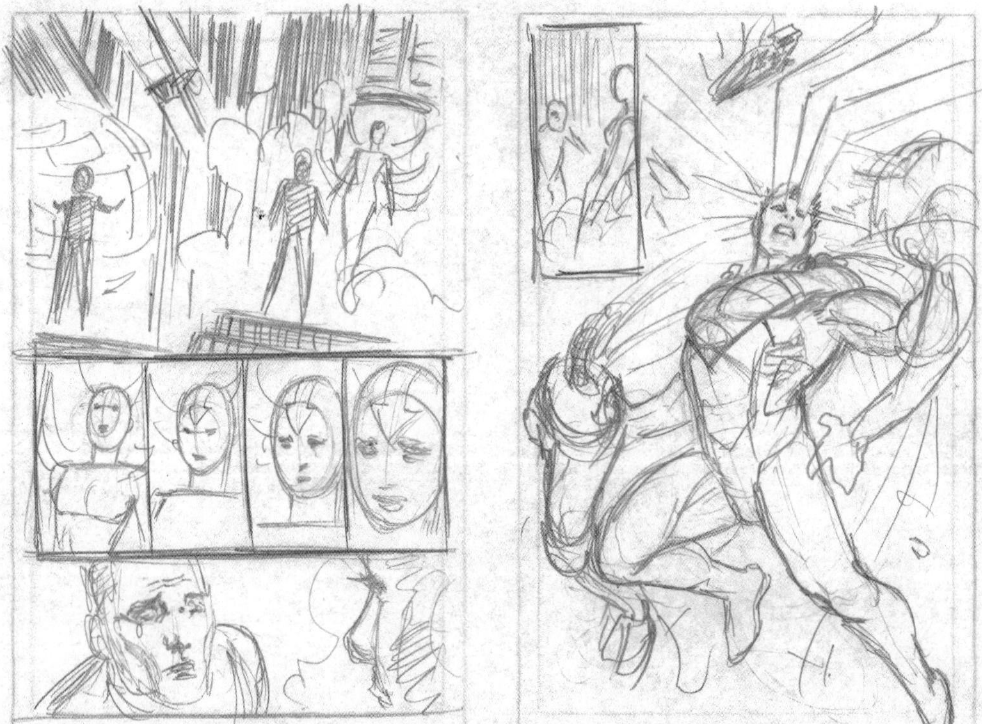

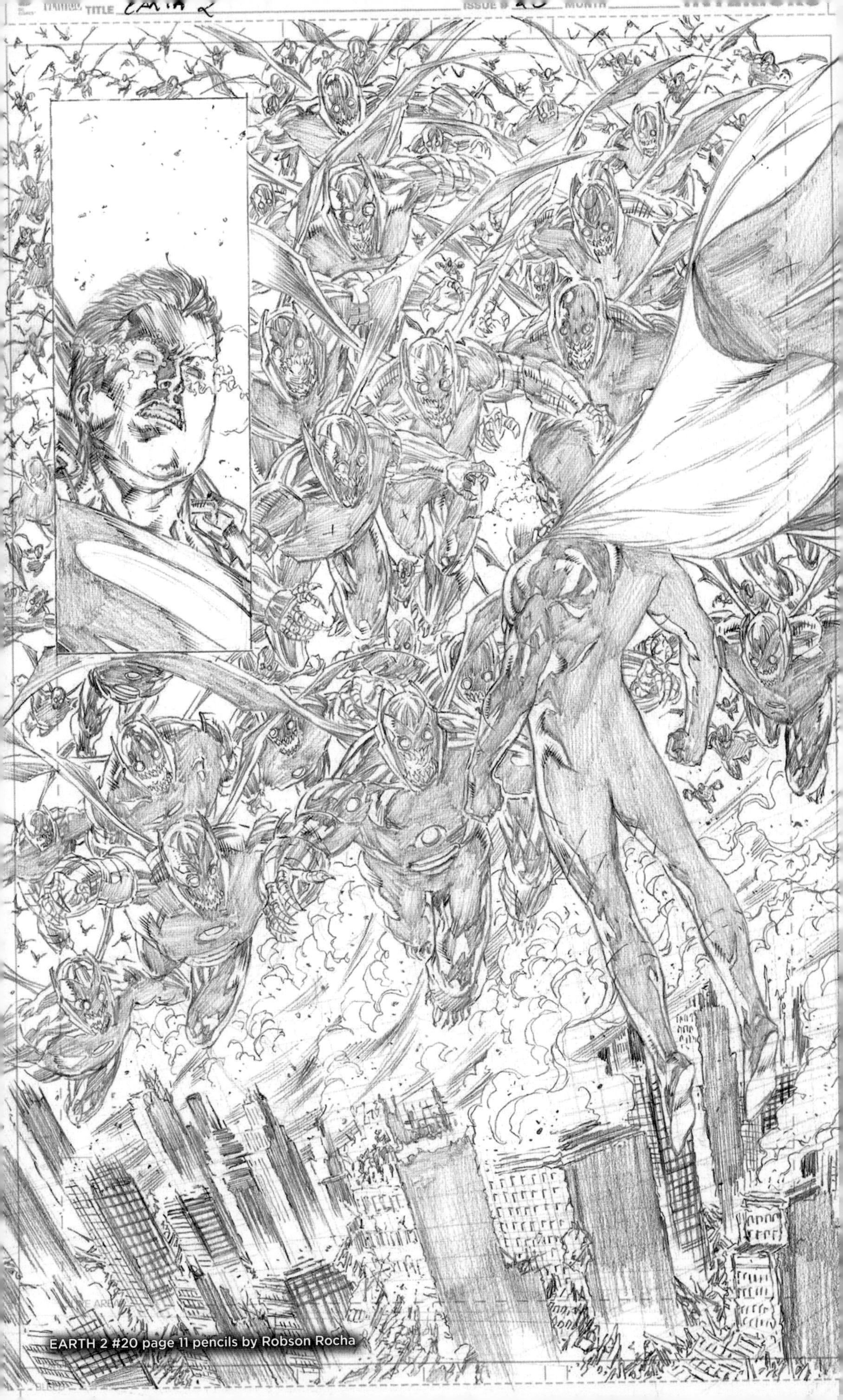

EARTH 2 #20 page 11 pencils by Robson Rocha

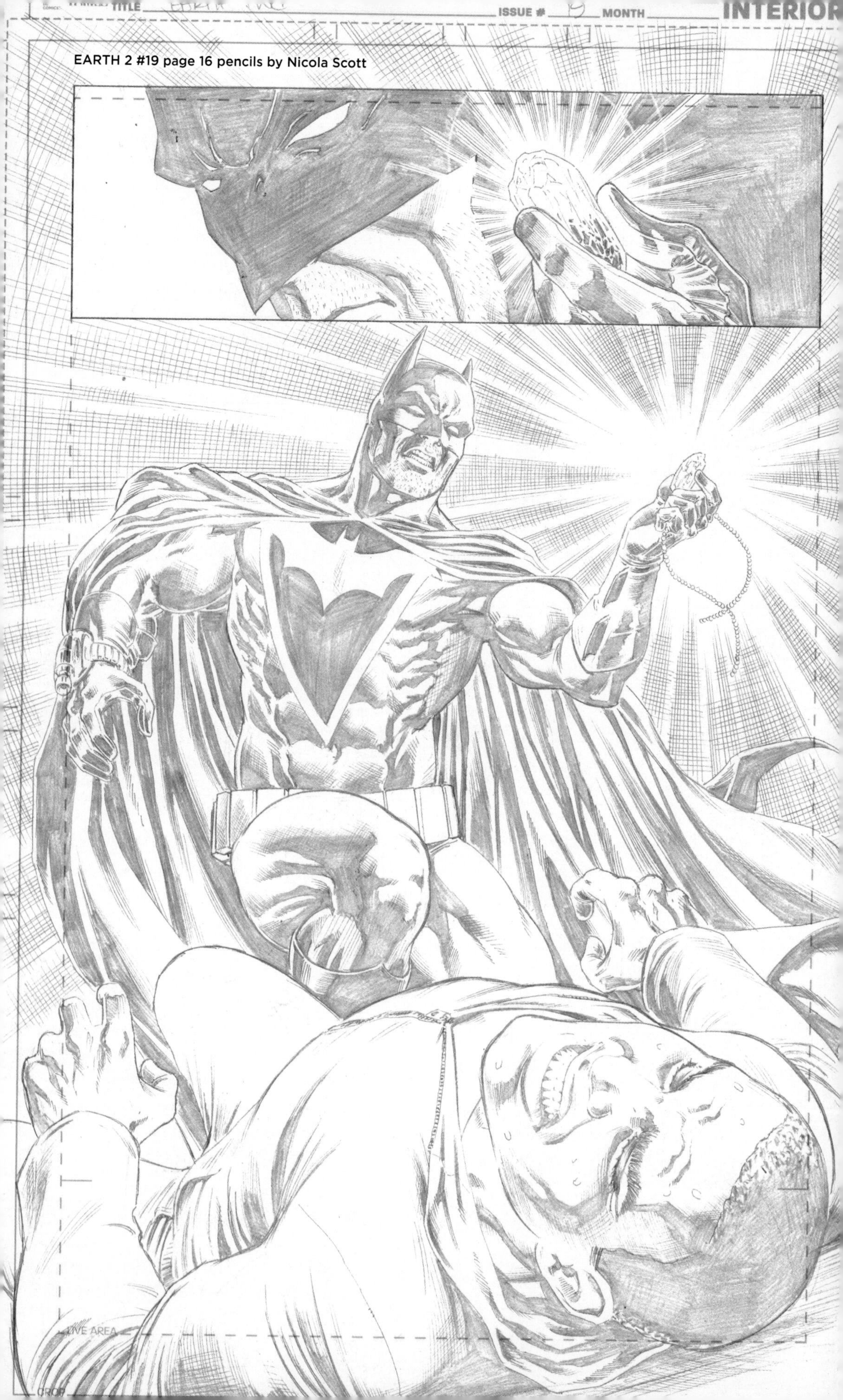
TITLE
ISSUE #
MONTH
INTERIOR
LIVE AREA
CROP

EARTH 2 #19 page 16 pencils by Nicola Scott